Every Child
Every School

Every Child
Every School

Success for All

Robert E. Slavin
Nancy A. Madden
Lawrence J. Dolan
Barbara A. Wasik

CORWIN PRESS, INC.
A Sage Publications Company
Thousand Oaks, California

For information address:

 Corwin Press, Inc.
A Sage Publications Company
2455 Teller Road
Thousand Oaks, California 91320
E-mail: order@corwin.sagepub.com

SAGE Publications Ltd.
6 Bonhill Street
London EC2A 4PU
United Kingdom

SAGE Publications India Pvt. Ltd.
M-32 Market
Greater Kailash I
New Delhi 110 048 India

Printed in the United States of America

Every child, every school: Success for all/ Robert E. Slavin . . . [et al.].
    p. cm.
   Includes bibliographical references (p.) and index.
   ISBN 0-8039-6435-8 (cloth: acid-free paper).—ISBN
0-8039-6436-6 (pbk.: acid-free paper)
   1. School improvement programs—United States. 2. Education, Elementary—United States. 3. Socially handicapped children—Education (Elementary)—United States. 4. Language arts (Elementary)—United States. I. Slavin, Robert E.
LB2822.82 E84 1996
372.973—dc20   96-4474

This book is printed on acid-free paper.
98 99 10 9 8 7 6 5 4
Sage Production Editor: Gillian Dickens

Contents

Acknowledgments

We gratefully acknowledge the following for permission to reprint within this book:

Portions of Chapters 1-4, 6-7, and 9 are adapted from Slavin, Madden, Karweit, Dolan, and Wasik (1992), *Success for All: A Relentless Approach to Prevention and Early Intervention in Elementary Schools.* Reprinted by permission of Educational Research Service.

Portions of Chapter 9 are adapted from "Neverstreaming: Prevention and Early Intervention as an Alternative to Special Education" by Slavin, Madden, Karweit, Dolan, Wasik, Shaw, Mainzer, and Haxby, 1991, *Journal of Learning Disabilities, 24*(6), 373-378. Copyright 1991 by PRO-ED, Inc.

Portions of the description of the Roots and Wings program described in Chapter 5 are adapted from "Roots and Wings: Inspiring Academic Excellence" by Slavin, Madden, Dolan, and Wasik, 1994, *Educational Leadership, 52*(3), 10-13.

Portions of research methods and results described in Chapter 8 and Tables 8.1-8.6 are adapted from "Success for All: A Summary of Research" by Slavin, Madden, Dolan, Wasik, Ross, Smith, and Dianda, (in press), *Journal for the Education of Students Placed at Risk, 1,* 41-76.

Figure 2.1 on page 15 and *Fang* on pages 29-33 were illustrated by Jennifer Clark, story by Laura Burton Rice. © 1994 *Roots and Wings,* The Johns Hopkins University.

Figure 2.2 on page 15 and *A Farm in China* on pages 34-40 were illustrated by Jackie Branch McAfee, story by Wendie Old. © 1994 *Roots and Wings,* The Johns Hopkins University.

Preface

Every child can learn. Every school can ensure the success of every child. Statements to this effect appear in goals statements, commission reports, and school district offices. They are posted in school buildings and appear as mottoes on school stationery. But does our education system behave as if they are true? If we truly believed that every child could learn under the proper circumstances, we would be relentless in the search of those circumstances. We would use well-validated instructional methods and materials known to be capable of ensuring the success of nearly all children if used with intelligence, flexibility, and fidelity. We would involve teachers in constant, collaborative professional development activities to continually improve their abilities to reach every child. We would frequently assess children's perform-ance to be sure that all students are on a path that leads to success, and to be able to respond immediately if children are not making adequate progress. If children were falling behind despite excellent instruction, we would try different instructional approaches, and if neces-sary, we would provide them with tutors or other intensive assistance. We would involve parents in support of their children's school success; we would check to see whether vision, hearing, health, nutrition, or other nonacademic problems were holding children back, and then we would find a solution to those problems. If we truly believed that all children could learn, we would rarely, if ever, assign children to special education or long-term remedial programs that in effect lower expectations for children. If we truly believed that all schools could ensure the success of all children, then the failure of even a single child would be cause for great alarm and immediate, forceful intervention.

Success for All and Roots and Wings are comprehensive restructuring programs for elementary schools designed to make the idea that all children can learn a practical, daily organizing principle for schools, especially those serving many children placed at risk. Success for All, first implemented in 1987, was created to show how schools could ensure that virtually all children can read and write. Roots and Wings, begun in 1991, extends similar principles to mathematics, social studies, and science. This book describes the programs in detail, presents the extensive research evaluating them, and discusses the implications of this research for policy and practice.

The development, dissemination, and evaluation of Success for All and Roots and Wings are the product of the dedicated efforts of hundreds of educators, developers, trainers, and researchers throughout the United States and other countries. Research and development of Success for All has been funded by the Office of Educational Research and Improvement, U.S. Department of Education (Grants No. OERI-R-117-R90002 and OERI-R-117-D40005), the Carnegie Corporation of New York, the Pew Charitable Trusts, the Abell Foundation, and the France and Merrick Foundations. Roots and Wings has been funded by the New American Schools Development Corporation, the Dana Foundation, and the Knight Foundation.

In addition to the authors of this volume, many other researchers have been involved in the development, evaluation, and dissemination of Success for All. These include Nancy Karweit of Johns Hopkins University; Barbara Livermon of Notre Dame College; Robert Stevens of Penn State University; Steve Ross, Lana Smith, Jason Casey, and John Nunnery of the University of Memphis; Marcie Dianda and John Flaherty of the Southwest Regional Laboratory; Bette Chambers and Philip Abrami of Concordia University in Montreal; and Yola Center of Macquarie University in Sydney, Australia. Assistance for data collection and analysis has come from Lois Hybl, Renee Kling, Gretta Gordy, and Ruth Palmer.

Development of Success for All and Roots and Wings has also involved many talented individuals. The overall director of all development has been Nancy Madden, who is also the developer of the reading, writing, and language arts programs with the help of Laura Burton Rice, Robert Stevens, Robert Petza, Alta Shaw, Dorothy Sauer, Barbara Livermon, Anna Marie Farnish, Judith Ramsey, Nancy Cummings, Margaret Livingston, Matt Bennett, Damien DeVille, Amy Martin, and Holly Coleman. Development of materials for prekindergarten and kindergarten has been led by Barbara Wasik, Nancy Karweit, Mary Alice Bond, and Irene Waclawiw. The Roots and Wings social studies/science program, WorldLab, is being developed by Cecelia Daniels, Stan Bennett, Angela Calamari, Coleen Furey, Susan Dangel, Clare von Secker, and Yael and Shlomo Sharan. MathWings, the Roots and Wings mathematics program, is being developed by Kathy Simons, Honi Bamberger, Barbara Luebbe, Pat Baltzley, and Melissa Sikorski. Family support and integrated services programs have been designed by Barbara Haxby, Lawrence Dolan, Maggie Lasaga-Flister, and Viola Cook. Editorial services for the development programs has come from Lois Hybl, Marguerite Collins, Holly Coleman, and Gretta Gordy.

The dissemination of Success for All and Roots and Wings has been carried out by an extraordinary corps of trainers who travel throughout the U.S. helping school staffs achieve their vision of success for every child. At present, this group consists of Anna Marie Farnish, Barbara Haxby, Margarita Calderón, Patrice Case-McFadin, Viola Cook, Nancy Cummings, Susan Dangel, Connie Fuller, Lydia Glassie, Suzi Grant, Carolyn Gwaltney, Tracy Heitmeier, Maggie Lasaga-Flister, Margaret Livingston, Barbara Luebbe, Carla Musci, Rachel Nicholas, Robert Petza, Judith Ramsey, Karen Rutledge, Dorothy Sauer, Alta Shaw, Norma Silva, Randi Suppe, Robin Thorson, and William Zangwill. Our trainers are assisted by adjunct trainers too numerous to name. Former trainers include Betty White, Lynne Mainzer, Elizabeth Lowry, Verian Dunbar, Mary Leighton, Leslie Jones, and Marshall Leavey. Support for materials distribution has come from Chris Kane, Gillian Edgehill, and Diane Diggs.

Perhaps most important of all are the many educators who have done the really hard work of making success for *all* a reality in their own schools and districts. There are too many to name, but some of the principals and district officials who have taken particular leadership roles in Success for All and Roots and Wings are as follows: Ardena Dixon, Alma Brown, Cornelius Johnson, Joyce Kavanagh, and Matthew Riley of the Baltimore City Schools; Joan Kozlovsky, Pat Richardson, Ronald Thomas, Charles Walsh, Mary Blakely, Elfreda Mathis, Janice Walthour, Janet Kellam, Kristin Berryman, Cindy Fletcher, Ann Schumaker, and Gail Holt of the St. Mary's County (MD) schools; Renee Yampolsky and Norris Eldridge of the Philadelphia schools; Gerry House, Marti Alberg, Charlene Parker, and Anna Borden of the Memphis (TN) schools; Enoch Peters and Gerry Karol of the Asbury Park (NJ) schools; Edward Hansberry and Sharon Yuille of the Flint (MI) schools; Cindy Burks and Teresa Miskell of the Montgomery (AL) schools; Joe Torres of the Kyrene (AZ) schools; Jerry Frye, Danny Cruz, Mark Lewis, and Jennifer Schindler of the Modesto (CA) schools; Susan Toscano of the Riverside (CA) schools; Diane Creekmore, Carolyn Allen, and Ruth Dimmick of the Aldine (TX) schools; Joe Stubbs, Phyllis Hunter, and James Ketelsen of Houston; Margaret Mastin and Sue St. Clair of Morton (TX); Nancy Cavanaugh of Cincinnati; Jane Harbert of the Charleston (WV) schools; Nereida Santa Cruz, Cynthia Clarke, and Aron Brumm of the Dade County (FL) schools; Margaret Brockmiller of the Palm Beach County (FL) schools; Debra Dimke of the Rockford (IL) schools; and Cornelia Shideler, Judy Diagostino, and Sharon Barnes, and Judy Ball of the Ft. Wayne (IN) schools.

About the Authors

Robert E. Slavin is co-director of the Center for Research on the Education of Students Placed at Risk at Johns Hopkins University. He received his BA in psychology from Reed College in 1972, and his PhD in social relations in 1975 from Johns Hopkins University. He has authored or coauthored more than 140 articles and 14 books, including *Educational Psychology: Theory Into Practice; School and Classroom Organization; Effective Programs for Students at Risk; Cooperative Learning: Theory, Research, and Practice;* and *Preventing Early School Failure.* He received the American Educational Research Association's Raymond B. Cattell Early Career Award for Programmatic Research in 1986, the Palmer O. Johnson award for the best article in an AERA journal in 1988, and the Charles A. Dana award in 1994.

Nancy A. Madden is the principal research scientist and co-director of the Elementary Program at the Center for Research on the Education of Students Placed at Risk at Johns Hopkins University, and is co-director of the Success for All program. She received her BA in psychology from Reed College in 1972 and a PhD in psychology from American University. She has authored or coauthored over 100 research articles and papers, including "Success for All: A Relentless Approach to Prevention and Early Intervention in Elementary Schools" and "Effective Programs for Students at Risk." She directs the curriculum development and dissemination of the comprehensive school reform programs, Success for All and Roots and Wings, now involving over 300 schools nationwide. She has reviewed

EVERY CHILD, EVERY SCHOOL

research on cooperative learning, mainstreaming and special education, effective programs for students placed at risk, and instruction for reading, writing, and mathematics. She is the primary author of instructional manuals for Cooperative Integrated Reading and Composition (CIRC), a reading program using cooperative learning; the *Reading Roots* manual of the Roots and Wings school reform; and the *Lee Conmigo* manual for the instruction of Spanish bilingual students in early reading in the Success for All program.

Lawrence J. Dolan is a research scientist for the Center for the Social Organization of Schools at Johns Hopkins University with research projects in the Center for Research on the Education of Students Placed at Risk and the Family Center. He serves as co-director of the Success for All and Roots and Wings elementary school reform programs. He received his PhD from the University of Chicago in educational psychology in 1980 and was a program officer for the Spencer Foundation and an assistant professor at the University of Rochester before coming to Johns Hopkins in 1984. At Johns Hopkins, he is also an associate professor for the School of Hygiene and Public Health. His research interests include the links between public education and public mental health, family-school connections, and effective elementary schools. He is presently the author of over 60 publications on these topics.

Barbara A. Wasik is a research scientist at the Johns Hopkins University Center for Social Organization of Schools. She works in the Center for Research on the Education of Students Placed at Risk, for the Early Education and Development program. She received her PhD in 1986 from Temple University. Her research interests include the effects of intensive birth-to-four interventions and early school-age programs. She is the author of almost 50 articles on these topics.

1

Success for All

The Promise and the Plan

Ms. Martin's kindergarten class has some of the brightest, happiest, friendliest, and most optimistic kids you'll ever meet. Students in her class are glad to be in school, proud of their accomplishments, certain that they will succeed at whatever the school has to offer. Every one of them is a natural scientist, a storyteller, a creative thinker, a curious seeker of knowledge. Ms. Martin's class could be anywhere, in suburb or ghetto, small town or barrio, it doesn't matter. Kindergartners everywhere are just as bright, enthusiastic, and confident as her kids are.

Only a few years from now, many of these same children will have lost the spark they all started with. Some will have failed a grade. Some will be in special education. Some will be in long-term remediation, such as Title I or other remedial programs. Some will be bored, or anxious, or unmotivated. Many will see school as a chore rather than a pleasure and will no longer expect to excel. In a very brief span of time, Ms. Martin's children will have defined themselves as successes or failures in school. All too often, only a few will still have a sense of excitement and positive self-expectations about learning. We cannot predict very well which of Ms. Martin's students will succeed and which will fail, but based on past experience we can predict that if nothing changes, far too many will fail. This is especially true if Ms. Martin's kindergarten happens to be located in a high-poverty neighborhood, in which there are typically fewer resources in the school to provide top-quality instruction to every child, fewer forms of rescue if children run into academic difficulties, and fewer supports for learning at home. Preventable failures occur in all schools, but in high-poverty schools failure can be endemic, so widespread that it makes it difficult to treat each child at risk of failure as a person of value in need of emergency assistance to get back on track. Instead, many such schools do their best to provide the greatest benefit to the greatest number of children possible, but have an unfortunately well-founded expectation that a certain percentage of students will fall by the wayside during the elementary years.

Any discussion of school reform should begin with Ms. Martin's kindergartners. The first goal of reform should be to ensure that every child, regardless of home background, home language, or learning style, achieves the success that he or she so confidently expected in kindergarten, that all children maintain their motivation, enthusiasm, and optimism because they are objectively succeeding at the school's tasks. Any reform that does less than this is hollow and self-defeating.

What does it mean to succeed in the early grades? The elementary school's definition of success, and therefore the parents' and children's definition as well, is overwhelmingly success in reading. Very few children who are reading adequately are retained, assigned to special education, or given long-term remedial services. Other subjects are important, of course, but reading and language arts form the core of what school success means in the early grades.

When a child fails to read well in the early grades, he or she begins a downward progression. In first grade, some children begin to notice that they are not reading adequately. They may fail first grade or be assigned to long-term remediation. As they proceed through the elementary grades, many students begin to see that they are failing at their full-time jobs. When this happens, things begin to unravel. Failing students begin to have poor motivation and poor self-expectations, which leads to continued poor achievement, in a declining spiral that ultimately leads to despair, delinquency, and dropout.

Remediating learning deficits after they are already well established is extremely difficult. Children who have already failed to learn to read, for example, are now anxious about reading, and doubt their ability to learn it. Their motivation to read may be low. They may ultimately learn to read but it will always be a chore, not a pleasure. Clearly, the time to provide additional help to children who are at risk is early, when children are still motivated and confident, and when any learning deficits are relatively small and remediable. The most important goal in educational programming for students at risk of school failure is to try to make certain that we do not squander the greatest resource we have: the enthusiasm and positive self-expectations of young children themselves.

In practical terms, what this perspective implies is that schools, and especially Title I, special education, and other services for at-risk children, must be shifted from an emphasis on remediation to an emphasis on prevention and early intervention. Prevention means providing developmentally appropriate preschool and kindergarten programs so that students will enter first grade ready to succeed, and it means providing regular classroom teachers with effective instructional programs, curricula, and professional development to enable them to see that most students are successful the first time they are taught. Early intervention means that supplementary instructional services are provided early in students' schooling and that they are intensive enough to bring at-risk students quickly to a level at which they can profit from good-quality classroom instruction.

The purpose of this book is to describe a program built around the idea that every child can and must succeed in the early grades, no matter what this takes. The name of this program is Success for All. The idea behind Success for All is to use everything we know about effective instruction for students at risk to direct all aspects of school and classroom organization toward the goal of preventing academic deficits from appearing in the first place; to recognize and intensively intervene with any deficits that do appear; and to provide students with a rich and full curriculum to enable them to build on their firm foundation in basic skills. The commitment of Success for All is to do whatever it takes to see that every child becomes a skilled, strategic, and enthusiastic reader by the end of the elementary grades.

Usual practices in elementary schools do not support the principle of prevention and early intervention emphasized in Success for All. Most elementary schools provide a pretty good kindergarten, a pretty good first grade, and so on. Starting in first grade, a certain number of students begin to fall behind, and over the course of time these students are assigned to remedial programs (such as Title I) or to special education, or are simply retained.

Our society's tacit assumption is that those students who fall by the wayside are defective in some way. Perhaps they have learning disabilities, or low IQs, or poor motivation, or parents who are unsupportive of school learning, or other problems. We assume that because most students do succeed with standard pretty good instruction in the early grades, there must be something wrong with those who do not.

Success for All is built around a completely different set of assumptions. The most important assumption is that every child can learn. We mean this not as wishful thinking or as a rallying cry, but as a practical, attainable reality. In particular, every child without organic retardation can learn to read. Some children need more help than others and may need different approaches than those needed by others, but one way or another every child can become a successful reader.

The first requirement for the success of every child is *prevention*. This means providing excellent preschool and kindergarten programs; improving curriculum, instruction, and classroom management throughout the grades; assessing students frequently to make sure they are making adequate progress; and establishing cooperative relationships with parents so they can support students' learning at home.

Top-quality curriculum and instruction from age 4 on will ensure the success of most students, but not all of them. The next requirement for the success of *all* students is *intensive early intervention*. This means one-to-one tutoring by certified teachers for first graders having reading problems. It means being able to work with parents and social service agencies to be sure that all students attend school, have medical services or eyeglasses if they need them, have help with behavior problems, and so on.

The most important idea in Success for All is that the school must relentlessly stick with every child until that child is succeeding. If prevention is not enough, the child may need tutoring. If this is not enough, he or she may need help with behavior or attendance or eyeglasses. If this is not enough, he or she may need a modified approach to reading. The school does not merely provide services to children, it constantly assesses the results of the services it provides and keeps varying or adding services until every child is successful.

Origins of Success for All

The development of the Success for All program began in 1986 as a response to a challenge made to our group at Johns Hopkins University by Baltimore's superintendent, Alice Pinderhughes, its school-board president, Robert Embry, and a former Maryland Secretary of Human Resources, Kalman "Buzzy" Hettleman. They asked us what it would take to ensure the success of every child in schools serving large numbers of disadvantaged students.

At the time, we were working on a book called *Effective Programs for Students at Risk* (Slavin, Karweit, & Madden, 1989), so we were very interested in this question. After many discussions, the superintendent asked us to go to the next step, to work with Baltimore's Elementary Division to actually plan a pilot program. We met for months with a planning committee, and finally produced a plan and selected a school to serve as a site. We began in September 1987 in an all-black school in which approximately 83% of students qualified for free lunch. Initially, the additional costs needed to fund the program came from a Chapter 2 grant, but the program was soon supported entirely by the same Chapter 1 funds received by all similar schools.

The first-year results were very positive (see Slavin, Madden, Karweit, Livermon, & Dolan, 1990). In comparison to matched control students, Success for All students had much higher reading scores, and retentions and special education placements were substantially reduced.

In 1988 to 1989, Success for All was substantially expanded in Baltimore, to a total of five schools. We also began implementation of Success for All at one of the poorest schools in Philadelphia, in which a majority of the students are Cambodian. This school gave us our first experience in adapting Success for All to meet the needs of limited-English proficient students. In 1990 to 1991, we developed a Spanish version of the Success for All reading program, called *Lee Conmigo,* and began to work in more bilingual schools. In 1992, we received a grant from the New American Schools Development Corporation (NASDC) to develop Roots and Wings, which adds constructivist math, science, and social studies to the reading and writing programs of Success for All. Roots and Wings is currently beginning to be disseminated widely.

In the course of developing and researching Success for All, we have learned a great deal about the process of change in schools serving disadvantaged students, as well as learning about the effects of the overall program and of many of its component parts. This book describes both our formal research and our informal hard-earned wisdom about elementary school reform. In more recent years, Success for All has grown exponentially. As of fall 1995, it is in about 300 schools in 70 districts in 23 states throughout the United States. The districts range from some of the largest in the country, such as Baltimore, Houston, Memphis, Philadelphia, Cincinnati, Cleveland, Chicago, New York, and Miami; to such middle-sized districts as Montgomery, Alabama; Rockford, Illinois; and Modesto and Riverside, California; to tiny rural districts, including two on the Navajo reservation in Arizona. Success for All reading curricula in Spanish have been developed and researched and are used in bilingual programs in California, Texas, Arizona, Florida, Illinois, New York, New Jersey, and Philadelphia. Almost all Success for All schools are high-poverty Title I schools, and the great majority are schoolwide projects. Otherwise, the schools vary widely.

Overview of Success for All Components

The elements of Success for All are described in detail in the early chapters of this book, but before we get to the particulars it is useful to see the big picture. Success for All has somewhat different components at different sites, depending on the school's needs and resources available to implement the program (adapted from Slavin, Madden, Karweit, Livermon, & Dolan, 1990). There is, however, a common set of elements characteristic of all.

Reading Program

Success for All uses a reading curriculum based on research and effective practices in beginning reading (e.g., Adams, 1990), and an appropriate use of cooperative learning (Slavin, 1995; Stevens, Madden, Slavin, & Farnish, 1987).

Reading teachers at every grade level begin the reading time by reading children's literature to students and engaging them in a discussion of the story to enhance their understanding of the story, listening and speaking vocabulary, and knowledge of story structure. In kindergarten and first grade, the program emphasizes development of basic language skills with the use of Story Telling and Retelling (STaR), which involves the students in listening to, retelling, and dramatizing children's literature. Big books, as well as oral and written composing activities, allow students to develop concepts of print as they also develop knowledge of story structure. Peabody Language Development Kits are used to further develop receptive and expressive language.

Reading Roots (Madden, 1995) is introduced in the second semester of kindergarten. This K-1 beginning reading program uses as its base a series of phonetically regular but meaningful and interesting minibooks and emphasizes repeated oral reading to partners as well as to the teacher. The minibooks begin with a set of "shared stories," in which part of a story is written in small type (read by the teacher) and part is written in large type (read by the students). The student portion uses a phonetically controlled vocabulary. Taken together, the teacher and student portions create interesting, worthwhile stories. Over time, the teacher portion diminishes and the student portion lengthens, until students are reading the entire book. This scaffolding allows students to read interesting literature when they only have a few letter sounds. Examples of shared stories appear in Appendix 2.1 and 2.2.

Letters and letter sounds are introduced in an active, engaging set of activities that begins with oral language and moves into written symbols. Individual sounds are integrated into a context of words, sentences, and stories. Instruction is provided in story structure, specific comprehension skills, metacognitive strategies for self-assessment and self-correction, and integration of reading and writing.

Spanish bilingual programs use an adaptation of *Reading Roots* called *Lee Conmigo* ("Read With Me") (Madden, Livermon, & Rice, 1994). *Lee Conmigo* uses the same instructional strategies as *Reading Roots,* but is built around the Macmillan *Campanitas de Oro* series.

When students reach the primer reading level, they use a program called *Reading Wings* (Madden et al., 1996), an adaptation of Cooperative Integrated Reading and Composition (CIRC) (Stevens et al., 1987). *Reading Wings* uses cooperative learning activities built around story structure, prediction, summarization, vocabulary building, decoding practice, and story-related writing. Students engage in partner reading and structured discussion of stories or novels, and work toward mastery of the vocabulary and content of the story in teams. Story-related writing is also shared within teams. Cooperative learning both increases students' motivation and engages students in cognitive activities known to contribute to reading comprehension, such as elaboration, summarization, and rephrasing (see Slavin, 1995). Research on CIRC has found it to significantly increase students' reading comprehension and language skills (Stevens et al., 1987).

In addition to these story-related activities, teachers provide direct instruction in reading comprehension skills, and students practice these skills in their teams. Classroom libraries of trade books at students' reading levels are provided for each teacher, and students read books of their choice for homework for 20 minutes each night. Home readings are shared via presentations, summaries, puppet shows, and other formats twice a week during "book club" sessions.

Materials to support *Reading Wings* through the sixth grade (or beyond) exist in English and Spanish. The English materials are built around children's literature and around the most widely used basal series and anthologies. Supportive materials have been developed for more than 100 children's novels and for most current basal series (e.g., Houghton Mifflin, Scott Foresman, Holt, HBJ, Macmillan, McGraw Hill, Silver Burdett-Ginn, Open Court). Spanish materials (Madden et al., 1996) are similarly built around Spanish-language novels and the *Campanitas* basal program and other basal series.

Beginning in the second semester of program implementation, Success for All schools usually implement a writing/language arts program based primarily on cooperative learning principles (see Slavin, Madden, & Stevens, 1989/1990). The reading and writing/language arts programs are described in more detail in Chapter 2.

Students in Grades 1 to 3 (and sometimes 4 to 6, as well) are regrouped for reading. The students are assigned to heterogeneous, age-grouped classes with class sizes of about 25 most of the day, but during a regular 90-minute reading period they are regrouped by reading performance levels into reading classes of students all at the same level. For example, a 2-1 reading class might contain first, second, and third grade students all reading at the same level. The reading classes are smaller than homerooms because tutors and other certificated staff (such as librarians or art teachers) teach reading during this common reading period.

Regrouping allows teachers to teach the whole reading class without having to break the class into reading groups. This greatly reduces the time spent in seatwork and increases direct instruction time, eliminating workbooks, dittos, or other follow-up activities that are needed in classes that have multiple reading groups. The regrouping is a form of the Joplin Plan, which has been found to increase reading achievement in the elementary grades (Slavin, 1987).

Eight-Week Reading Assessments

At 8-week intervals, reading teachers assess student progress through the reading program. The results of the assessments are used to determine who is to receive tutoring, to change students' reading groups, to suggest other adaptations in students' programs, and to identify students who need other types of assistance, such as family interventions or screening for vision and hearing problems. This process is described further in Chapter 2.

Reading Tutors

One of the most important elements of the Success for All model is the use of tutors to promote students' success in reading. One-to-one tutoring is the most effective form of instruction known (see Slavin, Karweit, & Madden, 1989; Wasik & Slavin, 1993). The tutors are certified teachers with experience teaching Title 1, special education, primary reading, or all three. Often, well-qualified paraprofessionals also tutor children who have less severe reading problems. Tutors work one-on-one with students who are having difficulties keeping up with their reading groups. The tutoring occurs in 20-minute sessions during times other than reading or math periods.

In general, tutors support students' success in the regular reading curriculum, rather than teaching different objectives. For example, the tutor generally works with a student on the same story and concepts being read and taught in the regular reading class. Tutors, however, seek to identify learning problems and use different strategies to teach the same skills. They also teach metacognitive skills beyond those taught in the classroom program (Wasik & Madden, 1995). Schools may have as many as six or more teachers serving as tutors depending on school size, need for tutoring, and other factors.

During daily 90-minute reading periods, certified tutors serve as additional reading teachers to reduce class size for reading. Reading teachers and tutors use brief forms to communicate about students' specific problems and needs and meet at regular times to coordinate their approaches with individual children.

Initial decisions about reading group placement and the need for tutoring are based on informal reading inventories that the tutors give to each child. Subsequent reading group placements and tutoring assignments are made based on curriculum-based assessments given every 8 weeks, which include teacher judgments as well as more formal assessments. First graders receive priority for tutoring, on the assumption that the primary function of the tutors is to help all students be successful in reading the first time, before they fail and become remedial readers. Tutoring procedures are described in more detail in Chapter 3.

Preschool and Kindergarten

Most Success for All schools provide a half-day preschool, a full-day kindergarten, or both for eligible students. The preschool and kindergarten programs (Wasik, Bond, & Waclawiw, 1995) focus on providing a balanced and developmentally appropriate learning experience for young children. The curriculum emphasizes the development and use of language. It provides a balance of academic readiness and nonacademic music, art, and movement activities in a series of thematic units. Readiness activities include use of the Peabody Language Development Kits and Story Telling and Retelling (STaR) in which students retell stories read by the teachers (Karweit & Coleman, 1991). Prereading activities begin during the second semester of kindergarten. Preschool and kindergarten programs are described further in Chapter 4.

Family Support Team ·

Parents are an essential part of the formula for success in Success for All. A Family Support Team (Haxby, Lasaga-Flister, Madden, Slavin, & Dolan, 1995) works in each school, serving to make families feel comfortable in the school and become active supporters of their child's education as well as providing specific services. The Family Support Team consists of the Title I parent liaison, vice-principal (if any), counselor (if any), facilitator, and any other appropriate staff already present in the school or added to the school staff.

The Family Support Team first works toward creating good relations with parents and increasing their involvement in the schools. Family Support Team members may complete "welcome" visits for new families. They organize many attractive programs in the school, such as parenting skills workshops. Many schools use a program called "Raising Readers" in which parents are given strategies to use in reading to their own children.

The Family Support Team also intervenes to solve problems. For example, they may contact parents whose children are frequently absent to see what resources can be provided to assist the family in getting their child to school. Family support staff, teachers, and parents work together to solve school behavior problems. Also, family support staff are called on to provide assistance when students seem to be working at less than their full potential because of problems at home. Families of students who are not receiving adequate sleep or nutrition, need glasses, are not attending school regularly, or are exhibiting serious behavior problems, may receive family support assistance.

The Family Support Team is strongly integrated into the academic program of the school. It receives referrals from teachers and tutors regarding children who are not making adequate academic progress, and thereby constitutes an additional stage of intervention for students in need above and beyond that provided by the classroom teacher or tutor. The Family Support Team also encourages and trains the parents to fulfill numerous volunteer roles within the school, ranging from providing a listening ear to emerging readers to helping in the school cafeteria. Family support and integrated services are described further in Chapter 6.

Program Facilitator

A program facilitator (Madden, Cummings, & Livingston, 1995) works at each school to oversee (with the principal) the operation of the Success for All model. The facilitator helps plan the Success for All program, helps the principal with scheduling, and visits classes and tutoring sessions frequently to help teachers and tutors with individual problems. He or she works directly with the teachers on implementation of the curriculum, classroom management, and other issues, helps teachers and tutors deal with any behavior problems or other special problems, and coordinates the activities of the Family Support Team with those of the instructional staff. The role of the facilitator is described further in Chapter 7.

Teachers and Teacher Training

The teachers and tutors are regular certified teachers. They receive detailed teachers' manuals supplemented by 3 days of inservice at the beginning of the school year. For classroom teachers of Grades 1 through 3 and for reading tutors, these training sessions focus on implementation of the reading program, and their detailed teachers' manuals cover general teaching strategies as well as specific lessons. Preschool and kindergarten teachers and aides are trained in use of the STaR and Peabody programs, thematic units, and other aspects of the preschool and kindergarten models. Tutors later receive 2 additional days of training on tutoring strategies and reading assessment.

Throughout the year, additional inservice presentations are made by the facilitators and other project staff on such topics as classroom management, instructional pace, and cooperative learning. Facilitators also organize many informal sessions to allow teachers to share problems and problem solutions, suggest changes, and discuss individual children. The staff development model used in Success for All emphasizes relatively brief initial training with extensive classroom follow-up, coaching, and group discussion. Training and monitoring procedures are described further in Chapter 7.

Advisory Committee

An advisory committee composed of the building principal, program facilitator, teacher representatives, parent representatives, and family support staff meets regularly to review the progress of the program and to identify and solve any problems that arise. In most schools existing site-based management teams are adapted to fulfill this function. In addition, grade-level teams and the Family Support Team meet regularly to discuss common problems and solutions and to make decisions in their areas of responsibility. See Chapter 7 for more on this.

Special Education

Every effort is made to deal with students' learning problems within the context of the regular classroom, as supplemented by tutors. Tutors evaluate students' strengths and weaknesses and develop strategies to teach in the most effective way. In some schools, special education teachers work as tutors and reading teachers with students identified as learning disabled, as well as with other students experiencing learning problems who are at risk for special education placement. One major goal of Success for All is to keep students with learning problems out of special education if at all possible, and to serve any students who do qualify for special education in a way that does not disrupt their regular classroom experience (see Slavin, 1996; Slavin et al., 1991). Implications of Success for All for special education are described in Chapter 9.

Relentlessness

Although the particular elements of Success for All may vary from school to school, there is one feature we try to make consistent in all: a relentless focus on the success of every child. It would be entirely possible to have tutoring and curriculum change, and have family support, and other services, yet still not ensure the success of at-risk children. Success does not come from piling on additional services but from coordinating human resources around a well-defined goal, constantly assessing progress toward that goal, and never giving up until success is achieved.

Roots and Wings

In 1991, we received a grant from New American Schools Development Corporation (NASDC) to create a comprehensive elementary school design for the 21st century. We call the program we designed under NASDC funding Roots and Wings (see Chapter 5). Roots and Wings incorporates revisions of all of the elements of Success for All—reading, writing, and language arts programs, prekindergarten and kindergarten programs, tutoring, family support, and so on—but adds to these a completely new program in mathematics, Math-Wings, and a new program that integrates social studies and science, which we call WorldLab.

WorldLab

WorldLab is an integrated curriculum for science, social studies, and writing, used in Grades 1 through 5. In it, students take on roles as people in history, in other countries, or in various occupations. For example, fifth graders learn about the American Revolution by participating in the writing of their own "declaration of independence" and by serving as delegates to the Constitutional Convention. Fourth graders learn about physics by creating and testing inventions. Third graders learn about the culture of Africa and about simple machines by serving as a council of elders in an African village trying to design a system for irrigating their fields. First and second graders learn scientific method by becoming scientists collecting and integrating information about trees. WorldLab units incorporate writing, reading, math, fine arts, and music, as well as science and social studies. Children work in small, cooperative groups, and carry out experiments, investigations, and projects.

MathWings

Roots and Wings schools use a constructivist mathematics program called MathWings in Grades 1 through 5. In this program, based on the standards of the National Council of Teachers of Mathematics, students work in cooperative groups to discover, experiment with, and apply mathematical ideas. The program builds on the practical knowledge base with which all children enter school, helping children build toward formal representations of such familiar ideas as combining and separating, dividing into equal parts, and parts of a whole. It incorporates problem solving in real and simulated situations (including WorldLab), skill practice, calculator use, alternative assessments, writing, and connections to literature and other disciplines. Children learn not only to find the right answer but to explain and apply their new understandings.

None of the elements of Success for All or Roots and Wings are completely new or unique. All are based on well-established principles of learning and rigorous instructional research. What is most distinctive about them is their schoolwide, coordinated, and proactive plan for translating positive expectations into concrete success for all children. Every child can complete elementary school a confident, strategic, and joyful learner and can maintain the enthusiasm and positive self-expectations they had when they came to first grade. The purpose of Success for All and Roots and Wings is to see that this vision becomes a practical reality in every school.

2

Reading and Writing/
Language Arts Programs

Although Success for All and Roots and Wings ultimately incorporate reform in most of the elementary school curriculum and instruction, the heart of the instructional program is reading. The reason for this is obvious; in the early grades, success in school is virtually synonymous with success in reading. Very few primary grade students are retained or assigned to special education solely on the basis of deficits in math performance, for example. A child who can read is not guaranteed to be a success in elementary school, but a child who cannot is guaranteed to be a failure.

The amount of reading failure in the early grades in schools serving disadvantaged students is shocking. In our studies of Success for All, we have consistently found that at the end of first grade about a quarter of students in our control schools cannot read and comprehend the following passage:

> I have a little black dog. He has a pink nose. He has a little tail. He can jump and run. (Durrell & Catterson, 1980, p. 1)

On the 1989-1990 National Assessment of Educational Progress, only 34% of African American 9-year-olds and 41% of Hispanic 9-year-olds could read at the "basic" level, compared to 66% of whites (National Center for Education Statistics, 1993). In many urban districts, retention rates for first graders have topped 20% in recent years. What these statistics mean is that despite some improvements over the past 20 years, the reading performance of disadvantaged and minority children is still seriously lacking, and the deficits begin early. The consequences of early reading failure are severe. A child who is not reading adequately by the end of third grade is headed for serious trouble.

11

The philosophy that guides the development of the reading curriculum in Success for All emphasizes the need for reading instruction to work for *all* students. We recognize that different children learn to read in different ways, so our approach emphasizes teaching reading many different ways at the same time. For example, each beginning reading lesson has students reading silently and aloud, singing, tracing letters with their fingers, writing, making visual and auditory discriminations, discussing stories, making predictions, using context clues, and engaging in many other activities. Teaching the same concepts and skills in many different ways both provides reinforcement and allows the curriculum to use the learning strengths of every child.

Grouping

Homeroom classes in Success for All/Roots and Wings are fully heterogeneous. To have enough instructional time to be able to teach reading in many different ways, however, students are regrouped for reading across grade lines according to reading level, so that all reading classes contain just one level. For example, a reading class working at an early second grade level might contain first, second, and third graders all reading at the same level. During reading time (90 minutes per day), additional teachers are available to teach reading because certified tutors (and in some schools, media specialists, special education or ESL teachers) teach a reading class. This means that reading classes are smaller than homeroom classes. On the basis of regular curriculum-based assessments given every 8 weeks, reading group assignments are constantly reexamined (see the following). Students capable of working in a higher-performing group are accelerated, whereas those who are not performing adequately are given tutoring, family support services, modifications in curriculum or instruction, or other services to help them keep up.

There are many reasons for cross-class and cross-grade grouping for reading in Success for All. First, having all students at one reading level avoids any need for the use of reading groups within the class. The problem with reading groups is that when the teacher is working with one group, the other groups are at their desks doing seatwork or other independent tasks of little instructional value. To have a full 90 minutes of active, productive, instruction, having only one reading group is essential. Research on cross-grade grouping for reading, often called the Joplin Plan, has shown that this method increases student achievement (Slavin, 1987).

In addition, use of cross-class and cross-grade grouping allows the use of tutors and other certified staff as reading teachers. This has many benefits. First, it reduces class size for reading, which has small but consistent benefits for achievement in the early grades (Slavin, 1994). Perhaps of equal importance, it gives tutors and other supplementary teachers experience in teaching the reading program, so that they know exactly what their students are experiencing. When a student is struggling with Lesson 37, the tutor knows what Lesson 37 is, because he or she has taught it.

Eight-Week Assessments

A critical feature of reading instruction in Success for All at all grade levels is assessment of student progress every 8 weeks. These assessments are closely linked to the curriculum. In the early grades they may include some written and some oral assessments; in the later grades they use written assessments keyed to novels (if the school uses novels) or may use "magazine tests" or other assessments provided with basal series (if the school uses basals). Eight-week assessments usually include assessments of skills above students' current level of performance to facilitate decisions to accelerate students to a higher reading group.

Eight-week assessments are used for three essential purposes. One is to change students' reading groupings, to identify students capable of being accelerated. A second is to decide which students are in the greatest need for tutoring and which no longer need tutoring (see

Chapter 3). Finally, the 8-week assessments provide an internal check on the progress of every child. They can indicate to school staff that a given student is not making adequate progress, and lead them to try other strategies.

The 8-week assessments are given and scored by reading teachers but are collated and interpreted by the facilitator, who uses them to review the progress of all children and to suggest changes in grouping, tutoring assignments, or other approaches to the reading teachers. See Chapter 6 for more on this topic.

Reading Approaches

The Success for All reading approach is divided into two programs. Reading Roots (Madden, 1995) is usually introduced either in the middle of kindergarten or the beginning of first grade, depending on the district's goals for kindergarten. Reading Roots continues through what would usually be thought of as the first reader, and is usually completed in early spring or by the end of first grade. Reading Roots replaces the usual basals and workbooks with a completely different set of materials. Bilingual schools choosing to teach beginning reading to their Spanish speaking students in Spanish use Lee Conmigo, which uses the same instructional strategies and processes as Reading Roots but is built around stories and materials in Spanish.

Starting at the early second grade level, students go on to what we call Reading Wings, which continues through the fifth or sixth grade. Reading Wings (Madden et al., 1996) uses the district's usual basals, anthologies, novels, or all three but replaces workbooks and other supplementary materials with a student-centered cooperative learning process that focuses on developing comprehension skills. Reading Wings involves students in many kinds of active interaction with reading, discussion, and writing. The Reading Wings process can also be used with Spanish novels or basals.

Reading Roots, Lee Conmigo, and Reading Wings are described in the following sections.

Reading Roots

There is both magic and method in learning to read. Students come to school knowing that learning to read will be their most important task, and that it will be an exciting step in growing up. Taught with effective methods, every child can experience the magic of reading and become a confident, joyful, and strategic reader by the end of first grade.

The Reading Roots program (Madden, 1995) used in Success for All is based on research that points to the need to have students learn to read in meaningful contexts and at the same time to have a systematic presentation of word attack skills (see Adams, 1990). Three basic components, reading of children's literature by the teacher, "shared story" beginning reading lessons, and systematic language development, combine to address the learning needs of first graders in a variety of ways. Teachers read to students every day using children's literature to expose them to the joy and meaning of reading as well as concepts of print.

Building Listening Comprehension

A major principle of Reading Roots is that students need to learn comprehension strategies at a level *above* their current independent reading level. What this means is that the teacher reads children's literature to students and engages students in discussions, retelling of the stories, and writing. The idea is to build reading comprehension skill with material more difficult than that which students could read on their own, because in the early grades material children can read independently does not challenge their far more advanced comprehension skills. This process begins in preschool and kindergarten with the Story

Telling and Retelling (STaR) program, and STaR continues through part of the first grade. At that point, students begin a Listening Comprehension program (Stevens & Shaw, 1990) in which teachers continue to read to children and teach them to identify characters, settings, problems, and problem solutions in narratives; to visualize descriptive elements of stories; to identify sequences of events; to predict story outcomes; to identify topics and main ideas in expository selections, and so on. The STaR process is described in more detail in Chapter 4.

Building Reading Strategies

Before entering Reading Roots, or early in the program, we expect that students have developed basic concepts about print, are beginning to understand that letters and words represent speech and are meant to communicate a message with meaning, that print progresses from left to right, that spoken and written words are made up of sounds, and so on. These concepts continue to be developed with story telling (STaR) and are reinforced as students begin to take on the task of reading for themselves in Reading Roots lessons. More specific knowledge of auditory discrimination, hearing sounds within words, knowledge of the sounds associated with specific letters, and blending letter sounds into words are developed in Reading Roots lessons so that students understand the phonetic nature of language and can independently use phonetic synthesis to help them read.

The shared story beginning reading curriculum emphasizes immediate application of skills to real reading. For example, students read an entire book in the first lesson. Reading Roots lessons are structured and fast-paced, involving activities that enable students to learn the new sounds and words introduced in the story thoroughly and quickly. In addition, the lessons develop general strategies for facilitating both word recognition and text comprehension so that students become independent, thinking readers who experience the joy of reading. These strategies include using context and pictures to unlock words and meaning, building knowledge of the purposes for reading, and previewing, self-questioning, and summarizing, which allow students to monitor their own comprehension.

The activities in Reading Roots are built on the following concepts:

Shared Stories. Shared Stories allow students to read complex, engaging, and interesting stories when they only know a few letter sounds. Each page in a Shared Story has both a teacher section and a student section. Beginning in Lesson 4, the students' portions of the shared stories use a phonetically regular vocabulary, so that the skills students are learning will work in cracking the reading code. The student sections use only the letter sounds and words students have learned and a few key sight words and "Readles," words represented by pictures. The teacher sections provide a context for the story and include predictive questions that are answered in the student sections. In the earliest stories, the teacher text adds a great deal to the meaning of the stories; but over time, the student sections increase while the teacher sections diminish. This "scaffolding" method allows children to read meaningful and worthwhile stories from the first weeks of their beginning reading instruction. As they learn systematic strategies for finding the meaning of words, sentences, and stories, students take increasing responsibility for their reading. Soon they are able to unlock the reading code and join the wacky world of Matt and his dog, Sad Sam, the world's most phonetically regular hound dog; Miss Sid, the pesky parrot; Nan and her cat, Pit-Pat; and many other engaging characters. Later, students meet Lana and her huge dog, Fang; Paco and his mischievous friend, Bob; finally, they experience a world of fairy tales and stories from many cultures. By the end of the Shared Story sequence, pictures within the text and adult text are no longer used. A sample page from a shared story presented in the early part of the sequence and another presented in the latter part are shown in Figures 2.1 and 2.2, and complete shared stories appear in Appendixes 2.1 and 2.2 at the end of this chapter.

2   Scott and Tanya look for the ball in the bushes while Lana looks on the other side of the playground. Suddenly, Scott sees something. What is it?

"Look, Tanya!" gasps Scott.

Tanya looks.

She sees a big fat dog.

The dog runs fast.

It bumps into Tanya.

She sits in the mud.

Figure 2.1.

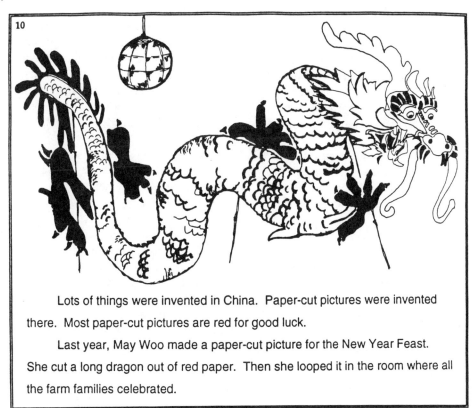

Lots of things were invented in China. Paper-cut pictures were invented there. Most paper-cut pictures are red for good luck.

Last year, May Woo made a paper-cut picture for the New Year Feast. She cut a long dragon out of red paper. Then she looped it in the room where all the farm families celebrated.

Figure 2.2.

The shared stories in Reading Roots are organized into four thematically related sections. Level 1, stories 1 through 15, is built around a first grader named Matt, his dog Sad Sam, and his friends in the neighborhood. Level 2, stories 16 through 25, describes the experiences of a group of students in Ms. Stanton's first grade class. Level 3, stories 26 through 37, focuses around a group of city children, and their visits to relatives in the country as the seasons change throughout the year. Level 4, stories 38 through 48, takes students around the world as it introduces both traditional folk and fairy tales and expository text. Expository narratives present facts about Sweden, Benin (Nigeria), China, Colombia, and the United States. Each factual story is followed by a tale from that country. Level 4 presents a very challenging reading experience that is designed to make the transition between the carefully sequenced Reading Roots lessons and the novels or basals that students will use in Reading Wings.

Cooperative Learning. Working cooperatively with other students provides children with an opportunity to discuss the concepts and skills they are learning with someone very close to their own level of understanding. In Reading Roots, students confer with their partners as they think of words that begin with a certain sound, as they predict the next event in a story, and as they orally read and reread new and familiar stories. These cooperative learning activities provide opportunities for students to explain their understanding to someone else, thus requiring them to organize their own thoughts. Simple peer practice routines are used throughout the lessons as a means of reinforcing and building mastery of basic reading skills. Students read and discuss their stories with partners and work with partners on reading practice activities. These activities increase the amount of time that each student can be actively engaged with text rather than passively listening as other students read. Opportunities for partner discussion of the story and of story-related writing increase the active thinking time for students.

Metacognitive Strategies Instruction. Metacognitive skills are emphasized throughout Reading Roots to help students think about the process of reading, to predict what is going to happen in a story, to assess their own comprehension, and to know how to find meaning when they experience difficulties. Four main strategies used to enhance text comprehension are taught and practiced in the context of the Shared Stories: understanding the purposes for reading, previewing to prepare for reading, monitoring for meaning to ensure that the text is understood, and summarization or retelling of the main ideas or events of a story.

Choral Response Games. During direct instruction, students are involved in games in which the class responds as a whole to questions. The students have a great deal of fun with these activities, and are all involved in thinking and responding. Students need not spend time waiting while others respond one at a time.

Auditory Discrimination and Sound Blending. The activities in these lessons are designed to build auditory discrimination (hearing the separate sounds in words) and sound-blending skills in a developmental sequence, so that students will be able to use sound blending as a strategy to aid them in word recognition. With systematic teaching, students become adept at using sound-blending strategies in addition to memory, context, and pictures to unlock the meaning of words and stories. Sound-blending instruction gives a real boost to the many students whose visual memory skills are not strong, a group that often includes students who would fail in reading without this kind of systematic approach to unlocking the reading code.

Writing. Students are encouraged to write to reinforce their learning and to express their response to stories. Writing activities may vary from completing simple letter and word writing activities that reinforce letter shapes and sounds, to answering specific questions about a story, writing personal experiences similar to those in a story, sharing feelings about characters, and summarizing story events. Sound-based spelling is explicitly taught, and teachers are encouraged to respond to the meaning of the ideas students express rather than to errors in spelling or punctuation. Peers assist one another in the writing process as they share their plans and drafts with one another, revise based on peers' suggestions, and celebrate each others' writing.

A Reading Roots Lesson

A 90-minute Reading Roots lesson has three major parts—a STaR or Listening Comprehension unit, the shared story lesson, and a Peabody unit. Each day begins with a 20-minute STaR lesson, in which the teacher reads and discusses a story. An example of a STaR lesson appears in Chapter 4. The 50-minute shared story lesson (description follows) would be followed by a 20-minute Peabody lesson, also described in Chapter 4. The activities in a shared story lesson would usually be completed over 2 or 3 days of reading instruction, depending on the time needed by the particular group to master the story.

The goals for specific activities in Reading Roots are discussed later, along with some specific instructions on effectively implementing the program. As students progress through the sequence, some of the activities described will no longer be used, but the basic parts of the lesson will remain. The materials and activities for each lesson are explained in detail in the actual lessons. Lessons are presented over 2 or 3 days, depending on the levels and abilities of the students.

Showtime (Reading Rehearsal and Letter Formation Review)

Review and practice are essential elements in acquiring proficiency in any skill area. Review segments are spread throughout the Reading Roots lesson because this structured practice is essential for the development of fluency with letters, sounds, and words.

Reading Rehearsal. In Reading Rehearsal, students reread a familiar story either in pairs or in a whole-class choral reading. The purpose of this Reading Rehearsal is to reinforce the concept that *real reading* is what reading instruction is all about. Children need to learn early that the essence of reading is the whole act of reading, not a series of unconnected skills. The Reading Rehearsal segment allows students to master reading through repeated practice, to learn words in context rather than through reading word lists, and to master the flow and phrasing of reading necessary to comprehend what is being read.

Letter Formation Review. Introduced in Lesson 2, Letter Formation Review provides practice in sound and name recognition, and in formation of known letters, by using standard cue phrases (e.g., "One stroke down, lift and cross. The sound for 't' is /t/."). This provides the practice needed to assist students in making an automatic association between the formation of the letter and its name and sound. In later lessons, as students become fluent in individual letters, words and even sentences are used as the basis for a brief written review.

Metacognitive Strategies

Thinking About Reading. The focus of Thinking About Reading is to teach students why, when, and how to use metacognitive reading strategies that will help them ask themselves whether they are understanding what they read, recognize if they are not, and know how to find the meaning. Metacognition is the awareness and comprehension of one's own thinking.

Successful readers use metacognitive strategies to help them effectively read and comprehend. The four strategies presented in Reading Roots include the following: understanding the purpose for reading, previewing to prepare for reading, monitoring for meaning, and summarization. These strategies are presented in the context of reading.

Presenting the Story

Setting the Stage. The teacher reads the story to the class as the first presentation of the story. As a part of the initial reading, the teacher provides a broad context for the story by giving background information, adding comments and questions, and requesting predictions to guide students' thoughts about the story.

Sound, Letter, and Word Development Activities

The focus of these activities is to teach students to discriminate sounds in language and to know the shapes of the letters and the sounds that they represent. The lessons are designed to begin with the isolation of specific sounds within the context of meaningful language; then, to teach sound/letter correspondence using a wide variety of practice techniques; and finally, to apply those techniques directly to the words to be read in the story. The steps involved in the presentation and practice of each sound and letter are now described.

Alphabet Song. Sound/letter/word activities center around a character named Alphie, who brings messages and materials each day to help the class learn letters and sounds. The class sings the alphabet song to entice Alphie, a puppet, to come out of his box each day. The repetition of the alphabet song motivates and gives students an opportunity to hear the names of the letters regularly, and thus to become familiar with them and with the order of letters in the alphabet. The alphabet song chosen should be brief.

Letter Presentation

The following activities are used to present the letter's name and sound.

Two-Picture Game. In this game, students practice hearing the new sound through the use of pictures. Two pictures are presented at once, and students as a group are asked to say the names of the pictures and identify which picture starts with the letter or letter combination being taught. This game again develops the skill of hearing a specific sound in a meaningful word, and separating it from other sounds in the word.

Hearing the Sound. Each sound is introduced with a sentence, called the Tongue Twister. It is presented as a message from Alphie, which uses that sound in several words. For instance, you will introduce the "/d/" sound by having the teacher reading Alphie's note: "Today, Alphie has written a silly note about dogs like Sad Sam. Many words begin with the sound /d/: Dizzy dogs dig doughnuts during December."
Students enjoy this procedure and learn that they can use the strategy of saying the word with the first sound separated as a way of hearing how a word starts. It is important to note that sounds are presented as parts of meaningful words, so that students use their own knowledge of language as a basis.

Introducing Pictures and Objects. Next, Alphie provides a set of pictures or objects that begin with the sound being taught. For the "/d/" sound, Alphie presents the pictures: Dad, dog, duck, and dishes, as well as any actual objects the teacher provides. Students name the pictures or objects, and identify the beginning sound for each one.

Making the Sound. The shape of the mouth while producing the sound is identified next. Focusing on the shape of the mouth gives students another cue to help them hear and "see" the separate sounds. As they learn to feel the changes in the shape of their mouths and watch the teacher's mouth, they will more clearly understand the concept that words are made up of groups of sounds. This understanding is crucial for decoding. Later, as they begin to write words, students will be able to use the feeling of change between sounds as an important way to recognize separate sounds.

Introducing the Shape. Finally, after many different kinds of practice in hearing and separating the sounds that have been learned, the students are ready for the introduction of the letter shape that identifies the sound. Up to this point, the letter name has not been used. Words have been referred to as having the "/d/" sound.

Practicing the Shape. The shape of the letter is practiced using several multisensory routines. Each letter has a verbal pattern associated with it that guides the student through the formation of the letter. For instance, the pattern for the "/d/" sound is: "Circle left, way up, back down."

Using a large letter on the board as a model, students use their "magic pencils" (their index fingers) to practice writing the letter in the air, on their desks, and on a partner's hand, arm, or back. The verbal pattern is repeated with each practice.

Letter Games

The following activities present a variety of game formats that focus on the letter sound being taught.

Say-It-Fast. This component gradually introduces the concept that letters represent sounds and sounds make words. The objective of this activity, also called "auditory sound blending" is to sharpen auditory awareness while helping students develop the ability to synthesize the sounds they hear into meaningful words. If a student cannot connect /b/-/e/-/d/ with the familiar word bed, then he or she will not be able to blend sounds into recognizable words. The activity has a game format and uses sentence context practice, along with a variety of familiar words. It prepares students for future work using sounds for reading and spelling.

Students' Words. In this step, students are asked to connect the sound concept they are learning to their own language and experience. Students are asked to select a word they know that starts with the sound they are studying.

Yes/No Game. The Yes/No Game provides a different kind of practice for students in separating sounds within real words. Students are shown a card and asked whether the name of the object on that card begins with the sound being studied. When students have mastered this they are given a word orally and asked whether the word begins with the letter being studied.

Matching Games. The Matching Games provide practice in sound/letter matching and auditory discrimination. The games begin simply and become more complex as the students gain proficiency. Four levels of games are used in teaching each letter. In each level, three sounds are represented and pictures or words using those sounds must be matched to them.

Story Activities

Word Presentation. In this segment, story words are introduced. The phonetically regular words are presented using Stretch and Read, and the sight words are presented using repetition or the context of the sentence in which the word is presented in the story.

Stretch and Read. Students learn that saying the sounds for letters in order (left to right) produces real words. This is done in a slow, exaggerated fashion at first and then, as students become proficient in letter/sound matching, becomes more of a rapid drill activity. Because the words presented in Stretch and Read are the words that students will use to read the story, the skill presented is immediately applicable in a meaningful reading situation. The Stretch and Read strategy will be familiar to them if they need to use a strategy besides memory and context to unlock a word as they read.

Quick Erase. This activity gives students an opportunity for a fun and fast-paced drill using letters and sounds they know from having practiced Stretch and Read. It involves changing one letter of a word at a time to create a new word—Tad becomes mad, mad becomes dad, and so forth. Quick Erase provides a way to explore word patterns and helps students generalize from known words to new words.

Say-Spell-Say. This is simply a repetition procedure to aid in memorization of important sight words. Sight words presented with the Say-Spell-Say process are pronouns, articles, prepositions, and so on.

Using Context. Students use context to unlock the meaning of some story words by analyzing the sentences in which they are found. Sight words commonly presented through context are nouns, verbs, adverbs, and adjectives.

Guided Group Reading. The story has been read to the group before; now the goal is to assist students in learning to read it by themselves. Students read the story first as a whole class. The teacher reads the story script again to add meaning to the students' text and to keep students focused on understanding what they are reading. Also, metacognitive strategies are reviewed during this segment.

Partner Reading. Students now reread the story with a partner. Each partner reads a page independently, receiving help from his or her partner if it is needed. Students are encouraged to use appropriate expression as they read. Students practice metacognitive strategies in this segment.

Share Sheets. Share Sheets are reading and writing activities designed to be used by pairs of students for practice and feedback on their reading and writing. Again, this partner practice increases the opportunities for giving and receiving explanations, as well as for oral reading and writing with feedback. All of the activities are story related. Share Sheets are practiced more than once. Eventually, they are taken home to be practiced further with parents and family members.

Spelling. After students have learned to say and read the new letter sound in words, sentences, and the shared story, they learn the correct spelling of the phonetic words.

Stretch and Count. This activity is a preliminary step in the spelling process. After students have had some practice with hearing individual sounds and sound blending, the concept of *auditory* sound/symbol correspondence is introduced. Students are taught to "stretch" simple words into their component sounds, and to make a count of the number of sounds in a word.

Stretch and Spell. This lesson segment develops the concept of spelling and using sounds to assist in spelling. Students stretch a word, identify the sounds one at a time, and write the letters they hear.

Celebration. At the end of each day, progress in reading is celebrated by having two students read a portion of a familiar story that they can read with expression.

A teacher's guide to Reading Roots Lesson 18 is included in Appendix 2.2 at the end of this chapter. Lesson 18 would be taught in the 2nd or 3rd month of the program.

Lee Conmigo

Lee Conmigo is built on the same principles as Reading Roots and uses the same lesson structure and instructional processes. The reading materials used for the original version of Lee Conmigo are the first grade materials for the Macmillan *Companitas de Oro* reading series. This series took advantage of the fact that written Spanish is highly phonetic, and developed stories that built on letter sounds and syllables one at a time, as do the Reading Roots stories. The stories are again enhanced by context provided in a teacher read portion of the story. Lee Conmigo lessons built around these stories teach both metacognitive and word attack skills using the same presentations, games, routines, and strategies as Reading Roots. As of this writing, a new version of Lee Conmigo is under development. This version will use a series of Spanish shared stories written specifically for Lee Conmigo.

The one significant difference between Lee Conmigo and Reading Roots lies in the frequent use of syllables (rather than individual letters) as the major unit of sound in Lee Conmigo. Within the Spanish language, words are essentially made up of groups of syllables rather than groups of individual letters. The games and activities in Lee Conmigo have been adapted to take advantage of this. For instance, in Stretch and Spell, words are stretched a syllable at a time (lla ma) rather than a letter at a time as in English (c a t). Lesson 19 of Lee Conmigo is included as Appendix 2.4 at the end of the chapter.

Reading Wings

Reading Wings (Madden et al., 1996) is the reading approach used in Success for All and Roots and Wings from the first reader level (usually spring of first grade) to the end of elementary school. It is an adaptation of Cooperative Integrated Reading and Composition (CIRC), a cooperative learning program that encompasses both reading and writing/language arts. Studies of CIRC have shown it to be effective in increasing students' reading, writing, and language achievement (Stevens, Madden, Slavin, & Farnish, 1987).

The curricular focus of Reading Wings is primarily on building comprehension and thinking skills, fluency, and pleasure in reading. Reading Wings assumes that students coming out of Reading Roots have solid word-attack skills, but need to build on this foundation to learn to understand and enjoy increasingly complex material.

As in Reading Roots, students in Reading Wings are regrouped for reading across grade lines, so a 3-1 reading class could be composed of second, third, and fourth graders. In addition, students are assigned to four- or five-member learning teams that are heterogeneous in performance level, sex, and age. These teams choose team names and sit together at most times. The teams have a responsibility to see that all team members are learning the material being taught in class. Each week, students take a set of quizzes. These contribute to a team score, and the teams can earn certificates and other recognition based on the team's average quiz scores. Students also contribute points to their teams by completing book reports and writing assignments, and by returning completed parent forms indicating that they have been reading at home each evening. Figure 2.3 shows a sample score sheet.

The main activities of Reading Wings are described in the following section (adapted from Madden et al., 1996).

TEAM SCORE SHEET

Team: **Reading Champs**   Week of: **February 6 -10**

Team Members	Story Test	Word Meaning Test	Words Out Loud Test	Reading Comp. Test	Adventures in Writing	Team Work Points	Book Report 1	Book Report 2	R & R Form	Average
Mary	100	95	100	90	90	90	95			94.3
Juan	90	90	100	85	95	90	100			92.9
Tamika	80	85	100	90	90	90	95	115 (95+20)	20	95.6
Roger	85	100	80	95	100	90	100		20	95.7

Monday	Tuesday	Wednesday	Thursday	Friday
20	20	15	20	15

Team Cooperation Points   *Supertan!*

TEAM TOTAL **378.5**

TEAM SCORE **94.6**

Figure 2.3. Sample Team Score Sheet

Story-Related Activities

Students use their regular basal readers, novels, anthologies, or whatever materials are available in the school. Guides, called Treasure Hunts, to accompany a large number of current basals and novels, including Spanish basals and novels, have been developed.

Stories are introduced and discussed by the teacher. During these lessons, teachers elicit and provide background knowledge, set a purpose for reading, introduce new vocabulary, review old vocabulary, discuss the story after students have read it, and so on. Presentation methods for each segment of the lesson are structured. For example, teachers are taught to use a vocabulary presentation procedure that requires a demonstration of understanding of word meaning by each individual, a review of methods of word attack, repetitive oral reading of vocabulary to achieve automaticity, and use of the meanings of the vocabulary words to help introduce the content of the story. Story discussions are structured to emphasize such skills as making and supporting predictions about the story and understanding major structural components of the story (e.g., problem and solution in a narrative).

After stories are introduced, students are given a series of activities to do in their teams when they are not working with the teacher in a reading group. The sequence of activities is as follows:

a. *Partner Reading.* Students read the story silently first, and then take turns reading the story aloud with their partners, alternating readers after each paragraph. As their partner reads, the listener follows along and corrects any errors the reader makes.

b. *Story Structure and Story-Related Writing.* Students are given questions related to each narrative story emphasizing the story structure (characters, setting, problem, and problem solution). Halfway through the story, they are instructed to stop reading and to identify the characters, the setting, and the problem in the story, and to predict how the problem will be resolved. At the end of the story students respond to the story as a whole and write a few paragraphs on a topic related to the story (e.g., they might be asked to write a different ending to the story).

c.   *Words Out Loud.* Students are given a list of new or difficult words used in the story that they must be able to read correctly in any order without hesitating or stumbling. These words are presented by the teacher in the reading group, and then students practice their lists with their partners or other teammates until they can read them smoothly.

d.   *Word Meaning.* Students are given a list of story words that are new in their speaking vocabularies and asked to write a sentence for each that shows the meaning of the word (i.e., "An *octopus* grabbed the swimmer with its 8 long legs," not "I have an *octopus*.") At higher grade levels, students are asked to look some of the words up in the dictionary and paraphrase the definition.

e.   *Story Retell.* After reading the story and discussing it in their reading groups, students summarize the main points of the story to their partners. The partners have a list of essential story elements that they use to check the completeness of the story summaries.

f.   *Spelling.* Students pretest one another on a list of spelling words each week, and then work over the course of the week to help one another master the list. Students use a "disappearing list" strategy in which they make new lists of missed words after each assessment until the list disappears and they can go back to the full list, repeating the process as many times as necessary.

Partner Checking. After students complete each of the activities listed previously, their partners initial a student assignment record form indicating that they have completed the criterion, achieved the criterion on that task, or both. Students are given daily expectations as to the number of activities to be completed, but they can go at their own rate and complete the activities earlier if they wish, creating additional time for independent reading (see later discussion).

Tests. At the end of three class periods, students are given a comprehension test on the story, are asked to write meaningful sentences for certain vocabulary words, and are asked to read the word list aloud to the teacher. Students are not permitted to help one another on these tests. The test scores and evaluations of the story-related writing are major components of student's weekly team scores.

The energy and excitement in Reading Wings comes from the teamwork. Students become very involved with their team members, and want to ensure that they are all succeeding. As students become more skilled, the discussion between partners and among team members becomes rich and challenging. Students no longer simply look for the right answer, they demand reasons and evidence to support answers. Books and stories come alive for students as they engage in meaningful discussion with their peers about their responses to their reading. Their enjoyment of reading grows at the same time as their skill and fluency with more and more complex material.

The teacher's edition of a sample Treasure Hunt for Chapter 1 of a story titled *Jumanji* is included in Appendix 2.5. The Reading Wings process for students reading in Spanish is the same as for students reading in English. The teacher's edition of a sample Spanish Treasure Hunt for Chapter 1 of a novel titled *Un Hatillo de Cerezas,* is included in Appendix 2.6.

Direct Instruction in Reading Comprehension

Students receive direct instruction from the teacher in reading comprehension skills such as identifying main ideas, drawing conclusions, and comparing and contrasting ideas. A special curriculum was designed for this purpose. After each lesson, students work on reading comprehension worksheets, games as a whole team, or both first gaining consensus on one set of worksheet items, then practicing independently, assessing one another's work, and discussing any remaining problems on a second set of items.

Independent Reading

Every evening, students are asked to read a trade book of their choice for at least 20 minutes. In most schools, classroom libraries of paperback books are established for this purpose. Parents initial forms indicating that students have read for the required time, and students contribute points to their teams if they submit a completed form each week. In a twice-weekly "book club," students discuss the books they have been reading and present more formal book reports, trying to entice others to take home the same book. "Book reports" can take many forms, from the completion of a brief summary form, to an oral summary, advertisements, puppet shows, or whatever other form the reader and teacher wish to use. Independent reading and book reports replace all other homework in reading and language arts. If students complete their story-related activities or other activities early, they may also read their independent reading books in class.

Listening Comprehension

Listening Comprehension provides an additional opportunity to stretch students' ability to understand more and more complex language in a variety of texts. Each day, the teacher reads to students from a novel, anthology, newspaper, magazine, or other source of text at students' interest level but above their current reading level. The teacher then uses the reading as an opportunity to present a lesson focusing on comprehension skills, such as visualization of story characters and settings; identification of problems and attempts to solve problems; story mapping; or sequence of events in narratives. More advanced lessons deal with aspects of authors' craft such as similes and metaphors, the creation of mood, character development, and the use of information from expository texts.

Writing and Language Arts

Writing and language arts are critical elements of the Success for All and Roots and Wings programs, particularly because writing is the opposite side of the reading coin. In prekindergarten, kindergarten, and first grade, emergent literacy strategies such as journal writing, shared writing, and sound-based spelling are used to build students' interest in expressing their ideas in writing. In Reading Roots and Lee Conmigo, students regularly write to respond in some way to the story, or to give their answers to questions about the story. In Reading Wings, students exercise their writing skills in responses to Treasure Hunt questions and in creative story-related writing activities.

All of these activities use writing to support the learning of reading while providing opportunities to write. Students, however, also need specific instruction in how to improve their writing. A formal writing/language arts instructional program is usually introduced in Success for All when most teachers are comfortable with the reading program. In practice, this usually means that the writing/language arts program is introduced in the spring of the first implementation year or in the fall of the second year.

Writing/language arts instruction in Success for All and Roots and Wings is provided to students in their heterogeneous homerooms, not in their reading groups. The basic philosophy behind the writing/language arts programs is that writing should be given the main emphasis and that language arts, especially mechanics and usage, should be taught in the context of writing, not as separate topic.

There are two levels in the Success for All/Roots and Wings writing and language arts approach. Both are based on the ideas of writing process (Calkins, 1983; Graves, 1983), which emphasizes writing for a real audience, writing for revision, and gradually building spelling and mechanics in the context of writing. Writing From the Heart, used in Grades 1 and 2, uses an informal version of writing process, while CIRC Writing, used in Grades 3 through 6, uses a more formal writing process model with regular four-member peer response groups and students working compositions through from plan to draft to revision to editing to publication. These programs are now described.

Writing From the Heart

A young child thinks of writing as an extension of oral communication. Most, given the undivided attention of an audience, will talk endlessly about their experiences. Young authors rarely have a problem of too little to say; their problem is overcoming the barriers they perceive to putting their ideas down on paper.

The goal of Writing From the Heart (Madden, Wasik, & Petza, 1989), the writing/language arts program used in Grades 1 through 2 in Success for All, is to tap students' innate desire, energy, and enthusiasm for communication and to move them to the next step of sharing their ideas with others through writing. When writing is seen as mastery of spelling and mechanics, it is a formidable task. Students will ultimately need to master these skills, but first they need to develop pleasure and fluency in putting their thoughts on paper. Most important, students need to see writing as a personal expression, not an ordinary school task. They must put their hearts into their writing, not just their minds.

Writing From the Heart uses a writing process model, which means that students write for a real audience and learn to revise their writing until it is ready for "publication." Students do not work in formal writing teams (that will come in third grade), but they do work informally with partners while they are writing.

The main elements of Writing From the Heart are as follows:

1. *Modeling and motivating writing.* At the beginning of each lesson, the teacher provides a model or motivator for writing. For example, the teacher may read a story that is like what students will be writing, or may ask students to describe experiences that relate to a particular kind of writing. The teacher may introduce formats to help students plan their writing. For example, in writing about "myself," students are given a set of questions to answer about themselves that they then use to put into a story.

2. *Writing a "sloppy copy."* Students are encouraged to write a "sloppy copy," a first draft of their composition. They are taught to use "sound spelling" (invented spelling) if they cannot spell a word. For example, DINASR is a way a student might write dinosaur.

3. *Partner sharing.* At several points in the writing process students share their writing with partners and receive feedback and ideas from them.

4. *Revision.* Beginning after several weeks of the program, students learn to revise their compositions using feedback from partners and from the teacher. Specific revision skills are taught and modeled in the lessons.

5. *Editing.* In preparation for publication, the teacher helps each child prepare a perfect draft of his or her composition, complete with pictures.

6. *Publication.* Final drafts of students writings are "published" in a class book, read to the class, and recognized in as many ways as the teacher can think of.

7. *Sharing and celebration.* At many points in the writing process students have opportunities to share their writing with the class. The teacher sets up a special "author's chair" from which the "authors" present their latest works. Authors are taught to ask three questions of their audience:

> What did you hear? Can you tell me about my story?
> What did you like about my story?
> What else would you like to know about my story?

The teacher models use of the author's chair by presenting his or her own writing and models answers to the author's questions.

Writing From the Heart prepares students for the CIRC Writing program starting in Grade 3 by convincing students that they are authors and have something to say; by teaching them that writing is a process of thinking, drafting, revising, and polishing ideas; and by letting them know that writing is fun. They are then ready to learn more about the craft of writing with more formal instruction in tricks of the trade, style, mechanics, and usage.

CIRC Writing/Language Arts

The writing/language arts program used in the upper elementary grades is one developed earlier as part of Cooperative Integrated Reading and Composition (CIRC) for Grades 3 and up (Madden et al., 1996). In this program, students are assigned to four- or five-member heterogeneous writing teams. CIRC Writing/Language Arts has two major instructional formats. About 3 days each week are used for writing process activities, and 2 for language arts instruction.

Writing Process Activities

Writing Concept Lessons. Each writing process day begins with a brief lesson on a writing concept. For example, the first lesson is on "mind movies," visualization of events in a narrative to see where additional detail or description is needed. Other lessons include organizing imaginative narratives, using observation to add life to descriptions, writing personal narratives, mysteries, persuasive arguments, explanatory writing, and so on. The writing concept lessons are meant to spark ideas and help students expand on their writing and evaluate their own and others' compositions.

Writing Process. Most of the writing/language arts period is spent with students writing their own compositions while the teacher circulates among the teams and conferences with individual students. Students draft many compositions and then choose a smaller number they would like to carry all the way through the steps to publication. The steps are as follows.

1. Prewriting. Students discuss with their teammates a topic they would like to address and an audience for their writing. They then draft a plan, using a "skeleton planning form," an "idea net," or other forms to organize their thinking.

2. Drafting. After the student prepares a plan in consultation with teammates, he or she writes a first draft, focusing on getting ideas on paper rather than spelling and mechanics (they will come later).

3. Team response and revision. Students read their drafts to their teammates. The teammates are taught to rephrase the main idea of the story in their own words, to mention two things they liked about the story, and to note two things they'd like to hear more about. The teacher may also conference with students at the revision stage to applaud students' ideas and suggest additions and changes. Specific revision guides for specific categories of writing assist students in responding usefully to their teammates writing. For instance, as students learn to enrich their narratives with rich description, they use a team response guide that asks them to tell the author (their teammate) their favorite descriptive words. As they look at the writing of their teammates, they learn to look for those features in their own writing. Students make revisions based on their teammates' responses.

4. Editing. Once the author is satisfied with the content of the writing, he or she is ready to correct the mechanics, usage, and spelling. Students work with a partner to go through an editing checklist. The checklist starts with a small number of goals (e.g., correct capitalization and end punctuation), but then adds goals as students complete language arts lessons. For example, after a lesson on subject-verb agreement or run-on sentences, these may be added to the checklist. The author first checks the composition against the checklist, then a teammate does so, and finally the teacher checks it.

5. Publication. Publication involves the creation of the final draft and celebration of the author's writing. Students carefully rewrite their work incorporating all final corrections made by the teacher. They then present their compositions to the class from a fancy "author's chair," and may then contribute their writing to a team book or a team section of a class book. These books are proudly displayed in the class or library. In addition, students may be asked to read their compositions to other classes, or to otherwise celebrate and disseminate their masterpieces!

A sample presentation guide for a writing lesson focusing on rich expression in a personal narrative is included in Appendix 2.7. This guide covers the development of the concept and the planning, drafting, and team response sections of the writing process. The other steps would be completed later.

Revision and Editing Skills Lessons

About 2 days each week the teacher teaches structured lessons on language mechanics skills. These are presented as skills for revision and editing, because their purpose is to directly support students' writing. The teacher determines the order of lessons according to problems students are experiencing and skills they will need for upcoming writing. For example, the teacher may notice that many students are having problems with complete sentences, or may anticipate that because students are about to write dialogue they may need to learn how to use quotation marks.

Students work in their four-member writing teams to help one another master the skills taught by the teacher. The students work on examples, compare answers with each other, resolve discrepancies, explain ideas to each other, and so on. Ultimately, students are quizzed on the skill, and teams can earn certificates or other recognition based on the average performance of all team members. As noted earlier, immediately after a revision and editing skills lesson the new skill is added to the editing checklist, so language arts skills are immediately put into practice in students' writing.

CHAPTER APPENDICES

Appendix 2.1. Reading Roots
Shared Story 18: *Fang*

Story by: Laura Burton Rice
Illustrations by: Jennifer Clark
© *Roots and Wings.* The Johns Hopkins University

Scott and Tanya practice kicking her ball during recess. Lana joins them. What will happen to the ball?   1

Scott rolls the ball.

BAM!

Tanya kicks it.

She fast.

Lana says, "The ball is off the field!"

2   Scott and Tanya look for the ball in the bushes while Lana looks on the other side of the playground. Suddenly, Scott sees something. What is it?

"Look, Tanya!" gasps Scott.

Tanya looks.

She sees a big fat dog.

The dog fast.

It bumps into Tanya.

She sits in the mud.

Poor Tanya! How do you think she feels about being pushed into the mud?   **3**

"Ick!" says Tanya. "Mud is not fun.

Go, dog!"

The big dog sits.

He pants.

4   Paco starts to shake. He turns pale. What has Paco seen that has scared him?

Paco says, "See the dog's fangs!"

"FANGS!!" says Tanya.

The big dog says, "RUFF!"

The kids climb up the jungle gym.

"Can we fit?" asks Paco.

5

Lana fast.

"Fang!" Lana says.

She skids to a stop.

"Fang is not bad," says Lana.

6   Lana explains that Fang is her St. Bernard. He is gentle, even though he has big teeth. He follows her to school when he gets lonely. What will the other children do now?

Lana says, "Fang is a fun dog.

He likes kids."

The kids get off the 🏗 .

All of a sudden, Derrick has an idea. What do you think it is?   **7**

Derrick says, "Dogs can sniff.

Can Fang sniff the ball?"

Lana nods.

"Get the ball, Fang," says Lana.

8   Fang puts his nose to the ground. Do you think he can find the ball?

Fang  .
runs

He sniffs.

He digs fast in a stack of .
leaves

The kids say, "Fang got the ball back!"

Fang is a hero. He has found the missing ball!

Appendix 2.2. Reading Roots Shared Story 42:
A Farm in China

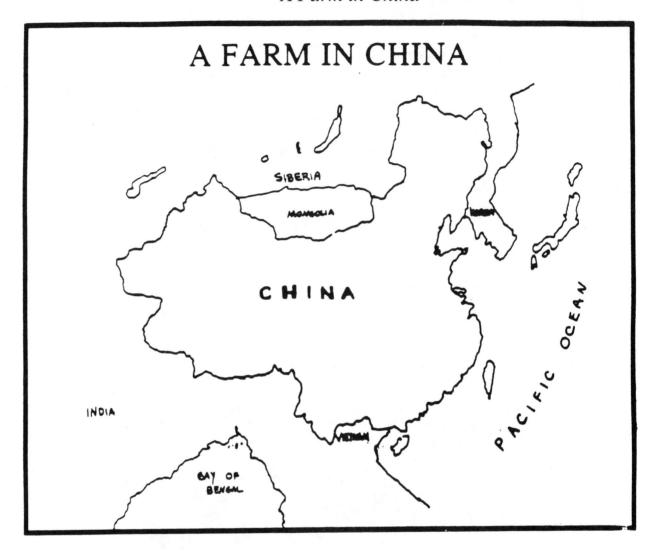

Story by: Wendie Old
Illustrations by: Jackie Branch McAfee

©1994 *Roots and Wings.* The Johns Hopkins University

Chen May Woo lives in the north of China. In China they say the last name first.

Chen May Woo's dad's name is Chen Ji Ling. Her mom's name is Chen Ling Ha. Her grandma's name is Chen Eu Fong.

May Woo lives on a big, big farm. Many families share the work on this farm. They plant wheat and beans. They raise this food to eat and to sell. May Woo's family has a pig, a duck, and a goose.

Most of the food May Woo eats is raised on the farm. Her mom makes meals. She chops small bits of meat and vegetables. May Woo helps chop the food. May Woo does not need a fork. She scoops her food with a spoon and chopsticks. She drinks green tea, instead of milk, with meals.

May Woo has a big class at school. Fifty children are in her room. She goes to school six days a week. The children are learning to read and write.

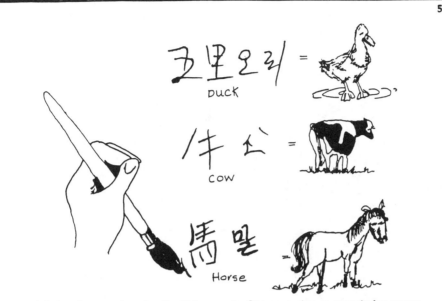

It is hard to read and write Chinese. In China, a picture stands for every sound. The Chinese alphabet has more than 5,000 pictures. May Woo and her classmates must learn all of these pictures. They will write the picture with a brush and ink.

Once, May Woo's class went to the zoo. May Woo liked to see the pandas. Wild pandas live in the west of China. They stay in the big bamboo forests. Pandas like to eat bamboo.

7

May Woo and her class also visited the Great Wall of China. It is tall and made of thick stone. It is very, very long. It swoops up hills deep into China. It would stretch from New York all the way to California. It is so big, it can be seen from space!

8

May Woo does fun things after school with her classmates. They eat lunch by the goldfish pool. Then they play Chinese jump rope, ping pong, five stones, and hopscotch. They like to kick a small bean bag, too. They must try to keep it in the air.

May Woo also likes to fly kites. Kites were invented in China! They are made of silk and paper in all shapes and sizes.

Some big kites are 16 feet high. More than one person is needed to fly them. Soft wing kites have wings that flap. In China, most kite sticks are made of bamboo.

Lots of things were invented in China. Paper-cut pictures were invented there. Most paper-cut pictures are red for good luck.

Last year, May Woo made a paper-cut picture for the New Year Feast. She cut a long dragon out of red paper. Then she looped it in the room where all the farm families celebrated.

After the feast, there were fireworks. Fireworks were invented in China, too! May Woo held her grandmother's hand as she looked up at the bright fireworks. At the end of the display, a big red dragon lit up the sky. Everyone cheered and clapped.

The fireworks were finished. May Woo got into bed. She liked to think of the fireworks. She liked to think of all the other things that were invented in China, too. She was very glad to live here!

Appendix 2.3. Lesson 18: *Fang*

OBJECTIVES

1. *Reinforce:* Monitoring for meaning strategy (see Guided Group Reading).
2. *Letter/Sound:* "f."
3. *Special Story Skill:* Identify and describe new story characters (see Story Discussion).
4. *Review:* Using context to find meaning (see Guided Group Reading).

PREPARATION

1. *Tongue Twister:* Fang found five fat fish by the fence.
2. *Pictures and Objects:* Fang, feet, fish, five
3. *Student Picture Cards:* Have one student picture card for each student.
4. *Key Picture:* feet
5. *Two-Picture Game:* football [fork]-dog, feather-bus, firefighter [foxes]-tiger, five-six
6. *Yes-No Game Pictures:* fish-bug, fan-cat, fire-tie, five-door
7. *Matching Games:* (letter cards) **"f," "b," "s"** (key picture cards) feet, balloon, sun (picture cards), fan, bed, feet, soap, fire, sun, sock, book
8. *Readles:* runs, jungle gym, leaves
9. *Stretch and Spell:* fun, fast, fit, fat
10. *Letter and Word Formation Review:* (letter cards) **"s," "u," "b"**

A. SHOWTIME

1. Reading Rehearsal. Create a brief motivation for students to reread a familiar story with whole group choral reading or partner reading. Be sure to motivate students and allow time to scan the story and do a "word check" before beginning.

2. Letter and Word Formation Review. Using the letter cue cards for the last three letters learned, **"s," "u,"and "b,"** have students quickly make each letter in the air three to five times, saying the cue phrase as they do so. Use additional letter cue cards to quickly review about four other letters previously learned, "writing" each letter once. Challenge students to write words during review, if they are able. Review letters and words on a daily basis, at appropriate times during the lesson.

B. SETTING THE STAGE

1. Introduction. Distribute the Shared Story. Say: *"We are going to read another story about the school friends we have already met. This time, we will meet a new friend, Lana, who causes a commotion during recess."*

Preview the story. Say: *"Let's preview the story by looking at the title and the cover picture. Remember, we learned that this way we will understand the story better when we read it. The title of this story is* Fang. *What is a fang?"* (Pause and discuss students' responses.) *"A fang is a very long and sharp tooth. Wolves have fangs. Why do you suppose this story is called* Fang?" (Pause and discuss students' responses.) *"Let's look at the picture on the front cover. What do you see?"* (Pause and discuss students' responses.) *"The picture shows a very large dog. Could this be why the story is called* Fang?" (Pause and discuss students' responses.)

Allow one minute for students to look through the book to enjoy and become familiar with the pictures.

2. Background Questions. Say: *"Do you have a pet? What other stories have we read about pets?"* (Pause and discuss students' responses.)

3. Predictive Question. Ask: *"What will the big dog do?"* (Pause and discuss students' responses.)

4. Teacher Script. Read to page 4. Ask the predictive question and have students respond. Encourage students to support their predictions. Then finish reading the story. Read slowly, with expression. Stop to comment and question (see the Teacher Script below for a model). Model the Monitoring for Meaning strategy as you read by stopping at the end of each page and asking aloud, "Did I understand what I read?" Then briefly paraphrase aloud what you just read.

---

1   Scott and Tanya practice kicking her ball during recess. Lana joins them. What will happen to the ball?
Scott rolls the ball.
BAM!
Tanya kicks it.
She **runs** fast.
Lana says, "The ball is off the field!"

---

2   Scott and Tanya look for the ball in the bushes while Lana looks on the other side of the playground. Suddenly, Scott sees something. What is it?
"Look, Tanya!" gasps Scott.
Tanya looks.
She sees a big fat dog.
The dog **runs** fast.
It bumps into Tanya.
She sits in the mud.

---

3   Poor Tanya! How do you think she feels about being pushed into the mud?
"Ick!" says Tanya. "Mud is not fun.
Go, dog!"
The big dog sits.
He pants.

---

4   Paco starts to shake. He turns pale. What has Paco seen that has scared him?
Paco says, "See the dog's fangs!"
"FANGS!!" says Tanya.
The big dog says, "RUFF!"
The kids climb up the **jungle gym.**
"Can we fit?" asks Paco.

Make a Prediction: *What will the dog do? Will the children be all right?* (Pause for student's predictions. Have students discuss predictions. Encourage them to support their predictions.)

---

5 Lana **runs** fast.
"Fang!" Lana says.
She skids to a stop.
"Fang is not bad," says Lana.

---

6 Lana explains that Fang is her St. Bernard. He is gentle, even though he has big teeth. He follows her to school when he gets lonely. What will the other children do now?
Lana says, "Fang is a fun dog.
He likes kids."
The kids get off the **jungle gym.**

---

7 All of a sudden, Derrick has an idea. What do you think it is?
Derrick says, "Dogs can sniff.
Can Fang sniff the ball?"
Lana nods.
"Get the ball, Fang," says Lana.

---

8 Fang puts his nose to the ground. Do you think he can find the ball?
Fang **runs.**
He sniffs.
He digs fast in a stack of **leaves.**
The kids say, "Fang got the ball back!"
Fang is a hero. He has found the missing ball!

---

5. Story Discussion. Direct students to identify and describe new characters introduced in the story. Have them think about and discuss how the children changed the way they felt about Fang in this story. Encourage them to focus on what they think the Purpose of Reading the story was. Collect the Shared Stories (or have students put them away). Then, tell the students that they are going to learn all the sounds, letters, and words they will need to read this story by themselves.

C. LETTER ACTIVITIES

1. Alphabet Song. Have students sing an alphabet song to invite Alphie to come out.

2. Letter Presentation.

a. Hearing the Sound. Introduce the tongue twister by reading today's "note" from Alphie: *"Many words contain the sound /f/.* Pretend that you are detectives so that you can discover where you hear this sound in words as you listen to Alphie's note about Fang." Read Alphie's tongue twister with as much expression as you can:

Fang found five fat fish by the fence.

Say the first **/f/** word and have students repeat it. Then, say the word again, stretching the beginning sound. Have students repeat it. Repeat this process for each **/f/** word in the tongue twister.

b. Introducing **/f/** Pictures and Objects. Tell students that now Alphie wants to show them some things that start with **/f/**. Have students name each picture or object as you pull it from Alphie's box. Stretch the **/f/** sound in the word as you say it. Show each one again, asking, *"What sound can you hear at the beginning of _____?"* Have the group respond by stretching the **/f/** sound.

Fang	**feet**	**fish**	**five**

c. Two-Picture Game. Tell the students that you are going to show them some pictures on cards. After you have shown each pair of cards you have placed on either side of the chalkboard, prompt students to point to the picture which starts with **/f/**. If the students make an error, name the correct picture and have them repeat it. Continue until students achieve fluency.

football [fork]	**feather**	**firefighter [foxes]**	**five**
dog	**bus**	**tiger**	**six**

d. Making the **/f/** Sound. Say: *"Our Key Picture for* **/f/** *is* **feet**.*"* Have everyone in the group make the **/f/** sound. Ask: *"How do your mouths make this sound?"* After students have thought about and discussed making the sound, continue: *"Place your upper teeth lightly over your lower lip. Pull your lip in a little bit. Blow out in a steady stream.* **/F/** *is a breathy sound."* Have all students practice the sound **/f/**.

e. Introducing the Shape. Pull Alphie's pennant out of his box and introduce the letter's name: *"The letter that goes with* **/fff/** *is* **'f'**. *Let's go over our letter's pictures and objects."*

Display the **"f"** pictures, or objects you presented, one at a time. Try to choose items that are related to the story. As students name them, write each one on the board in a vertical list, emphasizing the sound/letter match. Say the cue phrase, *"If we hear it with our ears, we'll see it with our eyes."*

Fang	**feet**	**fish**	**five**

f. Practicing the **"f"** Shape. Write the upper-and lowercase **"f"** on the chalkboard. Discuss their similarities and differences with the students.

Introduce the verbal pattern for **"f"**. **"Curve left, straight down, lift and cross."**

Have students use the lower case **"f"** on the board for a model as they make an **"f"** in the air and say the cue phrase. Have them make the letter, repeating the cue phrase in unison each time:

> on their desks, as big as they can.
> on their desks, as small as they can.
> on a partner's hand, arm, back, and so on.

Instruct students to trace the letter with you several times on their Letter Practice Sheet while they say the cue phrase in unison. When students have mastered the shape, add the sound to the cue phrase: **"Curve left, straight down, lift and cross. The sound for 'f' is /f/."** Then have students practice **"f"** several more times as they say the entire cue phrase.

3. Letter Games.

a. Students' **/f/** Words. Have students tell their partners all the **/f/** words they can think of. Highlight the theme of school friends playing together at recess in *Fang*. Challenge them to think of **"f"** words related to the story. Allow several students to share their favorite words. As they respond, write their words on the board and give each student a Student Picture Card as a reward.

b. (Visual) Yes-No Game. Tell students that you are going to show them more pictures on cards. Have students say the name of each picture as you show it, then have them point to the sign (*Yes* or *No*) to indicate whether or not it starts with "**f**". Assess individual students, as needed, after the group has achieved fluency.

fish	**fan**	**fire**	**five**
bug	**cat**	**tie**	**door**

c. (Auditory) Yes-No Game. Say each of the words in the list below, one at a time and then have students point to *"Yes"* or *"No"* to indicate whether the word begins with "**f**". Assess individual students, as needed after the group has achieved fluency.

fat	**fold**	**fawn**	**fox**
bucket	**jacket**	**hat**	**lamb**

d. Matching Games. Use pictures selected during the lesson preparation that begin with the sounds **/f/**, **/b/**, and **/s/**.

   ▨ Have students match pictures of objects with Letter Cards *with* Picture Cards attached. (Use a pocket chart or chalkboard ledge.)

Give your students a few seconds to think, and then, at your signal, have them point to the side of the board that indicates the letter with which the word starts. Continue until students are fluent.

fan	**bed**	**feet**	**soap**

   ▨ Have students match spoken words with Letter Cards with Student Picture Cards attached.

Say the words below one at a time. Give your students a few seconds to think, and then, at your signal, have them point to the side of the board that indicates the letter with which the word starts. Continue until students are fluent.

big	**fat**	**fast**	**back**

   ▨ Have students match pictures of objects with Letter Cards without Student Picture Cards attached.

Remove the Key Pictures. Go through the set of pictures, one at a time. This time, have students point to the Letter Card only. Continue until students are fluent.

fire	**sun**	**sock**	**book**

   ▨ Have students match spoken words with Letter Cards *without* Student Picture Cards attached.

Say the following words to the class, one at a time. Have them point to the correct beginning letter. Continue until students are fluent.

sick	**fun**	**bin**	**fist**

Now, tell students that they are going to read the story for themselves. Remind them that it has many words that start with the **/f/** sound. Ask them to put on their listening ears so they can hear this special new sound in the story. Redistribute the Shared Story (or have students take out their Shared Story).

D. STORY ACTIVITIES

1. Word Presentation.

a. Stretch and Read. Have the students stretch and read the story's new phonetic words. Have them use the starred words in a sentence, then share the sentences with their partner. Discuss the meaning of the starred words in the context of the story. Guide students as needed.

fit	***fast**	**fun**	***sniff**	**Bam**
fat	***fangs**	**off**	***stack**	***bumps**
				dog

b. Quick Erase. Start with **fat,** finish with **sun,** changing one letter at a time. Help student Stretch and Read as needed. Use the words in sentences as needed to make sure that students recognize them as words they know.

fat→fast→fist→fit→fin→fun→sun

c. Say-Spell-Say. Say-Spell-Say the story's new sight word, **go,** and have students soft-clap it three times, by letters. Have students Say-Spell-Say (spelling rhythmically, by letters) the sight word.

Introduce the story's readles, **runs, jungle gym,** and **leaves.**

d. Using Context. Have students use the context of the story to read the following words. When presenting each word, say "Let's see if we can use the whole sentence to figure out a word." (Write the sentence on the chalkboard, leaving a blank for the context word.) Read the sentence without the word. Ask: "What word could go in the blank?" (Guide children to use the picture and the rest of the sentence to figure out the word.)

Page 1.   *Scott_____(***rolls***) the ball.*
            *_____(***Lana***) says, "The ball is off the _____(***field***)!"*

Page 4.   *The big dog says "_____(***Ruff***)!"*
            *The kids_____(***climb***) up the (jungle gym.)*

2. Guided Group Reading. Review how to use the previewing strategy. Read the introductory script and the story again (see the Teacher Script for the Story Presentation) with expression, while students read along in a low voice. On page 3, remind students that they can use context to figure out word meaning and usage. They have already learned to read **pants** as an article of clothing. Present it as a verb:

Page 3.   *The big dog sits. He pants.*

Model the Monitoring for Meaning strategy as you read by stopping at the end of each page and asking aloud, *"Did I understand what I read?"* Then briefly paraphrase aloud what you just read. For example:

Page 1.   Say: *"Did I understand what I read? Yes, Scott, Tanya, and Lana kick a soccer ball off the field."*

Continue to model self questioning and paraphrasing for each page. Read each story sentence twice to help students build fluency.

3. Partner Reading. Encourage students to use the previewing strategy. Direct students to take turns with their partner to read alternate pages of the story aloud, with expression, and to help each other.

a. Monitoring for Meaning. Reinforce the importance of using the Monitoring for Meaning strategy. Have students read each page and then ask, *"Did I understand what I read?"* Have them explain what they read to their partner before going on to the next page.

b. Story Comprehension. When students have finished the partner reading, read the questions aloud. Have them discuss their answers as partners, and then as a group. Encourage them to use the book to find specific clues to the answers.

How did the ball get lost?
Why did the children climb up the jungle gym?
Why did the dog bark at the children when they yelled "FANGS!"?
Who found the ball?
What happened to change how the children felt about Fang?

Have the group gather together to write a short answer to one or more of the questions. Explain again how they must ask themselves if what they read makes sense to comprehend the story. Model the process by writing what the group wants to answer on the board. Have students attempt to write a short answer to one of the questions on their own, using sound spelling. Encourage partners to give each other feedback.

5. Shared Treasure. This Share Sheet focuses on story comprehension and sentence reading practice. Have students complete the Share Sheet with their partner, then have partners share with the group. Have students take home the Share Sheet to read to as many people as they can. Ask them to have their listeners initial the Share Sheet in the box to indicate that they have heard the students read. Allow students to color in a star for each successful reading they accomplish.

6. Story-Related Writing. This Share Sheet focuses on writing about a topic generated by the story that relates to students' own experiences. Have students complete the Share Sheet with their partner, then have partners share with the group. Allow students to take home their writing to share with as many people as they can.

7. Stretch and Spell. Distribute scrap paper. Say each word, stretching if needed, and have students write it on their paper. If your students are ready, use large, lined primary writing paper. Introduce them to numbering their papers when it is appropriate. Have the group Say-Spell-Say the word before they proceed to the next one.

fun   **fast**   **fit**   **fat**

E. CELEBRATION

1. Performance. At the end of each day, have two students read, with expression, a page or more from a story they have mastered. Have the entire class provide applause and praise. (You may wish to send home a certificate.) Also, let students take their Share Sheets home to read to parents and other family members when these have been mastered fairly well. Send a form for listeners to sign and have students return both the Share Sheet and the form. Enjoy your celebration!

2. Letter Sound Review. Summarize the day's lesson by reviewing all sounds quickly, using flash cards. Ask students to look for and think about lots of **"f"** words for tomorrow's lesson.

> Teachers, please remember: Using flash cards and Share Sheets, work in a quick review at some point in each day's lesson. Frequent but brief reviews of sound and words will increase your students' reading fluency, as will repeated readings of stories and share sheets.

Appendix 2.4. Lee Conmigo Teacher's Guide:
Lesson 19: *va, ve, vi, vo, vu*

Teachers, please note: Individual Letter Cards will be used in the Stretch and Spell activity. You may wish to have your students, a parent volunteer, or other assistant prepare the letters.

A. SHOWTIME

Create a brief motivation for students to reread any stories previously read. The story may be student selected or teacher selected, with a whole group choral reading or partners reading. Be sure to motivate students and allow time to scan the story and do a "word check" before beginning.

B. LETTER FORMATION REVIEW

Using the Letter Cue Cards for the last three letters learned, have students quickly make each letter in the air three to five times, saying the cue phrase as they do so. Use additional Letter Cue Cards to quickly review about four other letters previously learned, "writing" each letter once. Review letters on a daily basis.

C. THINKING ABOUT READING

1. Strategy Presentation. Present the Monitoring for Meaning strategy. Explain, *"Cuando ustedes leen, hay que asegurarse que entiendan lo que están leyendo. La manera para fijarse si entienden es leer una oración y preguntarse a si mismo, '¿Comprendo lo que he leido?' Luego, en sus palabras, cuéntense a si mismo lo que han leido. Acuérdense de que una de los razones de leer es para aprender."* Reinforce the rationale that it it important to read for meaning, and therefore, students must monitor the meaning of what they read.

2. Strategy modeling. The strategy modeling is done in the context of reading. See the Teacher Script in Section D, Story Presentation.

3. Practicing the strategy. This is presented in the Partner Reading section.

D. STORY PRESENTATION

1. Introduction. Discuss with students how we can help a person or an animal who is sick or hurt. What do we do for them? Where can we take them? Say: *"Vamos a leer un cuentito acerca de una niña que ayuda un ave. El título del cuento es ¡Qué ave tan linda!"*

Preview the story by asking students to think about what the story might be about based on this title.

2. Background Questions. *"Describa algunos problemas que pudiera tener un ave. ¿Cómo se le puede ayudar?"* (Pause for students' responses. Discuss students' responses.)

3. Predictive Questions. *"¿*Qué ha pasado al ave de la niña del cuento? ¿La encuentra Eva? ¿Cómo le va a ayudar?" (Pause for students' responses. Discuss students' responses.)

4. Teacher Script. Read the story slowly, with expression. Stop to comment and question. Model the Monitor for Modeling strategy as you present the story (see questions incorporated in the script below). The Make a Prediction question follows page 52.

AUTHORS' NOTE: The page numbers referred to in the text are from *Osito, Osito* published in 1987 by Macmillan.

Una mañana, sale una niña de su casa. Escuchen lo que pasa (page 50):
　　–¡Qué mañana tan linda!
　　–dice Eva.
¿Qué he leido? ¿Quién es Eva? (Pause for students' responses. Discuss students' responses.)
　　Eva de paseo.
　　–¿Qué es eso? –dice Eva.
A ver, ¿qué he leido? He leido que Eva va de paseo. Ella pregunta algo. ¿Por qué? (Reread the passage above, explaining that sometimes you need to reread to understand.) *¿Es posible que ella ha visto algo? ¿Qué ha visto ella?* (Pause for students' responses. Discuss students' responses.) Tell students that because you do not know yet what has surprised Eva, you will continue reading to learn this information. You are modeling for the children how to ask questions about the meaning of what they read as they go through the story.

Miren el dibujo de la página 51. ¿Qué pasa? (Pause for students' responses. Discuss students' responses.) *Escuchen* (page 51):
　　Eva mire y dice:
　　–¡Qué ave tan linda!
　　¿Está viva?
¿Qué he leido? Eva pregunta si el ave está viva. ¿Por qué pregunta ella eso? (Pause for students' responses. Discuss students' responses.)
　　El ave la mira.
　　–Sí, está viva –dice Eva.
¿Comprendo lo que he leido? ¿Qué hace el ave? (Reread the previous passage, reminding students that sometimes you need to reread to understand. *¿Cómo sabe Eva que sí está viva el ave?* (Pause for students' responses. Discuss students' responses.)

Miren el dibujo de la página 52. ¿Qué hace Eva? ¿Por qué no se mueve el ave? (Pause for students' responses. Discuss students' responses.) *Los animales salvajes no dejan que las personas se les acercan tanto si no están enfermos o heridos. Si el ave no se mueve, ¿es posible que esté enferme o herida?* (Pause for students' responses. Discuss students' responses.)
　　Escuchen lo que pasa (page 52):
　　Eva dice:
　　–¿Qué tengo para el ave tan linda?
　　Mira.
　　Tengo pan.
　　Toma.
¿Comprendo lo que he leido? ¿Qué hace Eva? Sé que ella le da algo al ave, pero no recuerdo lo que es. Voy a leerlo otra vez para saberlo. (Reread the previous passage.) *¿Lo va a tomar?* (Pause for students' responses. Discuss students' responses.)

Haz una predicción: *¿Va a dejar el ave que Eva le ayude?* (Pause for students' predictions. Discuss students' predictions.) Finish reading the story and briefly comment on its outcome.

Miren el dibujo de la página 53. ¿Qué pasa? (Pause for students' responses. Discuss students' responses.) *Escuchen* (page 53):

> *Eva le da el pan.*
> *El ave mira el pan.*
> *Se lo come.*
> *–¿Qué bien! –dice Eva.*
> *Te veo mañana.*

¿Comprendo lo que he leido? Pues, Eva le da el pan al ave y el ave se lo come. (Explain that it is good to think about what you read so that you can make sure that you understand it.) *¿Cómo se siente Eva? ¿Por qué dice que va a ver el ave mañana?* (Pause for students' responses. Discuss students' responses.)

¿Va a ver Eva el ave mañana? ¿Qué va a pasar? (Pause for students' responses. Discuss students' responses.) *Escuchen* (page 54):

> *Eva visita el ave todos los días.*
> *Todos los días le da pan.*
> *Todos los días el ave se lo come.*

¿Qué he leido? Me parece que algunos días han pasado. Voy a leer otra vez para asegurarme lo que he leido. (Reread the previous passage, explaining again that when you don't understand what you have read, you reread to help you understand.) *Pues, el ave se lo come todos los días. ¿Qué significa eso? ¿Qué va a pasar al ave?* (Pause for students' responses. Discuss students' responses.)

Miren el dibujo de la página 55. ¿Dónde está el ave? (Pause for students' responses. Discuss students' responses.) *Escuchen* (page 55):

> *Una mañana, Eva visita al ave.*
> *Mira y mira.*
> *No la ve.*
> *–¡El ave ya no está –dice Eva!*
> *¡Qué bien!*
> *¡El ave ya está bien!*

¿Por qué no está el ave por ahí? (Reread the previous passage, if needed. Tell students that rereading helps you to catch details you might have missed the first time you read.) *La niña dice que el ave está bien. ¿Cómo se siente Eva? ¿Por qué se seinte así?* (Pause for students' responses. Discuss students' responses.) Have students think about and discuss Eva's character. How does the story demonstrate that she is a kind and thoughtful girl? Would Eva make a good friend? Ask students to think about how Eva showed that she could do things on her own. Have students describe what they have learned about the Purpose of Reading from this story.

Now, tell your students that they will learn all the letters, sounds and words they will need to read this story by themselves.

E. LETTER PRESENTATION

   1. Alphabet Song. Invite students to sing the alphabet song.

   2. Tongue Twister. Introduce the tongue twister by reading today's *"carta"* from Alfi: *"Muchas palabras empiezan con el sonido de /v/. Escuchen: **Vendo veinte verduras verdes.**"* Say, then stretch and read each word that starts with "v."

   3. Introducing /v/ Pictures and Objects. Have students name each picture or object as you pull it from Alfi's box. Stretch the /v/ sound at the beginning of the word as you say it.

Show each one again, asking, *"¿Qué sonido pueden oir al principio de___?"* Have the group respond by stretching the /v/ sound.

4. Making the /v/ Sound. Have everyone in the group make the /v/ sound. Ask: *"¿Cómo hacen sus bocas este sonido?"* Help students to see that /v/ is made by pressing the upper teeth over the lower lip and forcing the air out in a steady stream. Have them stretch the sound to sustain it: /v v v v/.

5. Introducing the "v" Shape. Introduce the letter's name: *"Vamos a ver que letra va con /v v v/. La letra que va con el sonido /v/ es la 'v.' Repasaremos nuestras Cartas de Dibujos."*

Display the Key Pictures, or choose objects that start with "v," one at a time. As students name them, write each one on the board in a vertical list, emphasizing the sound/letter match. Say the cue phrase, *"Si las orejas oyen, los ojos ven."*

| *vaca* | *vela* | *vidrio* | *voleibol* |

6. Practicing the "v" Shape. Write the upper- and lowercase "v" on the chalkboard. Discuss their similarities and differences with the students.

Introduce the verbal pattern for "v": ***"Rayita en medio hacia abajo, un puntito, y una rayita hacia arriba. (Rayita inclinada a la izquierda y una rayita inclinada a la derecha.)"***

Have students use the lower case "v" on the board for a model as they make a "v" in the air and say the cue phrase. After they have done this several times, have them continue to say the cue phrase as they practice writing the shape in a variety of sizes and places.

Instruct students to trace the letter with you several times on their Letter Practice Sheet while they say the cue phrase in unison. When students have mastered the shape, add the sound to the cue phrase: ***"Rayita en medio hacia abajo, un puntito, y una rayita hacia arriba. (Rayita inclinada a la izquierda y una rayita inclinada a la derecha.) /V/ es el sonido para la 'v.'"*** Then have students practice "v" several more times as they say the entire cue phrase.

7. ¿Cuál Es? (Two-Picture Game). After you have shown each pair of cards you have placed on either side of the chalkboard, prompt students to point to the picture that starts with /v/. If the students make an error, name the correct picture and have them repeat it. Continue until students achieve mastery.

| *vaso* | *venado* | *volante* | *vela* |
| *gusano* | *lupa* | *nudo* | *yeso* |

8. Students' /v/ Words. Have students tell their partners all the /v/ words they can think of. Highlight the theme of learning to do things on your own. Challenge them to think of "v" words related to *¡Qué ave tan linda!* Allow several students to share their favorite words. As they respond, write their words on the board and distribute the Student Picture Cards.

9. ¡Ésto Es! (Yes-No Game)

a. *¡Ésto Es!* (Visual Yes-No Game). Have students say the name of each picture as you show it, then have them point to the sign (*Sí* or *No*) to indicate whether or not the name's initial sound is /v/. Assess individual students, as needed, after the group has achieved mastery.

| *vidrio* | *venado* | *vaso* | *volante* |
| *sopa* | *tomate* | *sello* | *puma* |

b. *¡Ésto Es!* (Auditory Yes-No Game). Say each of the words in the list below, one at a time and then have students point to *"Sí"* or *"No"* to indicate whether the word begins with /v/. Assess individual students, as needed, after the group has achieved mastery.

vivir	*ver*	*visita*	*vuelo*
pan	*días*	*suerte*	*perder*

10. Hacer Juego (Matching Games). Use pictures selected during the lesson preparation that begin with sounds /v/, /b/, and /n/.

a. Match pictures with Letter Cards (accompanied by Key Pictures)

vidrio   *botas*   *voleibol*   *nariz*   *bebé*   *vaca*   *nube*   *vela*

b. Match words with Letter Cards (accompanied by Key Pictures)

borrador   *vida*   *brillante*   *viaje*   *níquel*   *visible*   *nuestro*   *venir*

c. Match pictures with Letter Cards

vaso   *ballena*   *vela*   *naranja*   *volante*   *nido*   *búfalo*   *venado*

d. Match words with Letter Cards

nombre   *viva*   *bañar*   *viejo*   *voz*   *baúl*   *viento*

11. Syllable Sounds. Review the syllable sounds by flashing Syllable Cards from past lessons. In a daily, 2 to 3 minute review practice previous syllables, rotating through the stack of known syllables so that all are reviewed at least once weekly. Develop a rhythmic pattern for the review, repeating syllables several times as appropriate to your students' needs.

Now introduce the new consonant in combination with the vowel sounds. Write "vo" on the board. Stretch and read "vo." Have students repeat after you. Then, tell them that they have said the first part of a word. Write "lar" next to "vo", and tell them the word, *"volar."* Continue with the remaining words below.

vo	vi	va	ve	vu
as in *volar*	as in *viva*	as in *vaso*	as in *veo*	as in *vuelta*

F. STORY READING ACTIVITIES

1. Word Presentation

a. Estira y Lee (Stretch and Read). Have students stretch and read the phonetic words, then have them use the words in a sentence. Guide students, as needed.

tan	*te*	*ave*	*pan*	*días*
viva	*veo*	*ve*	*visita*	*Eva*

b. *Cambio Rápido* (Quick-Erase Game). Erase one or more letters and substitute the desired letter(s) as you ask each question below.

- "Si *t-e* es *te*,   ¿qué es *v-e*?"
- "Si *a-v-e* es *ave*,   ¿qué es *E-v-a*?"
- "Si *t-a-n* es *tan*,   ¿qué es *p-a-n*?"
- "Si *f-e-o* es *feo*,   ¿qué es *v-e-o*?"

c. ***Di-Deletrea-Di*** (Say-Spell-Say). There are no sight words in *¡Qué ave tan linda!*
d. Review. Randomly review all the words on a chart. Have the group read in unison until each word has been reviewed several times and can be read fluently. Then, with the class, read each sentence that you have written on the board or on strips. Have the students, as a group, read each one aloud again. (Repeat this practice each day for the story being read.)

- *¡Qué ave tan linda!*
- *Eva visita el ave todos los días.*
- *El ave mira el pan.*
- *Se lo come.*

2. Guided Group Reading. Model how to use the previewing strategy. Read the introductory script and the story again (see the Teacher's Script for the Story Presentation, section C) with expression, while students read along in a low voice. Read each story sentence twice to help students gain fluency. Model the Monitoring for Meaning strategy as you read.
3. Partner Reading. Encourage students to use the previewing strategy. Direct students to take turns with their partner to read alternate pages aloud, with expression, and to help each other. At this point, model the Monitoring for Meaning strategy again and reinforce the importance of using it. Have one student read a page and then ask himself, *¿Comprendo lo que he leído?* Have them explain what they read to their partner.
a. Practicing the Strategy. Have the students take turns with their partner to read the last two pages of this story. Ask: "*¿Comprenden lo que han leído?*" Explain again how they must ask themselves if what they read makes sense to comprehend the story. Have them write one or two sentences, without concentrating on spelling, about the last two pages of the story. Have students share their writing with their partner.
b. Story Comprehension. When students have finished the partner reading, read the questions aloud. Have them discuss their answers as partners, and then as a group. Encourage them to use the book to find specific clues to the answers.

- *¿Qué encuentra Eva cuando va de paseo?*
- *¿Cómo sabe Eva que el ave no se siente muy bien?*
- *¿Cómo le ayuda Eva al ave?*
- *¿Por qué se va el ave?*
- *¿Cómo se siente Eva? ¿Por qué?*

Have the group gather together to write a short answer to one or more of the questions. Model the process by writing what the group wants to answer on the board. Have students attempt to write a short answer to one of the questions on their own, using sound spelling. Encourage partners to give each other feedback.
4. Tesoro Repartido (Shared Treasure). This Share Sheet focuses on story comprehension and sentence reading practice.
5. Estira y Deletrea (Stretch and Spell). Distribute Letter Cards in envelopes, adding one "d" and one "v" from the following page. Say, stretching if needed, each of the following

words and have students "build" it. Have them check with their partners on completion of each word. Then give the group the cue to Say-Spell-Say the word in unison. If your students are ready, challenge them to spell *visita*.

| *ave* | *viva* | *veo* | *días* | *visita* |

6. ***Escritura*** *(Story-Related Writing)*. At the end of each day, have two students read, with expression, sentences from their story. Have the entire class provide applause and praise. (You may wish to send home a certificate.) Also, let students take their Share Sheets home to read to parents and other family members when these have been mastered fairly well. Send a form for listeners to sign and have students return both the Share Sheet and the form. Enjoy your celebration!

> *Teachers, please remember: Using syllable cards, flash cards, and Share Sheets, work in a quick review at some point in each day's lesson. Frequent but brief reviews of words and syllables will increase your students' reading fluency, as will repeated readings of stories and Share Sheets.*

Stretch and Spell (19)

d	v	d	v
d	v	d	v
d	v	d	v
d	v	d	v
d	v	d	v
d	v	d	v

Lesson 19
Tesoro Compartido

Word Reading. Have students take turns reading aloud the phonetic words with their partner

tan	ave	días	veo	visita
te	pan	viva	ve	Eva

Sentence Reading. Have students take turns reading aloud the sentences with their partner. Encourage them to read with expression.

Eva va de paseo.
Mira un ave linda.
El ave no se mueve.
Eva le da pan.
¡El ave ya está bien!

Have a few students read out loud to the class, with expression.

Comprehension.   Ask the question: "¿ Qué pasó en el cuento?" Have students read each phrase aloud then point to the correct answer that completes the phrase, alternating with their partner. Students may write the phrase in the blank space after each incomplete sentence if they are able. Have students take turns orally answering the last questions. Challenge students to write their answers.

1. Eva visita al _____.
   ave   sapo

2. El ave se come el _____.
   tomate   pan

3. ¿Qué mira Eva?

   _____

4. ¿Dónde va el ave?

   _____

5. ¿Ayuda Eva al ave?

   _____

Practicing Concepts. Have students color a star in the box every time they read the words and sentences or share their ideas with their partner. Once Share Sheets have been mastered, have students take them home. Tell students to read their Share Sheets to as many people as possible. Each listener should write their initials and the date in the designated box.

Lesson 19
Escritura

Letter Writing. *Have students stretch and read the letter, then write it three times.*

V

Stretch and Spell. *Have students take turns with their partner stretching the word for each picture. After they have said the word, direct students to try to spell the whole word. If students are not able, have them write the first letter.*

(vaca) _____   (vaso) _____

Writing Ideas. *Have students think about and discuss how Eva visited the bird every day. Read the first two sentences aloud, then have students take turns with their partner reading them aloud. Tell students to finish the next sentence by describing or drawing someone they might visit frequently. Challenge them to write about what they do when they visit.*

Eva visita al ave. Le da el pan.
Visito _____

_____

_____

_____

Have students share their writing with their partner, and have a few students share with the class.

Appendix 2.5

Cooperative Integrated Reading and Composition

Jumanji

by

Chris van Allsburg

Production Team:
Anna Marie Farnish
Pamela Cantrell

Center for Social Organization of Schools
3505 North Charles Street
Johns Hopkins University
Baltimore, MD 21218
Phone: (410) 516-0370 Fax: (410) 516-6370

Note: The Houghton Mifflin Company edition of *Jumanji* was used to prepare this Treasure Hunt. The page references may differ in other editions or in the hard cover book.

Story Summary: *Jumanji* tells how two children, out looking for adventure, find a mysterious board game in the park. After Peter and Judy's parents leave for the opera, the children tire of playing their old games and messing up the house. Looking for excitement, they journey to the park where they find a game called Jumanji under a tree. They take the game home and read the instructions that explicitly state that once the game is started, it must be finished. They soon find out what this direction means, as everything that is happening in the game also happens in real life. Soon Peter and Judy are sitting in their living room with monsoon rains pouring down, a lion in the bedroom, and monkeys making a mess in the kitchen. Anxious to finish the game, they are relieved when Judy finally reaches Jumanji, a city of golden buildings and towers, and all of the animals and confusion disappear into a cloud. The two children quickly return the game to the park. When the parents return home from the opera, they do not believe the story of the day's adventures. Peter and Judy, however, know that the trouble isn't over when they see two of their friends running through the park, carrying Jumanji.

✍ **About The Author:** Chris Van Allsburg received his BA from the University of Michigan and his MA from Rhode Island School of Design. Currently, he lives in Providence, Rhode Island, with his wife Lisa, and his cat Cecil. He has received numerous awards for his illustrations and is praised for his off-beat stories, loved by both children and adults. Van Allsburg likes to include a drawing of a dog in each of his books and he describes himself as "a writer who is motivated by the images that I see in my mind."

☆ **Listening Comprehension/Read Aloud Connections** ☆

Every author has a unique style and students can learn about that style by studying story elements and the craft used by the author. *Jumanji* has many examples of foreshadowing, or hints and clues that certain events will occur later. Select a book or story that has examples of foreshadowing for examination during the Listening Comprehension. Call attention to how these techniques support the author's style and reinforce the students' ability to construct meaning while reading. Examples of other stories with foreshadowing include: *Night Noises* by Mem Fox, *The Snow Queen* retold by Joan Collins, *The Firebird* by Selina Hastings, and *The Headless Horseman* by Washington Irving.

Building Background: To prepare students for reading *Jumanji,* discuss the following topics with them.

- *Jumanji,* is a fantasy. Ask students if they know what a fantasy is. What are the differences between a fantasy and realistic fiction?

- Ask the students how a board game is played. What are some examples of board games? What makes a board game fun? Do you ever get "bored" with board games? Why?

- Jumanji is an African game that brings the wild animals of Africa into Peter and Judy's house. Using the know-want to know-learned (K-W-L) learning model, make a list of what the students already know about the wild areas of Africa. What is an African safari like? What kinds of animals live there? What kinds of animals live in African jungles? Make another list of the things that students might like to find out about these places. As students learn about Africa while reading the book, create a third list of what they have learned. Ask students to include in their lists the things that they might see, hear, and do in a jungle.

- It has been speculated that the adventures of the board game Jumanji are related to the opera "Aïda." The opera is set in Africa and while the parents were seeing it, the children have an African adventure of their own. Consult with the music teacher and play a selection from this opera for the class. Ask the class what images the music gives them, and later, discuss how this relates to the tone of the story. *Aïda* by Leontyne Price tells the story of the opera and may be used to compare illustrations, setting, and tone with *Jumanji.*

♀ **Preview/Predict/Purpose:** Have students read and think about the title of the book, look at the illustrations and read the first two pages. Have students predict what might happen in the story. Then have them use their predictions to set a purpose for reading such as, "I'm going to read to find out what happens when the children play the game."

♀ *Jumanji* may be coupled with the following reading/ ♀
listening comprehension/study skills exercises:

✔Drawing conclusions (RC)   ✔Fact and fantasy (RC)
✔Character traits (RC/LC)   ✔Cause and effect (RC/LC)
✔Following directions (SS)   ✔Problem solving with failed attempts (LC)
✔Foreshadowing (LC)   ✔Mood (LC)

📖 *Read the first three pages aloud to the students* 📖

✧ Word Mastery List ✧

agreed 3	opera 1	laughter 1	silence 1
revealing 5	slouched 1	sweater 3	board 5
gasping 9	horror 7	piano 7	whisker 9
instant 11	stampede 17	rumble 17	interrupted 25
relief 23	exhaustion 23	lava 21	erupts 21
volcano 21	guide 15		

TREASURE HUNT

Section I. Read through page 13. Discuss the answers to the questions with your partner. Then write your answers, while your partner answers separately.

1. Describe the main characters in this story. Peter and Judy were the main characters in this story. Judy was a determined, bossy, older sister. Peter was a follower.

2. What did the children do when their parents left? Why? Peter and Judy made a mess in the house and then went looking in the park for adventure. They were bored with their games at home.
🎵 **How is this different from what you would have done?**

3. What did the children find in the park? Peter and Judy found a game called Jumanji. The mysterious way that they found the game, the fact that the game is designed for the bored and restless, the phrase "fun for some but not for all," and the direction that states that the game, once started, must be finished, all indicate that playing Jumanji will be an adventure.
🎵 **What clues did the author give to help you predict that Jumanji will be an exciting game?**

4. Explain how the game, Jumanji, is special. When Peter landed on a square, the animal appeared, just like the game said. The events of the game were occurring in real life.

5. Why do you think that the author wrote the words for Instruction D in capital letters? Why must the children continue playing the game? Instruction D was written in capital letters to show that it was the most important instruction. The game's directions stated that the game would not end until someone reached the city of Jumanji and won the game. The animals wouldn't go away until then.

Make a Prediction

What has happened in the story so far? How is that different from what you expected? What will happen next? Will Peter and Judy be able to finish playing Jumanji? Give reasons for your answers. (Discuss students' predictions. Have students give support for their predictions.)

Section II. Finish reading the story. Discuss the answers to the following questions with your partner. Then each of you should write your answers separately.

1. What has happened in the story that lets you know that this story is a fantasy and not realistic fiction? Each time that Peter or Judy landed on a new space, whatever was written in that game square would happen in real life.

2. How do you think the children felt when they played the game? How do you know? Peter and Judy were probably very scared that something bad would happen to them. They rushed to try to finish the game quickly. Judy begged to roll a 12 so the game would be over.

3. What did the children do with the game when they were finished? They rushed it back to the park so it wouldn't be in their house anymore.
🎵 **What would you have done in their situation? Why?**

4. Why did the adults laugh when the children tried to tell them about their day? The adults didn't believe Peter's story. They thought that the children were playing make believe.
🎵 **How might Peter and Judy have tried to convince them that they were telling the truth?**

5. What do you think the children learned? The children learned to read directions carefully. They also decided that their ordinary games weren't so boring after all.

6. What do you think the game maker meant by, "Free game. Fun for some but not for all." Did Peter and Judy have fun playing Jumanji? Why? (Answers may vary. Accept those that are supported.) The game is only fun if the players follow the directions. Otherwise, the animals will never leave. The game maker may also mean that the game is more scary than fun. Peter and Judy did not enjoy the game because they were very scared. They rushed through the game and wanted it to be over quickly, even though it had been an exciting experience to remember.

1. *How did Peter and Judy feel at the beginning of the story?* The two children were bored. They were tired of playing their games and making a mess in the house. They wanted to do something exciting.

2. *Explain what happened when the children played Jumanji.* Each time they landed on a space, something new would happen. Whatever was written in the game square happened in real life. Peter and Judy had to finish the game so that the wild animals would disappear and their house would return to normal.

3. *Compare how Peter and Judy felt about their old games at the start of the story to how they felt at the end.* At the beginning of the story, Peter and Judy were very bored with their old games and were anxious to find some excitement. After playing Jumanji, they were more appreciative of their old games.

4. *What conclusion did Peter and Judy's parents draw about Peter's tale of adventure? Why did they make this conclusion?* The parents laughed at the story, assuming that Peter was imagining the adventure. The parents had found Peter and Judy soundly asleep on the couch and probably could not imagine that such confusion could have taken place that evening in their own home.

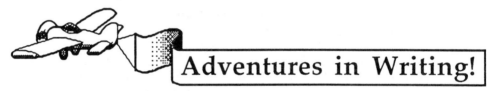

Adventures in Writing!

Choose one of the following:

1. At the end of the story, Daniel and Walter Budwig had found the game in the park. Mrs. Budwig said that the two boys did not read directions carefully. Write several paragraphs about Daniel and Walter. What will happen when they play Jumanji? What clues from the story let you know that this might happen? Will they finish the game? Describe their exciting adventures as they play Jumanji. Include a picture of the scene that Mr. and Mrs. Budwig might find if they arrive home in the middle of the game.

2. Imagine that Peter and Judy's parents arrived home in the middle of the Jumanji game. What would their parents have done? Would Judy and Peter have gotten in trouble? Would the game ever be finished? Pretending that you are Peter or Judy, write several paragraphs persuading your parents that the game must be finished.

✧ Story Test Answers ✧

1. **Why did Peter and Judy go to the park?** Peter and Judy were bored. They wanted to play in the park because it would surely be more exciting than their games at home.

2. **Why did Judy read the directions to Jumanji carefully?** There was a note taped to the box that said that they should read the directions carefully.

3. **What happened when Judy and Peter played Jumanji?** Everything that happened in the game happened in real life. There were wild animals all over the house.

4. **How did the adults react to Peter's story?** The adults laughed because they thought that he was making it all up.

5. **What was the new problem at the end of the story?** Walter and Daniel had found the game and they usually did not follow directions carefully. They might get hurt playing the game.

✎ Extension Activities ✎

1. **What's Your Game?** Using the game Jumanji as a model, create your own game in which you pretend that the things you include in the game really happen. Think about the rules that Van Allsburg used for Jumanji. Use things or places that interest you. How about a game about outer space, or about deep sea travel?

2. **African Experience:** The game of Jumanji takes place in an African jungle, but not all of Africa is a jungle like the one in the story. Africa has large cities, deserts, coastline, and grasslands. Research the continent of Africa. Once you have found enough information on the continent, create a tour brochure that highlights the important facts about Africa and describes major points of interest.

3. **Van Allsburg Illustrations:** Chris Van Allsburg's books are all well known for their exceptional illustrations. Pick another book of Van Allsburg and compare and contrast those illustrations to the ones found in *Jumanji*. Pick your favorite illustration from each book and write, along with your comparison, why you like those drawings the most. What does the author do to contribute to suspense through his illustrations?

4. **Volcano:** Research volcanoes. How are they formed? Where are major ones located? What are some famous volcanic eruptions? Whey are they considered to be dangerous? Write a report on your findings to present to your class, along with a diagram of a volcano.

5. **Games Alive!** Pick your favorite board game and imagine what would happen if that game came to life while you were playing, as they did in *Jumanji*. Are you alone or are you playing with a partner? Write several paragraphs telling what happens and how you react. How does the game end?

6. **Van Allsburg Interview:** Pretend that you will have the opportunity to interview Chris Van Allsburg. Write five questions for the author/illustrator about his life, his stories, or his illustrations. Then exchange your questions with a partner and pretend that you are Van Allsburg, answer the questions as you think that he would.

✳ So, You Want to Read More ✳

✍   by Van Allsburg? Look for *The Garden of Abdul Gasazi, The Polar Express, The Mysteries of Harris Burdick,* or *Ben's Dream.*

✍   fantasy books? Try *James and the Giant Peach* by Roald Dahl, *Mufaro's Beautiful Daughters* by John Steptoe, or *The Secret Garden* by Frances Hodgson Burnett.

Appendix 2.6

COOPERATIVE INTEGRATED READING AND COMPOSITION

Beyond the Basics
Reading Wings

UN HATILLO DE CEREZAS

BY
MARÌA PUNCEL

Center for Social Organization of Schools
3505 North Charles Street
Johns Hopkins University
Baltimore, MD 21218
Phone: (410) 516-8800   Fax: (410) 516-8890

EDICIÓN DEL MAESTRO

1995

Resumen del Cuento: Tema y enfoque de la selección

El cuento se desarrolla en un valle donde Antonio es ayudante de panadero. Un día al llevar el pan a vender al mercado se encuentra al tío Curro que le regala un hatillo de cerezas. A Antonio le encantaban las cerezas pero decidió llevárselas a la abuela Francisca porque sólo podía comer cosas blandas y jugosas. La abuela Francisca decidió dárselas a su hermana María. El hatillo de cerezas fue pasando de mano en mano hasta que llegó de nuevo a las manos de Antonio que se sorprendió de como fue que el hatillo de cerezas llegó de nuevo hasta él. Antonio disfrutó mucho de las cerezas pero le pidió a su madre que investigara porque le habían regresado las cerezas.

Sobre la Autora: Conozcamos a María Puncel.

Construyendo Conocimiento: Estrategias previas a la lectura

Explíqueles que *Un hatillo de cerezas* es el relato de un grupo de campesinos que se demuestran afecto y cariño haciéndose un regalo singular. Luego escriba en el pizarrón "Es mejor dar que recibir" y anime a los estudiantes a intercambiar ideas sobre lo que esa frase significa para ellos. Pídales que mencionen ocasiones en que le hayan dado un regalo singular a alguien o hayan compartido algo excepcional con otros. Pídales que expliquen cómo se sintieron y que discutan porqué los regalos hacen que una persona se sienta bien.

Muestre como se hace un hatillo:

- con un cuadro de tela se forma un hatillo
- un hatillo se puede formar con una servilleta
- las cerezas pueden ir dentro de un hatillo

Comprensión Auditiva/Conexiones de Lectura en Voz Alta: Todos los autores tienen un estilo único. Los estudiantes pueden aprender ese estilo al estudiar los elementos del cuento y la habilidad del autor. *Un hatillo de cerezas* es un **cuento de ficción.** Escoja otro **cuento de ficción** para leer en voz alta a los estudiantes. Asegúrese que los estudiantes se den cuenta de cómo las técnicas de los **cuentos de ficción** apoyan al estilo del autor y refuerzan la habilidad del lector para construir el significado mientras lee. Unos ejemplos de otros **cuentos de ficción** son: *Jugo de pecas* y *La princesa de papel.*

Previsión/Predicción/Propósito: Pídales a los estudiantes que lean y mediten sobre el título del cuento, que miren el dibujo de la portada, y que lean las primeras dos páginas. Haga que los estudiantes predigan lo que pueda pasar en el cuento. Después, pídale que se propongan un propósito para leer, tal como, **"Voy a leer para saber quién se comerá las cerezas."**

📖 **Lea las páginas 1-3 en voz alta a los estudiantes** 📖

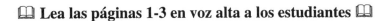

┌─────────────────────────────┐
│   ✧ **Palabras Retadoras** ✧   │
└─────────────────────────────┘

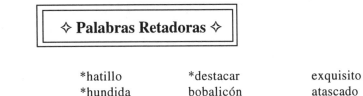

| *hogosas | *hatillo | *destacar | exquisito |
| serenos | *hundida | bobalicón | atascado |

BÚSQUEDA
DE TESOROS

Sección I. Lee las páginas 1 a5. Discute las respuestas a las preguntas con tu compañero. Luego, escribe tus respuestas, mientras que tu compañero contesta por separado.

1. *¿Por qué trabajaba Antonio desde la noche hasta el amanecer?* Antonio trabajaba desde la noche hasta el amanecer porque era ayudante de panadero.
   ♫ *¿Por qué tendría que llevar Antonio el pan que hacía a la panadería del mercado?*

2. *¿Por qué marchaba Antonio a los caseríos del valle?* Las respuestas varian.

3. *¿Por qué crees que el caballo se espantó?* Las respuestas varían.

4. *¿Cómo crees que le hicieron Antonio y Farina para quitar el carro del atolladero?* Las respuestas varían.

5. *¿Por qué le dio las cerezas el tío Curro a Antonio?* Antonio le ayudó al tío con su carro.

6. *Explica por qué se le hacía agua la boca de Antonio agua sólo de pensar en las cerezas.* Las respuestas varían.
   ♫ *¿Por qué se dice que se le hace uno "agua la boca" cuando piensa en algo sabroso?*

Haz una Predicció

¿Qué va a hacer Antoinio con las cerezas? Justifica tus respuestas. (Discuta las predicciones de los estudiantes. Pídales que apoyen sus predicciones con el texto.)

Sección II. Lee hasta la página 10. Discute las respuestas a las preguntas con tu compañero. Luego, escribe tus respuestas, mientras tu compañero contesta por separado.

1. *¿Por qué le dio Antonio a su abuela las cerezas?* Las respuestas varían.
   Discute lo que tú hubieras hecho con las cerezas.

2. *¿Por qué no se comió la abuela Francisca las cerezas para el almuerzo?* La abuela se las quería dar a su hermana María.

3. *¿Por qué iba ser mejor que María se comiera las cerezas, según la abuela?* María dice siempre tener un sabor amargo en la boca.
   ♫ *¿Cómo es que tiñen las madejas de lana?*

4. *¿Por qué crees que María quería darle las cerezas a Pedro?* Las respuestas varían.

5. *¿Por qué crees que Antonio tuvo que ir a llevarle a Pedro las cerazas?* Las respuestas varían.

6. *¿Crees que Pedro va a comerse las cerezas?* Las respuestas varían.

¿Recuerdas el Cuento?
Trabaja con tu Compañero

1. *¿Cuál era el trabajo de Antonio?* Antonio era ayudante de panadero. Trabajaba cada noche hasta el amanecer: preparaba la masa, calentaba el horno y cocía las hogazas. Antonio ponía los panes en grandes cestos y los llevaba por los caseríos del valle, para repartir el pan.

2. *¿Qué pasó una mañana?* Antonio encontró el carro del tío Curro atascado. El caballo del tío Curro se asustó y el carro se hundió en un hoyo. Antonio de muy buena voluntad le ayudó a sacar el carro del atolladero.

3. *¿Cómo recompensó el tío a Antonio?* El tío Curro le dio a Antonio unas cerezas. El tío Curro tomó una sevilleta e hizo un hatillo para que se las llevara. A Antonio se le hacía agua la boca sólo de pensar en ellas.

¡Aventuras con la Escritura!

Escoge una de las siguientes opciones:

1. *Antonio y Farina le ayudaron a su tío Curro con el carro. ¿Qué crees que tenían que hacer para sacar la rueda del hoyo? Descríbelo en dos o tres palabras.*

2. *¿Te gustan las cerezas? ¿Qué fruta te gusta mejor? ¿Por qué? Imagina que tienes un amigo que nunca ha probado esa fruta. Escribe dos o tres palabras que tratan de persuadirlo a probar la fruta.*

3. *¿Has recibido un regalo especial que alguien más quería? ¿Has compartido un regalo con un amigo para poder gozar juntos? Escribe un párrafo sobre cuando compartiste un regalo con alguien importante.*

✳ Respuestas del Examen del Cuento ✳

1. **¿Por qué trabajaba Antonio de la noche a la mañana?** Antonio trabajaba de la noche a la mañana porque era ayudante de panadero.

2. **¿Por qué marchaba Antonio a los caseríos del valle?** Las respuestas varían.

3. **¿Por qué le dio las cerezas a Antonio el tío Curro?** Las respuestas varían.

4. **¿Por qué no se comió Antonio las cerezas?** Las respuestas varían.

5. **¿Por qué no se comió la abuela las cerezas?** Las respuestas varían.

6. **¿Por qué no se comió María las cerezas?** Las respuestas varían.

Appendix 2.7. Sample Writing Lesson: Mind Movies

Lesson 1
CREATING MIND MOVIES

Objective: In this lesson, you will help students learn how to develop enough detail in their narrative to keep readers interested.

Writing Activity #1—"_____Made Me Furious"

Preparation: Write the following "skeleton," or planning form, on the board.

SKELETON PLAN

Assignment?
For whom am I writing?
What is it about?

QUESTIONS	ANSWERS	DETAILS

What happened first?
　　　　Second?
　　　　Third?
What happened last?

You may wish to make enough copies of this form for your students to use in planning three compositions. A full-page-sized copy of this form is included at the end of the lesson.

Teacher Presentation:

1. Explain the writing process. (Skip this step if your students are familiar with the writing process.) Explain to students that they are going to be authors. Show them the step-by-step process that authors go through as they develop each piece of writing. Explain each of the following steps:

Prewriting: Identifying the purpose, audience, and topic you will write about. Starting to plan the writing.

Drafting: Getting the ideas down on paper in some form. Focus on meaning, not mechanics.

Responding: Hearing what a reader has to say.

Revising: Using the reader's response and your own ideas about what will improve the writing to develop the ideas further. Focus again on meaning.

Editing: Checking for errors in sentence sense, spelling, punctuation, and capitalization.

Publication: Making a final *great* copy to keep and present to others.

2. *Explain the focus of the lesson.* Read the following personal narrative, or share a story of your own.

"How My Sister Made Me Furious"

You can imagine how furious I was when my sister, Joan, broke my new model train! Aunt Mary gave it to me for Christmas. I have wanted a train ever since I can remember. It was my most prized possession. Joan wanted to play with it and kept asking me for permission. She was bothering me, so I finally let her play with it. I showed her how to use the control box and told her to be very careful. Then she pushed the wrong button. The train went off the tracks and crashed into the wall. Now the control box doesn't work, the tracks are bent out of shape, and the train is smashed. I'm so mad at Joan that I haven't talked to her since she broke the train last Monday.

Ask your students if they found the story interesting. Explain that readers often like to read about personal experiences that writers have, things that happened in their lives. Explain that in this lesson they will be writing about experiences from their lives that they think will interest their audience, which will be their classmates.

3. *Prewriting.* Show students the planning form that you have written on the board. (Pass out copies of the form if you have made them. If not, have students copy the steps in the form as they work through it.) Tell your students that in this assignment you want them to share with their classmates something that made them so angry they could feel steam coming out of their ears. Fill in the first two sections of the planning form as you discuss the assignment with your students.

SKELETON PLAN

Assignment?
For whom am I writing?
What is it about?

QUESTIONS	ANSWERS	DETAILS

What happened first?
Second?
Third?
What happened last?

Take a few minutes to have students write down two or three things that have made them angry. Now, brainstorm some ideas for topics with the class all together.

If you need some warm-ups, try out starters like these:

- The day my mother made me do chores when the circus was in town.
- The day I was soaked by a bus going through a puddle.
- The day I lost a soccer game I had started out winning.
- I got sick opening night and I couldn't be in the play.

4. Discuss how to keep a reader interested. Point out that readers will stay interested in a piece of writing if an author includes enough information to let the reader share the experience. Tell your students to try to create a *mind movie* as they write. A mind movie is the ability of the reader to see a movie of the story in his or her mind. If the author includes lots of clear detail, the reader will be able to see a mind movie of the story. If the reader has to guess about details, the movie won't get rolling. Use the following story to illustrate how the movie begins to roll as the details are filled in. (This story provides an illustration of the developing movie. It is about a topic different than the one your students will use.)

Carol decided that she wanted to have a party, so she told her mother that her friends were coming over. They had a great time. They had a lot to eat.

Ask the class, "Can you see a movie in your mind or do you have to guess what happened?" Obviously, they have to guess. They do not know who came, how many came, what they ate, what everyone did, and so on. They have to write their own script for the movie if they are going to picture this experience in their minds.

Now try this story:

Carol decided that she wanted to have a roller skating party for her birthday. She invited 10 of her best friends from school. They had a blast. The most fun they had was making a chain.

Ask your students what additional information helped them to see a movie in their minds. Ask them what they still need to guess. They now know what kind of party it was and who came. They still need to guess what a chain is and what there was to eat.

Carol decided that she wanted to have a roller skating party for her birthday. She invited 10 of her best friends from school. They had a blast. The most fun they had was making a chain. Carol was the leader. Each person held hands with someone else as they skated around and around the rink together. They had lots of food to eat.

Ask your students what additional information helped them see a movie in their mind. Ask them what they still need to guess. They now know that the chain was a human chain of skaters, but they still have to guess what there was to eat.

Point out that the story and the mind movie were improved with each draft as the details were filled in so that the reader did not have to guess.

Complete a planning form for one of these topics to demonstrate how the form is used. A sample is given next:

SKELETON PLAN

Assignment? Share an event that made me *furious!*
For whom am I writing? Classmates.
What is it about? The day I got soaked by a truck going through a puddle.

QUESTIONS	ANSWERS	DETAILS
What happened first?	•Got ready for Halloween	•Witch costume
Second?	•Put on face makeup	•White powdered face, painted black lines
Third?	•Truck splashed mud	•Covered my face
What happened last?	•Had to go home	•Had to be a ghost

5. Invite teammate feedback on planning. Have students select a topic and complete their planning form. If students have difficulty identifying a topic, have them talk with teammates about things that have made them angry.

When some students have completed their planning forms, ask for a volunteer to discuss his or her plan with the class. Model with that student for the class how to help the author develop a plan by asking for more information about things readers have to guess to fill in their mind movies.

Now, have all your students present to a teammate what they wish to write about. Have the teammates try to visualize a mind movie and to ask for more details if they find they have to guess. *Have the responding teammate write his or her initials in the upper right corner of the planning form.*

6. Drafting the story. Have your students write their first draft on every other line so that they can make additions and changes as their story develops. Remind them that their goal is simply to get their ideas down. They need not worry about correct spelling or mechanics or even whether they have expressed their ideas as well as possible.

You may wish to have your students complete their draft during class or for homework. If you have time to allow drafting during class time, confer briefly (1 to 2 minutes) with as many students as possible, helping them to develop their mind movies.

7. Review the Team Response Guide. Before having students read their first stories to the class or to their team, review the Team Response Guide below. This guide will help the students learn how to provide one another with useful feedback by asking for the three kinds of responses listed next:

   a. Restate, in one sentence, what the author had to say. This gives important feedback to the author about whether his or her basic message got across.

   b. State what they liked or found interesting. This provides encouragement.

   c. Ask questions to find out more about the topic presented. These questions will tell the author what else the audience would like to know and may point out things that are not clear.

It is most important to encourage students to identify and share with the author what they like about a piece of writing. This kind of feedback is often very effective at developing an author's confidence.

TEAM RESPONSE GUIDE
CREATING MIND MOVIES—ACTIVITY #1

Reader:
1. Read your paper with expression.
2. Write a brief note about how your teammates responded after they have talked about your story.

Discussion leader (the person to the left of the reader):

Ask each of the following questions. You and your teammates can all offer answers to the questions. If no one starts off the discussion, you may ask someone to say what he or she thinks. Encourage everyone on the team to participate.

1. What did you hear? What was the story about?
2. What did you like most about the story?
3. Picture your mind movie. Do you have to guess about details? Ask questions to help the author fill in the picture.

Teammates:
Be thoughtful. Share your responses, especially your positive ones!

To help them read smoothly and clearly, have all the students practice reading their compositions out loud (in a murmur) before the class reading begins. Then have one student from each team read his or her writing to the class and have the class respond by using the team Response Guide. You should act as discussion leader for the first one or two readings to provide a model for the role and then ask a student to act as discussion leader. Model the way you want students to respond to the questions, especially how to provide positive comments and even how to phrase somewhat critical comments positively. Keep the tone very encouraging. Enjoy the readings with the class.

After the discussion, have the author write a brief note summarizing the responses, noting things the readers had to guess at the end of the draft. Help the first author or two, to again provide a model for the class.

8. *Team response.* Have the students who did not read their pieces to the class read them to their teams.

Your role during this time is to move around the room, listening and helping students respond usefully to their teammates' writing. Allow 3 to 4 minutes for each student to read and get teammate responses. Remind them to move on to the next question. Remind students to write a note about their teammates' responses at the bottom of the draft.

9. *Scoring.* Collect the drafts and planning forms. Give 100 team points to each student who hands in an initialed planning form and a draft with a note about teammate's responses at the end. Hand the drafts back to the students to keep in their writing folders.

3

Tutoring Programs

Tutoring is the most important means by which Success for All/Roots and Wings ensures that all students will succeed in reading. It is the most expensive element of the program, but also probably one of the most cost-effective, because it is tutoring, more than any other feature, that enables the school to reduce retentions and special education placements (see Chapters 8 and 9).

Tutors in Success for All/Roots and Wings are usually certified teachers with a background in reading or early childhood education. In some circumstances, highly trained paraprofessionals are used. In many schools moving away from traditional Title I pullout models, tutors were once the Title I teachers. Some tutors are special education teachers, in which case they primarily tutor special education students or students at risk for special education placement.

Tutors have a dual role. During reading period (usually 90 minutes per day), they teach a reading class, both to reduce class sizes for reading and to give them a thorough idea of what the regular reading program is. The rest of the day, tutors work one-on-one with children who are having the greatest difficulties learning to read.

Decisions about which students need tutoring are made based on students' scores on 8-week assessments (see Chapter 2), plus teacher recommendations. First graders receive priority for tutoring, although second and third graders can be tutored if enough tutoring services are available. A number of first, second, and third grade tutoring "slots" are set aside based on the number of tutors available and scheduling constraints, and then the lowest-achieving students at each grade level are assigned a tutor. Students leave tutoring when their performance no longer places them among the lowest achievers in their grade. The average student who receives any tutoring will meet with a tutor every day for a semester (18 weeks), but individual first graders have stayed in tutoring for as long as 1 ½ years—into midsecond grade.

Tutors meet with children 20 minutes each day. The school's schedule is set up so that tutors can work all day without ever taking students from reading, language arts, or math periods. Many schools reorganize their days to add 20 minutes each day to social studies, and then those students who receive tutoring are taken from social studies. In this arrangement, social studies periods are placed at different times for different classes and grades. Some schools have special resource periods or find other ways to schedule tutoring with minimum impact on students' other subjects. Before- and after-school tutoring can sometimes extend the hours available for tutoring when transportation is not a problem.

Basic Principles of Tutoring in Success for All/Roots and Wings

The tutoring program in Success for All/Roots and Wings is based on a set of fundamental principles. These are as follows (adapted from Wasik & Madden, 1995).

Tutoring Is One-to-One

One-to-one tutoring is the most effective form of instruction, especially for students with reading problems (Slavin, 1994; Wasik & Slavin, 1993). One reason for the effectiveness of one-to-one tutoring is that it allows tutors to teach to the individual student's needs. Tutors can make individual learning plans that fit the student's needs and can spend as much time as needed to teach a particular sound-blending or comprehension strategy.

Also, in one-to-one tutoring tutors have the opportunity to give constant, immediate feedback to a student. If a student makes an error when reading, immediate corrective feedback can be provided along with the instruction needed to prevent further errors. This on-line diagnostic assessment and feedback is not possible when working with an entire class, or even a small group.

Because tutors have the opportunity to have intensive instruction time with each student, they learn a lot about the student's strengths and weaknesses, and which approaches work best with each. Tutors capitalize on this knowledge and use it in presenting material in the best way that will help students learn and remember the information.

One-to-one tutoring increases the opportunity for reading. When it is just one tutor and one student, the student can read and reread until he or she has mastered words, comprehended the story, and can read fluently. These opportunities are extremely limited for poor readers during group instruction.

Tutoring Supports Classroom Instruction

Tutoring is closely coordinated with classroom instruction. The tutor works to support student success on the material that is presented in class, rather than teaching a separate program. For example, if the consonant /n/ is being taught in the student's reading class, then the tutor works on words and stories using this sound during tutoring. This helps students keep up with class instruction and helps accelerate their learning. The repeated practice with and exposure to the material presented in the classroom helps students solidify their reading knowledge.

Students Learn to Read by Reading

Students learn to read by reading. Reading is a complex process that involves decoding of words, tracking of words across the page, and constructing meaning from individual words as well as sentences and paragraphs. Success in reading requires the coordination of these complex activities. Therefore, teaching each of these activities in isolation will not teach a student to read and comprehend text. Reading connected text helps develop decoding skills, helps with fluency, and facilitates reading comprehension. Tutoring provides an opportunity for students to read and get on-line feedback on their reading.

Communication Between Tutors and Classroom Reading Teachers Is Essential

Tutors must communicate with the reading teacher of the students they are tutoring. It is essential that the tutors know how the students they are tutoring are performing in the classroom. They need to adapt their tutoring plan to the specific areas in which the student is having problems. The teacher also needs to be informed of the student's progress and other specific information that the tutor can provide that would help the teacher work better with the student.

The Tutoring Process in Reading Roots

Tutoring Goals

The primary focus of tutoring is to help the student learn to create meaning from the printed word. The tutor reinforces the Reading Roots lessons presented in the reading classroom, providing students with a number of strategies to figure out unknown words and to understand the meaning of sentences and paragraphs. These strategies include the following:

1. Mastering letter/sound relationships and using phonics to sound out unknown words;
2. Using pictures and context to figure out unknown words;
3. Using pictures and context to add meaningful information about what is happening in the story to promote comprehension; and
4. Using comprehension monitoring strategies to improve comprehension.

Diagnostic Assessment

Before the tutor begins working with a student, the tutor administers the Tutoring Diagnostic Assessment Checklist (see Figure 3.1). The assessment checklist helps tutors determine the specific problems and strengths of a student and to tailor the tutoring session to meet the specific needs of the student. The tutor can determine if the student is having problems sounding out words, recognizing specific letters, or understanding connected text, or has more basic problems with concepts about print.

A tutoring plan tailored to the needs of the particular student is made based on the information gained from the diagnostic checklist. The diagnostic assessment may show that a student has difficulty understanding basic concepts about print and tracking from left to right, as well as sounding out words. The tutor would then integrate opportunities to review and reinforce basic concepts about print into the basic tutoring activities such as rereading of a familiar story, and would ensure that as the student read, he or she used a finger or other tracking support strategy to assist in tracking. A second student might have difficulties with memory, comprehension monitoring, and fluency. Many strategies are in place in the basic tutoring model to address these difficulties, but the tutor's plan would set the priorities and specific strategies helpful in focusing on the specific student's difficulties. In this case, the

Tutoring Diagnostic Assessment Checklist—
Success for All/Roots and Wings

Student _____ Date _____ Tester _____

Book title _____

The Assessment Checklist is administered to each student in tutoring. Mark **yes** or **no** next to each statement to indicate if the student does or does not exhibit the behavior.

Yes responses indicate that the child has the behavior. It in not a problem. **No** responses indicate that the child does not have the behavior and therefore, it is something that should be worked on in tutoring.

ACTIVITY I: Place a familiar story in front of the student and ask him to point where he should start to read.

STUDENT BEHAVIOR	YES/NO	SKILL
1. Knows the back from the front of the book.		Concepts about print
2. Knows what the first page is.		Concepts about print
3. Points to words not to the pictures.		Concepts about print

ACTIVITY II: Ask the student to read aloud from a familiar story. Observe. (Second day of familiar story, Lesson 4 or beyond)

STUDENT BEHAVIOR	YES/NO	SKILL
4. Reads smoothly and fluently.		Fluency and tracking
5. Follows from one line to the next.		Tracking
6. Reads without losing track or skipping words.		Tracking
7. Tries to sound out words rather than just guessing.		Self monitoring
8. Asks for help, appropriately, with unknown words.		Self monitoring
9. Sounds out initial sounds.		Sounding out words
10. Sounds out ending sounds.		Sounding out words
11. Sounds out sound blends.		Sounding out words
12. Can put words together after sounding out letters.		Sounding out words

ACTIVITY III: Ask the student to continue to read, but to use his finger to follow each word.

STUDENT BEHAVIOR	YES/NO	SKILL
13. Reads from left to right.		Concepts about print
14. Points to the correct word as he reads.		Tracking
15. Reads more smoothly when using his finger.		Tracking

ACTIVITY IV: Have the student read three sentences in a row. Ask the student to tell you about what he read.

STUDENT BEHAVIOR	YES/NO	SKILL
16. Adequately explains what was read.		Memory and comprehension
17. Uses picture clues appropriately for comprehension.		Memory and comprehension
18. Gives adequate details when summarizing 2 or more sentences.		Memory and comprehension

Figure 3.1. Tutoring Diagnostic Assessment Checklist—Success for All/Roots and Wings

ACTIVITY V: Have the student continue to read. Observe what the student does when making errors.

STUDENT BEHAVIOR	YES/NO	SKILL
19. Rereads when meaning is unclear.		Comprehension
20. Uses context clues to help with unknown words.		Comprehension
21. Uses picture cues.		Comprehension
22. Attempts to sound out words.		Sounding out words
23. Describes a solution or strategy for how he reads.		Comprehension

ACTIVITY VI: Ask the meaning of some of the words that he has read.

STUDENT BEHAVIOR	YES/NO	SKILL
24. Understands the meaning of individual words.		Comprehension
25. Asks for help when the meaning of a word is unknown or unclear.		Self Monitoring

ACTIVITY VII: Read a page of the story aloud. Ask the student some comprehension questions about what you read.

STUDENT BEHAVIOR	YES/NO	SKILL
26.[a] Understands text when presented orally.		Comprehension

ACTIVITY VIII: As student continues to read, correct any errors the student makes and tell the student words he does not know. Observe how the student uses your feedback.

STUDENT BEHAVIOR	YES/NO	SKILL
27.[a] Can recall a word that you just told him.		Memory
28. Can recall sight words.		Memory

ACTIVITY IX: Have the student continue to read aloud. Listen for mispronounced or mislabeled words.

STUDENT BEHAVIOR	YES/NO	SKILL
29. Does not combine one letter from another word. For example: "The man sat on the **mat**." "The man sat on the **sat**."		Tracking
30. Reads with confidence.		Self-monitoring
31. Attempts to sound out words.		Self-monitoring Sounding out words

ACTIVITY X: Do this the next day. Have the student read aloud the same story he read yesterday.

STUDENT BEHAVIOR	YES/NO	SKILL
32. Able to remember sounds from one day to the next.		Memory
33. Able to remember sight words from one day to the next.		Memory
34. Able to remember word meanings from one day to the next.		Memory
35. Able to remember general meaning of the story.		Memory

NOTE: The order of common reading problems is as follows: concepts of print, sounding out words, tracking, memory problems, comprehension, fluency, self-monitoring.

a. If the child cannot understand information when presented orally, a language comprehension or learning problem may exist. Formal testing may be needed.

Figure 3.1. *Continued*

tutor may decide to focus on using the opportunity for rereading a familiar story as a time to allow the student to become fluent enough with a single story to allow that story to be read to a special audience, such as a group of kindergarten students or a special adult, to highlight fluency and expression and to celebrate a successful reading experience.

As the plan is developed, the tutor will identify backup strategies to implement if the initial strategies are not successful. The tutor will also plan a timetable for evaluation of progress to determine if the plan needs to be changed.

The *Tutoring Manual* (Wasik & Madden, 1995) contains considerable specific guidance for tutors in the analysis of errors on the diagnostic checklist, and on the strategies that tutors can use to address those errors.

Activities for Tutoring in Reading Roots

The following is a list of specific activities that are typically included in a 20-minute Reading Roots tutoring session. An explanation of these activities is also presented.

1. Rereading familiar stories;
2. Reading new stories;
3. Quick drills of letter/sounds, phonetic words, and sound blending; and
4. Writing.

Rereading Familiar Stories. Familiar stories are those which the student has read several times in class or in tutoring and has mastered fairly well. Rereading familiar stories helps the student develop rapid word recognition, expression in oral reading, and comprehension skills. When reading a story for the first time, a student will focus mainly on the individual words. In doing this, considerable effort is put into sounding the words out, so the student is not attending as well to the meaning of the individual words and sentences. When reading a story a second or third time, the student will have practiced pronouncing the words and will be able to direct his or her attention to understanding the story. The tutor plays an important role in this activity, asking the student questions about what he or she has read, teaching understanding of the message communicated in the story, and teaching metacognitive strategies to facilitate finding of the story's meaning (text follows).

Rereading a familiar story also helps develop fluency and confidence in reading. Repeated readings help the student practice familiar words and familiar sentence patterns. Also, through repeated readings, the student gets repeated opportunities to comprehend the material. Being able to read fluently and with expression indicates that the student does in fact comprehend what he or she is reading. It may take three, or four, or more readings of the same story before the student reads it with appropriate intonations and expression. Each time the student reads the story, however, he or she focuses on different parts of the reading process, which reinforces word recognition strategies and comprehension skills.

Students' rereading of familiar stories provides an opportunity for tutors to teach metacognitive comprehension monitoring skills, "tricks of the trade" that effective readers use to monitor their own reading and help make sense of it.

The purpose of this activity is to teach the student how to read for meaning and monitor comprehension at the same time. Often a student will read the words in a story but not understand the message being communicated in the text. For students with reading problems, comprehension monitoring is not a skill that comes automatically with reading. The tutor needs to teach this skill.

There are two parts to teaching comprehension monitoring skills. One is to help the student identify a problem in understanding what he or she has read. The tutor begins by explaining that a reader needs to get a message from the information being read, and then teaches self-monitoring strategies that will help the student determine if he or she understands the reading. The second part is to teach the student how to fix comprehension monitoring problems.

The tutor begins by teaching the student to ask questions that determine if he or she is understanding what is being read. First, the tutor models these self-monitoring strategies. After the student has read a section of a story, the tutor may ask a question that will assess his or her understanding, such as "Does what you have just read make sense to you; do you understand what happened in the story?" The student is asked to summarize in his or her own words what he or she just read.

The idea is to get students into a routine of asking themselves comprehension check questions. After the student reads a section of the text, the tutor continues to ask, "Did that make sense to you?" The student gets to the point where he or she knows what question to ask. As the student reads a section of the text, the tutor may ask, "What question do you ask yourself?" and the student will respond, "Did what I read make sense?" Early on, the tutor asks comprehension check questions very frequently, even after the student has read only one or two sentences. As the student progresses, these questions are asked only after key paragraphs or at critical points in the story.

As the student learns to ask general comprehension check questions, the tutor may teach him or her to ask more specific questions to check comprehension. These questions can be either explicit ("What did you find out from that sentence or paragraph?") or inferential ("Why do you think the main character did what he did?") comprehension questions.

If the student cannot answer the comprehension check questions correctly, or does not provide information to show that he or she understands the reading, the tutor demonstrates how to find the answer. The tutor may begin by instructing the student to orally reread the section that he or she has just read, explaining that rereading the story will improve understanding so the student will be able to tell if what he or she read makes sense.

After the student has reread the section of a story, the tutor may ask the comprehension check question again, "Does what you have read make sense?" If the student is still unable to answer the question, he or she may assess other obstacles that might be interfering with comprehension, such as inadequate vocabulary knowledge, word recognition skills, or insufficient background knowledge, and may help the student with any of these.

Reading New Stories. After reading a familiar story, the student usually works on stories containing words with sounds that have been presented in class but that have not yet been mastered. These stories can be the ones that the student is working on in class; stories that the tutor makes up, containing similar word sounds; or both. When learning new letter sounds, the student needs repeated practice with words that contain these sounds in the context of a story. The repeated practice and exposure to the sounds in different words help the student learn to recall the letter sounds. Also, presenting words in the context of a story helps the student attach meaning to these words while using letter/sound correspondences. Meaningful material is learned more quickly than isolated material.

Listening to the student's oral reading allows the tutor to understand precisely where he or she needs instruction. Frequently, it is the blending of individual sounds to make a recognizable word rather than the memory of individual sounds that is the most difficult task for the student. When the student is orally reading a real story, the tutor is able to model repeatedly how to solve the problem of an unknown word through the use of the sound-blending strategy, as well as through the use of context and pictures. Knowledge of sounds and sound blending is not an end in itself, but a tool to be used to read real texts. The use of oral reading in tutoring helps teach the student how to use his or her knowledge of sounds in reading. In addition, metacognitive comprehension monitoring strategies learned with familiar stories can be called on to understand new ones.

Drill. The student needs to get to the point where knowledge of the letter sounds is automatic, so that the student's attention can be free to focus on comprehension. Repeated practice of the letter sounds or phonetically regular words during a quick drill helps the student overlearn these sounds. When the student can automatically say letter sounds, this facilitates his or her ability to sound out words and makes reading more automatic. Important sight words are also briefly drilled.

Writing. Reading and writing are intricately connected. Having the student write a paragraph and read it promotes understanding of the relationship between the written word and reading. Also, being able to put the spoken word into writing teaches the student how to manipulate language. Connecting writing activities with reading builds comprehension skills. When writing, the student has the opportunity to practice making words with sounds, which helps the student gain fluency with letter sounds in a meaningful context.

Example of a Tutoring Session: Early in Reading Roots

The following script of a Reading Roots tutoring session shows how the tutoring activities and strategies described are used with a student.

Reading a Familiar Story

Terrell is a first grader in beginning reading. He is up to Lesson 18 and has selected *The Costume Party* (Shared Story No. 11) to read as his familiar story.

Tutor: Do you remember what this story, *The Costume Party,* is about? (The tutor begins with a brief discussion of the book to get the student to think about the story.)

Student: Yes, it's about dressing up.

T: What about dressing up?

S: Well, this boy wants to go to a costume party and doesn't know what he can be.

T: Yes, why can't he decide what he wants to be?

S: Because all his friends are the things he wants to be.

T: What does he want to be?

S: I'm not sure. I think he wants to be a fireman.

T: At first he wants to be a fireman. Let's read. Because this a familiar story, I won't read the teacher part. You read the story yourself smoothly and using expression.

S: *Matt sits on /Niiiccckkk/, Niiiccckk, Nick, Nick's cot. He says, "I am a cot,"* I mean *"cat."*

T: Good thinking, you corrected yourself. Keep reading.

S: *Tim's cap is on Nnnick's cot. Tim's bat is on Nick's cot. He says, "I am a baseball player." Nick looks at Tim and Matt. He says, "I can be a cat, I can."* Oh no, *"I can not be a cat, I can not be a baseball player."* He is says.

T: Hmmm. You read, "He is says." Does that make sense?

S: No!

T: Look at this word (points to the word *sad*). Try to sound out this word.

S: Saaa, Saaaa,

T: What sound does this letter make? (Points to the /d/.)

S: /d/

T: Try to sound out the word and put the /d/ sound on the end.

S: Saaaddd, sssaaaddd, sad.

T: Great job, the word is *sad.* Keep reading.

S: *He is sad. Tim says, "You can be a dragon! I cccaaann, can, put on the,* I mean, *I can pin on the tail." Don is a dragon.* What is this word? (Student points to the word *Nick.*)

T: I like the way you corrected yourself when you said *put* instead of *pin.* Try to sound out this word. (Tutor points to the word *Nick.*)

S: NNNiiiccckkk, Nnniiiccckkk, Nick, Nick. *Nick sits on the cat.* Wait that doesn't make sense. *Nick sits on the cot. He says, "I can not be a dragon." He is sad. Don says, "You can be a pirate! I can get a pirate cap."*

T: I like the way you asked yourself if what you read made sense and then reread when it didn't. Keep reading. You are doing a great job!

S: *Ann is a pirate. Nick sits on the cot. He says, "I can not be a pirate." He is sad. Nick says, "Dad is a policeman. I can be a policeman!" Nick gets Dad's jacket. Nick gets Dad's hat.*

T: *Helmet.* (This is a sight word so it is just stated, not stretched.)

S: *Nick gets Dad's helmet. Nick gets Dad's badge.*

T: You did a great job. Your reading gets smoother all the time and you are reading with a lot of expression. It really sounds like a good story when you read that way. Now let's do a quick drill.

Drill of Letters, Sounds, Sight Words, or All Three

This drill of letter, sounds, words, or all three should be no longer than one minute. The purpose of these drills is to give the student practice with specific words and sounds with which they are having difficulty. It is most beneficial to the student, however, to practice letter sounds and sight words in the context of written text so the drill is kept very brief.

In this tutoring session, the tutor has the student review words that he had difficulty with from the familiar story, such as "Nick" and "sad," as well as some sight words that are challenging. The tutor will also have the student review words that begin with the /f/ sound because the story being read in class, *Fang,* presents the /f/ sound.

T: What does this say? (Shows the word *Nick* on a small card.)

S: Nnniiiccckkk. Nick.

T: Good. (Shows *sad.*)

S: I remember this, *sad.*

T: (Shows the word *the.*)

S: The

T: (Shows the word *on.*)

S: In

T: This is *on.* Let's say/spell/say it.

S/T: On, "o" "n," on.

T: Good. (Shows the word, *be.*)

S: Did.

T: No. This word is *be.* Let's say/spell/say it.

S/T: Be, "b" "e," be.

T: (The tutor and student have been working on the distinction between *be* and *did.* These are two sight words that the student constantly confuses.) Look at the first letter of *be.* What is it?

S: /B/

T: Yes, remember the word *be* has only two letters and it begins with the /b/ sound. Now try this word (shows *Fang*).

S: /Fffaaannnggg/, /Fffaaannnggg/, Fang.

T: Yes, very good, the word is *Fang.* Let's change the beginning sound and see what other words we can say (the tutor puts a /s/ in front of /ang/). What is this word?

S: /Sss/ /ang/, sang.

T: Now try this. (Shows *fat.*)

S: Fffaaatt. Fat.

T: Great. (Shows *fit.*)

S: Ffffffiiiiitt. Fit.

T: Very smooth. This is hard. (Shows *fast.*)

S: Fffaaaatt. Fat.

T: Try it with me.

S/T: Ffffaaaasssstttt. Ffaasstt. Fast.

T: You did a great job! Let's read the current story you are working on in class.

Working on the Shared Story
Currently Being Read in Class

Terrell is having difficulty with decoding words and with comprehension.

The tutor introduces the story that Terrell is working on in class. This week Terrell is reading *Fang.* Reading the stories being studied in class during tutoring provides the opportunity to reinforce classroom instruction.

During this reading of the story, the tutor works on a variety of strategies including sounding out words and building comprehension strategies in the context of the current story.

T: Let's begin by reading this book. You have read this book before with your class. Can you tell me what the name of the book is?

S: I remember. It's *Fang.*

T: Right! Do you remember who Fang is? (The tutor is trying to activate the student's background knowledge.)

S: Yes.

T: Tell me who he is.

S: He's a dog.

T: Can you tell me anything else about him?

S: He's big and he's a Beethoven dog.

T: Yes, he is big and he's a St. Bernard! Good job remembering. Can you tell me who this little girl is? (Points to the girl next to Fang on the cover of the book.)

S: I think she is his owner, but I can't remember her name.

T: Yes, she is Fang's owner. Do you remember what this story is about? (Tutor asks comprehension questions that help the student think about the meaning of the text he has read and will read again.)

S: About Fang.

T: Yes, what about Fang? (She probes to see if the student can briefly tell the story, thus demonstrating his comprehension.)

S: The dog pushed the girl in the mud.

T: Right, that's a part of what happened. Let's read to remember what the whole story is. (Tutor begins reading the teacher part of the story.) *Scott and Tanya practice kicking her ball during recess. Lana joins them. What will happen to the ball?*

S: /Ssscott/ *Scott rolls the ball.* /Bbbbaaammm/. *Bam.* /Tttttaaa/ /Tttttt/.

T: Tanya. It is the little girl's name. (Tanya is a sight word and is stated quickly for the student if he is having difficulty with it.)

S: *Tanya kicks it. She runs fat.*

T: Does what you read make sense?

S: No.

T: Read it again.

S: *She runs far.*

T: Let's sound it out.

S/T: /Ffffaaaasssstttt/, /ffaasstt/?

S: /Fffaaasssttt/.

T: Now say it faster.

S: /ffaasstt/, *fast.*

T: Good. /fffaaasssttt/, *fast.* We will work on saying the words faster when we sound them out. (The tutor explicitly tells the student why he is doing certain activities and what he needs to work on. This builds metacognitive skills.) Keep reading.

S: *She runs fast. Lana says, "The ball is . . ."* What is this word?

T: This is a word that you can't sound out. It is a red word. The word is *off.* Do you know what it means? (Tutor checks comprehension of prepositions, which can be misunderstood and affect comprehension.)

S: *Off* means like not on, like off.

T: Good, keep going.

S: *Lana, says, "The ball is off the fence!"*

T: Does that make sense? *The ball is off the fence?* Look at the picture. Do you see a fence? (The tutor is asking the student to look at the context to help figure out what the sight word is.)

S: No. Oh, yeah, *field. The ball is off the field!*

T: (Tutor reads her part.) *Scott and Tanya look for the ball in the bushes while Lana looks on the other side of the playground. Suddenly, Scott sees something. What is it?*

S: *"Look!"* gggaaapppsss, *gaps Scott.*

T: Look at that word again. Good job sounding it out but there is one more sound. Try it with me.

S/T: Gggaaasssppppsss. Ggaassppss. Gasps.

T: Good job. Now can you tell me what the word *gasps* means? (This is a literal comprehension question.)

S: No, I'm not sure what it means.

T: A person gasps when they are surprised. (The tutor demonstrates what gasping would look like.) If you read a word and you don't understand its meaning either try to figure it out from the context of the story or ask someone to tell you what it means. (Tutor is explicitly instructing the student to not pass over words he does not understand and provides strategies for figuring out the meaning of words.)

S: *"Look Tanya!" gasps Scott. Tanya looks. She sees a big fat dog. It . . .* (The student looks to the tutor for help with the word.)

T: Try to sound out the word.

S: Bbbuuummmpppsss, bbuummppss, bumps.

T: Great! Now read these two sentences again so you understand what you are reading. (The tutor always gives the student the opportunity to read the entire sentence over after he has sounded out the words. This helps with fluency and comprehension.)

S: *The dog runs fast. It bumps into Tanya. She sits on the mud.*

T: Look and listen to what you read. (The tutor points to the text as she says what the student read.) She sits on the mud. Does that make sense?

S: Yes.

T: Can you sit on mud?

S: Well, yes.

T: Do you sit on top of mud or would you sit in the mud?

S: In the mud.

T: Yes, because mud is mushy. You would sink into it if you sat on it. Read the sentence again, and read this word carefully. (The tutor points to the word *in.*)

S: *She sits in the mud.*

T: Let's go on. I'll read this part. *Poor Tanya! How do you think she feels about being pushed into the mud?* (The tutor reads fluently and with expression as to model good reading for the student.)

S: What is this word? (The student points to the word "ick.")

T: Let's stretch this word.

S/T: */Iiiiccccckkkk/ /Iicckk/. Ick.*

T: Say it fast.

S: *Ick.*

T: Do you know what it means? (The tutor wants to be sure that the student understands the meaning of the word.)

S: Yes, when something is icky, it is not good or doesn't taste good.

T: Yes, *ick* means that you don't like something. Keep reading.

S: *"Ick!" says /TTT/ Tanya. Mud is not fun. Go, dog!*

T: Why do you think the mud is not fun?

S: Because the girl, Tanya, got all dirty.

T: Yes, the mud can be icky and make you all dirty. Good job. Keep reading.

S: *The /bbbiiiggg/ /bbbiiiggg/ the big dog says.* No that's not right the big dog can't talk. *The big dog /sssiiitttsss/ /sssits/ sits. The big dog sits. He pants?* This doesn't make sense either. He pants. He wears pants?

T: The word pants has two meanings. One is something you wear. The other means breathing heavily. It's what you do if you've been running fast. Fang is a big dog who breathes heavily. He pants.

S: Oh. OK. *He pants.*

T: Let me read the teacher part before you continue. *Paco starts to shake. He turns pale. What has Paco seen that has scared him?*

S: *Paco says, "See the dog's . . ."* What is this word?

T: Try to sound it out.

S: *Fffaaannngggg, fan?*

T: Look at the word again. Make sure you don't forget that last sound. (The tutor wants to encourage the student to independently sound out the word and say it fast, combining all the letters.)

S: */Fffaaannngggg/, fan?*

T: Try it with me.

S/T: */Fffaaannngggg/.*

T: Good, now put these sounds together.

S: */Fffaaannngggg/.*

T: Good, say it faster.

S: *Fang.*

T: Yes, *fang*. (The tutor repeats the word so the student can hear all the letter sounds in the word.)

S: *"Fangs!!" says Tanya. The big dog says* . . . What is this word?

T: *Ruff.* (This word is a sight word so the tutor simply states it for the student.)

S: *"Ruff!" The kids clim up, clim, clim/b/ up the jungle gym.*

T: The word is climb. It is a red word. (The tutor tells the student the sight word.)

S: *"Can we fit?" asks Paco. Lana runs fast. "Fang!" Lana says. She skips* (skids) *to a stop.*

T: Good, but let's take a look at this word. When you come to a word that you are not sure try to sound it out first before you guess at it. (The tutor has observed that the student guesses before he takes the time to sound out the words. Although the tutor does not want to totally discourage thoughtful guessing, the sounding out strategy should be tried first.)

S: *Skips?*

T: Look at the word. Do you see a letter that makes the /p/ sound?

S: No. There is a /d/ in the word.

T: That's right. Let's stretch it.

S/T: */Sssskkkkiiiiddddsss/. /Sskkiiddss/. Skids.*

S: */Sss/ kids, skids. She skids to a stop. "Fang is not bad," sits,* I mean, *says Lana.*

T: Good. You went back and corrected yourself. I'll read my part. *Lana explains that Fang is her St. Bernard. He is very gentle, even though he has big teeth. He follows her to school when he gets lonely. What will the other children do now?*

S: *Lana says, "Fang is a fun dog. He likes kids."* Kids is like skids.

T: That's right! It's good that you noticed. Continue to read. (The tutor reinforces the student's making the connection between one word and another.)

S: *The kids get off the jungle gym.*

T: *All of a sudden, Derrick has an idea. What do you think?*

S: I can not remember this name.

T: *Derrick.* (The tutor simply tells the student the sight word to continue the pace of the story.)

S: *Derrick says, "Dogs can /sssnnniiiffff/ sniff. Can Fang sniff the ball?"*

T: What do you think? Can Fang sniff the ball? (Tutor wants to check the student's comprehension.)

S: Yes, he has a nose, he can sniff.

T: Yes, good job, keep reading.

S: *Lana nots.* Oh, wait. *Lana nods. "Get the ball, Fang," says Lana.*

T: Good job correcting yourself! I'll read. *Fang puts his nose to the ground. Do you think he can find the ball?*

S: *Fang runs. He sniffs. He digs fast in a* (long pause) *stack.*

T: *Stack.* (The tutor repeats the word to confirm that the student is correct.)

S: *Stack of leaves. The kids say, "Fang got the ball back!"*

T: *Fang is a hero. He found the missing ball.* You did a great job. Now let's read the last page together so we can practice reading with expression.

T/S: *Fang runs. He sniffs. He digs fast in a stack of leaves. The kids say, "Fang got the ball back!"*

Writing Activity

When the student finishes reading the story, the tutor introduces the writing activity based on the story.

T: Now you are going to get a chance to write your own story. Let's pretend that Fang is your dog. Is there something fun that you can think of doing with Fang if he were your dog? (The tutor wants to give the student a chance to verbally express his ideas before he writes them. The tutor and student talk about Fang going to the park and the fun they would have at the park.)
Terrell writes the following:

> I have a dog call Fang.
> We go the parc
> He goes on the swing with me.
> He go on the seesz with me.
> He go on the tir with me. I lov my dog Fang.

Terrell reads the story he wrote to his tutor. He is proud of what he wrote. The tutor will put the story in his tutoring folder and have him read it at the next session. She will also go over some of the spelling errors when they rewrite the story as part of the writing process.

The Tutoring Process in Reading Wings

Tutoring Goals.

There are several goals in tutoring students in Reading Wings. One is to teach comprehension monitoring skills. The emphasis in Reading Wings is to teach students how to get meaning from what they have read. This involves getting meaning from individual words as well as connected text. Other goals in Reading Wings are to help students build their vocabulary, to develop fluency in reading, and to teach students to effectively express ideas in words.

The first step in working with a student in Reading Wings is to determine the reading problems of the student. The Tutoring Diagnostic Assessment Checklist (see Figure 3.1) is used to do this. After this diagnostic evaluation is made, a plan is made to target the areas on which the student needs to work. For example, a student may be having problems figuring out the meaning of specific words, and this may be interfering with his comprehension of the text. Another student may not understand how to answer the comprehension questions in the Treasure Hunts. A third student may be having trouble tracking what he is reading. Although all of these problems interfere with understanding what has been read, the ways these problems are dealt with in tutoring are very different.

Activities in Tutoring Reading Wings

These are the specific activities done in tutoring a student in Reading Wings.

Vocabulary Drill. The Vocabulary Drill gives the student the opportunity to practice pronouncing words with which he is having difficulty. Repeated practice of words that the student encounters frequently when reading will help reinforce correct pronunciation of these words. In addition, the student has the opportunity to clarify the definitions of words.

Reading Sections of Basal Stories. Reading stories helps develop comprehension monitoring strategies. Poor readers often have difficulty monitoring their comprehension as they read. When reading sections of the basal stories, the student can be taught comprehension monitoring skills. As the student reads sections of the story, the tutor asks questions that check understanding of the parts that he or she has read. If the student is unable to answer the questions, the tutor provides the student with helpful strategies. For example, the tutor may guide the student to reread a section of the text where the answer is located, or may guide his thinking through a response to an inferential question. In both cases, the tutor is modeling comprehension strategies that facilitate comprehension.

Rereading Familiar Stories. Rereading familiar stories helps even older readers read with fluency and expression. Rereading also helps the student gain a sense of mastery over reading. This repeated practice builds confidence in the student's self-perceptions as a reader.

Reviewing a Treasure Hunt. Reviewing the answers to the Treasure Hunts helps develop comprehension skills. Using the specific Treasure Hunt questions from a story being studied in class provides direct support and reinforcement for classwork. If the student does not know an answer, the tutor will work with him or her on the strategies needed to find the answer, such as looking back in the text, thinking beyond the literal meaning of a section, and so on. Tutor and student will also work to develop comprehension monitoring while reading so that the information will be absorbed on subsequent first readings. The student receives immediate feedback on the quality of his or her answers to Treasure Hunt questions in the tutoring situation and can learn to develop more complete answers.

Reviewing the Treasure Hunts also teaches the student how to work with them. The tutor explicitly explains how the Treasure Hunts are set up and what is expected of the student.

Writing. During tutoring, the students and teacher work on written expression primarily through developing high-quality answers to the Treasure Hunts. Writing the answers requires the student to express his thoughts clearly in a short sentence. The tutor provides immediate feedback, modeling, and instruction as the students work.

Tutor and student can also work on story-related writing activities. The one-to-one tutoring situation once again provides an opportunity for feedback, modeling, and guidance that is tailored specifically to the individual student's needs.

Sample Tutoring Session: Reading Wings

This script of a tutoring session with a student who is beyond Reading Roots demonstrates the activities and strategies used at that level.

Vocabulary Drill

The following is an example of a tutor working with a student on the vocabulary drill. The tutor is working on 10 words with which the student is having difficulty. The tutor selects some words in which the student is having difficulty recalling meaning and some that he is unable to pronounce. These words can be words from the Word Mastery List of the Treasure Hunt or other words with which the student is having difficulty. The tutor writes each word on a 2 × 2 card and presents them individually to the student.

The following is a sample vocabulary drill. These words are ones that the tutor has been noting with which the student has been having difficulty. The tutor will select some of these words to keep the drill brief and to leave more time for reading connected text. (Note: The words with asterisks are words from the Word Mastery List of the Treasure Hunt.)

Fern	straw	in
weather-vane*	peered	under
apple-blossom	tunnel	crawled

T: (Shows the word *Fern.*) What is this word?

S: FFFern, Fern.

T: Good! What is this word? (Shows the word *weather-vane.*)

S: Weather-van.

T: Close, you got the first part of the hyphenated word correct, now look at the second part. There is an /e/ end that changes the sound of the /a/. Try it.

S: /Vvvaaannneee/, van.

T: What is this word? (The tutor writes the word *cane.*)

S: Cane.

T: Good! Now put a /v/ sound in front of the /ane/. What does it sound like?

S: Vane.

T: Good! What is the whole word?

S: Weather-vane.

T: What is a weather-vane?

S: I don't know.

T: It's a device that indicates the direction of the wind. Here is a picture of one. (The tutor shows the student a picture of a weather-vane.) This can have other kinds of things on top like a rooster or a whale, but the purpose of the thing is the same. It helps tell what direction the wind is blowing. Let's look at this next word. (The tutor shows the word, *apple-blossom.*)

S: Apple-blossom.

T: Good! (Because this is quick drill, the tutor does not probe the meaning of every word presented.) How about this word? (Shows the word *straw.*)

S: Straw.

T: Good! Do you know what straw is?

S: It's like hay and it is on a farm.

T: Great! You really know that word. It is also something you drink from. Here is the next word. (The tutor shows the word, *peered.*)

S: Peeped.

T: No, peered. Do you know what it means. (The tutor tells the student the word because the /ee/ sounds in this case sounds like /i/.)

S: Yes, like looking at someone.

T: Yes, it means to look at something closely. What is this next word? (The tutor shows the word *under.* The student has had difficulty remembering this word, which is why it is included in the list.)

S: Under?

T: Are you sure?

S: Yes, it is *under* and it means like when you step on something, it is under your foot.
See like this. (The student demonstrates for the tutor what he means.)

T: Great! We'll do more tomorrow. Let's go on to reading a section of the novel you are working on in class.

Reading a Portion of a Novel

To provide a thorough, yet concise example of a tutor working with a student on reading, a portion of a chapter is presented in the following section. During a session, the tutor may work on a portion or the entire chapter of a story.

The following is an example of a tutoring session with a student who is working on comprehension skills. The stories can be taken from the basal readers, novels, or both. The story (*Charlotte's Web* by E. B. White) was read in the student's reading group that day and they are working on it in the afternoon tutoring session. This rereading and discussion of what was read will assist a student who is having fluency or comprehension problems.

T: You read Chapter 2 of *Charlotte's Web* in class today. Before we begin to reread that chapter, can you tell me a little of what you know about the story so far?

S: Well, the girl, I can't remember her name . . .

T: Fern

S: Yes, Fern, the little girl named Fern wanted this pig so her dad let her keep it.

T: Why did her dad let her keep it? (This is an inferential question.)

S: I am not sure. It didn't say why.

T: After reading about Fern and her dad, why do you think her dad let her keep the pig? (The tutor wants the student to go beyond what is explicitly stated in the story and make inferences about what he read.)

S: Because she asked him?

T: Yes, she did ask him, but we don't always get things because we ask for them. Do you think maybe he knew how much it meant to Fern to have the pig and didn't want to see her sad?

S: Yes, he knew if she didn't have the pig that she would be sad.

T: Let's start to read.

S: *Chapter 2 /Wwwiillbbb/, /Wiilbbbuuurrr/, Wilbur.*

T: Good job stretching the word out. *Wilbur.*

S: *Fern loved Wilbur more than anyone.*

T: Look at this word. (The tutor points to the word, *anything,* which the student has called *anyone.*) What is this word?

S: *Anyone.* No wait, it is *anything.*

T: Continue to read and read carefully so you read the correct words.

S: *She loved to stroke him, to feed him, to put him to bed.*

T: Do you know what the word, *stroke,* means? (The tutor takes what often is assumed to be a simple word that the student should know and asks its meaning.)

S: Hit?

T: Let's look at the way the word is used to see if we can figure out what it means. *She loved to stroke him.* Would that mean that she loved to hit him?

S: No, she liked the pig. *Stroke* means to touch nicely.

T: Yes, stroke means to gently touch like this. (The tutor demonstrates on the stuffed pig that she uses as a prop when they are reading *Charlotte's Web.*) Continue to read.

S: *Every morning, as soon as she got up, she warned* (warmed) *his milk, tied his bib on, and held out the bottle for him.*

T: (The tutor allows the student to finish the sentence first to see if the student recognizes that he has made an error.) Let me read what you read and see if it make sense. *She warned* (warmed) *his milk, tied his bib on, and held out the bottle for him.*

S: No. She didn't warn him.

T: Look at this word. (The tutor points to the word, *warmed.*) What is this word?

S: Warmed.

T: Yes, now read the sentence.

S: *Every morning, as soon as she got up, she warmed his milk, tied his bib on, and held out the bottle for him.*

S: *Every afternoon, when the school bus stopped in* . . . What is this word?

T: *Front.* The tutor will tell the student the word when the tutor is trying not to interrupt fluency.

S: *Stopped in front of her house, she jumped out and run,* I mean, *ran to the* (long pause) *kitchen to fix another bottle for him. She feed him again at supper time, and again before going to school.*

T: Look at this word. (The tutor points to the word *fed.*) What is this word?

S: Feed.

T: There is only one /e/ in this word, the word is fed. Go back and reread that sentence. (The tutor wants the student to learn to go back and read when she misreads words in a sentence.)

S: *She fed him again at supper time and again before going to bed. Mrs. Able . . .*

T: *Arable.* (The tutor simply tells the student this word to maintain the flow of the reading.)

S: *Mrs. Arable gave him a feeding around noontime each day, when Fern was away in school. Wilbur loved his milk, and he was never happier than when Fern was warming up a bottle for him. He would stand and gaze up at her with /aaadddd/, /aadddooorrriiinnng/, /adoorrriinnggg/, adoring eyes.*

T: Good job! Before we go on with the story, let's talk about what you have read so far. Who is Wilbur? (This is a literal comprehension question. It is important when working with students who have problems with comprehension monitoring to get them to stop and think about what they have read. Initially this is done frequently. Asking questions about the story makes the students aware that they need to understand what they read as they go along. Also, it provides the students with the opportunity to immediately repair any misunderstandings that could interfere with their overall comprehension.)

S: A pig.

T: He is a pig. How does Fern treat him? Does she treat him like a pig?

S: No, she treats him like a baby.

T: Yes, she does treat him like a baby. What did you read that made you think that Fern treated the pig like a baby?

S: Well, she gave him a bottle.

T: Yes, she gave him milk in a bottle and she cuddled him like a baby. Let's keep reading and see what else happens with this pig.

S: *For the first few days of life, Wilbur was allowed to live in a box near the stove in the kitchen. Then, when Mrs. Arable com /cccc/ . . .*

T: Try breaking the word into parts. Read this (covers the last syllable of the word).

S: *Com.*

T: Right. Now this (covers only the "ed.")

S: *Plain.*

T: Put it together.

S: *Complain.*

S: *Complained, he was moved to a bigger box in the woodshed. At 2 weeks of age, he was moved outdoors. It was apple-blossom time, and the days were getting warmer. Mr. Able, I mean Arable, Mr. Arable fixed a small yard especially . . .*

T: *Specially.* (The tutor corrects the student.)

S: *Specially for Wilbur under an apple tree, and gave him a large wooden box full of /ssttrraaww/, /ssttrraaww/, straw with a doorway cut in it so he could walk in and out as he pleased.*

T: I like the way you went back and corrected yourself when you misread *Mrs. Arable*. Where did Wilbur live for the first few days of his life?

S: In the barn.

T: No, it wasn't the barn. How can you find out? (The tutor wants to encourage the student to reread when he doesn't recall or understand what he read. The tutor is also indicating an opportunity to read silently.)

S: (Reads the passage he just read silently.) Wilbur lived in a box in the kitchen for the first few days.

T: Yes, why was he moved? (A literal comprehension question.)

S: Because Mrs. Arable complained.

T: Why do you think she complained? (The tutor wants to ask questions which check inferential and explicit knowledge.)

S: It didn't say.

T: Yes, I know it did not say exactly, but why would you think that Mrs. Arable would complain about a pig in the kitchen? Think about how your own mom and how she would feel about a pig in her kitchen. (The tutor wants the student to go beyond the specific text.)

S: Well, the pig was probably messy and she didn't want him in the house.

T: Very good! Creating a mind-movie while you read helps you think about the feelings and thoughts of the characters you are reading about. Let's keep reading.

S: *"Won't it be cold at night?" asked Fern. "No," said her father. "You watch and see what he does." Carrying a bottle of milk, Fern sat down under the apple tree inside the yard. Wilbur ran to her and she held the bottle from him while he sucked. When he finished the last drop, he . . .* What is this word?

T: Try to figure it out. (The word asked about is phonetically regular, so the tutor has the student sound it out.)

S: /Gggrrruuttt/, /grut/.

T: Good try. Stretch it with me.

S/T: /Gggrrruunnnttt/, /ggrruunntt/, grunt.

T: Yes, do you know what *grunt* means?

S: No.

T: It is the sound that the pigs make. Pigs grunt. (The tutor takes the stuffed pig and make the grunting sound.) Keep reading.

S: *He grunted and walked sleepily into the box. Fern peered through the door. Wilbur was poking the straw with his /ssnnnoootttt/, snote.*

T: Look at the word and cover the /sn/. What do you see?

S: *Out.*

T: Right. Now put the /sn/ sound on the beginning of this word.

S: */SSSnnnout/. Snout.*

T: Good, do you know what a snout is?

S: No.

T: The snout is the pig's nose. Continue to read.

S: *In a short time he had dug a tunnel in the straw. He crawled into the tunnel and disappeared from sight, completely covered with straw. Fern was excited . . .*

T: *Enchanted.* (The tutor states the word rather than asking him to sound it out because it is not clear whether the student knows the meaning of the word.)

S: *Enchanted. It relieved her mind to know that her baby would sleep covered up, and would stay warm.*

T: Summarize briefly what you just read. (The ability to summarize is a good indicator of comprehension.)

S: The little girl Fern had a pig and it stayed in the house and then it went outside in the box filled with straw.

T: Good! You had trouble with this word. (The tutor points to the word, *enchanted.*) What is this word?

S: Enchanted.

T: Good! Do you know what it means?

S: No.

T: What is another word that might fit with the sentence?

S: Maybe happy. Fern was happy Wilbur liked his house.

T: Good. That's close to the meaning of enchanted. Enchanted means delighted. Fern was delighted that Wilbur liked his house. Fern was totally enchanted by Wilbur. You did a great job reading today.

Working on a Treasure Hunt

The following is a sample tutoring session with a third grader who is reading the story, *Charlotte's Web,* and who is working on Treasure Hunts in his reading class. This student has completed up to Chapter 6 of the story. He is having difficulty understanding the relationship between the questions and the information in the story. Because this activity is focusing on comprehension, the responses to the Treasure Hunts are oral and not written.

T: We're going to work on the Treasure Hunts that go with *Charlotte's Web.* Before we get started, let's think about what we have read so far. (The tutor begins by asking questions that activate background knowledge about the story.)

S: Yes, the story is about a pig, Wilbur, and he wants to have a friend. His only friend was a little girl but she didn't live in the barn. So he found another friend. This friend was a spider.

T: That was great! You really know this story. Let's work on some Treasure Hunt questions. (The tutor and the student have been working on summarizing the chapters and the tutor positively reinforces the student for this good summary.) Let's go over some of the Treasure Hunt questions. Let's start. (The tutor reads the first question from the Treasure Hunt. *What upset Fern about her father's wanting to kill the runt of the litter?*

S: She liked the pig and didn't want to see it die.

T: Yes, but why was her dad going to kill the runt?

S: Because it was small.

T: Yes. How did Fern feel about this?

S: Not good.

T: Yes, but let's read a section of the story that would explain how she felt. (The tutor wants the student to learn to return to the text when he is unsure or unclear about an answer to a question. The tutor turns to the page in the story where Fern is upset with her dad.)

S: (Reads silently.) Fern didn't think it was fair to kill the runt of the litter. She didn't think it was fair to kill something because it was small.

T: You are right. How about this next question. Why did Fern answer the capital of Pennsylvania was "Wilbur?"

S: Oh, I remember this because it was funny. Fern was thinking about the pig when she was called on to answer. Instead of giving the answer, she called out Wilbur's name.

T: Good job! How about this next question. *How did Wilbur stay warm when he was outside?*

S: He would sleep in the barn.

T: Before he went to live in the barn, he lived outside at Fern's house. (The tutor creates the context for the student to remember information from the story.) How did he keep warm there?

S: He would go into a box. I remember the picture of the box in the book.

T: Yes, and what did he have inside the box that would help keep him warm? Think about what he would bury his snout in.

S: Straw. He had straw in his box and he would bury himself in the straw.

T: Good job. *What evidence was there that Mr. Arable didn't really want to get rid of Wilbur?*

S: I don't understand that question because Mr. Arable wanted to get rid of the pig.

T: Did he sell the Wilbur like the other pigs? (The tutor is trying to get the student to understand how Mr. Arable treated Wilbur differently.)

S: No.

T: What did he do with Wilbur when it was time to leave Fern's house?

S: He sold Wilbur to Fern's uncle.

T: You see he did treat Wilbur differently. Do you think he liked Wilbur and wanted him to stay close by?

S: Maybe.

T: Let's try the question again. *What evidence was there that Mr. Arable didn't really want to get rid of Wilbur?*

S: He sold him to Fern's uncle so Fern could still see him.

T: Let's go to the next question. (The tutor helps the student to state clear detailed answers to several questions orally and then moves to writing.) Let's spend some time writing about the story. (The tutor can either have the student work on writing the answers to the Treasure Hunts or work on writing a short paragraph about the story.)

Working on Writing Activities in Reading Wings

Writing is important in tutoring. As mentioned previously, the tutor can work with the student on answers to the Treasure Hunts. In addition, the tutor can work with the student on writing paragraphs about the story. This tutor asked the student to write a short paragraph on what he would do if a pig like Wilbur lived in his house.

S: If i had pig, i would let it sleep in my closet. Becaus my closet is safe and dry. He caud not sleep in my bed. I wood feed him Trixs lik I eat for brakfas.

T: This is good. Can you read it to me?

The student reads the paragraph. After the student reads the paragraph, the tutor works on correcting spelling and punctuation. This is all part of the writing process.

4

Prekindergarten and Kindergarten Programs

One of the key emphases of Success for All and Roots and Wings is *prevention,* doing everything possible to ensure that students succeed in school the first time they are taught so that they will never need remediation. Learning problems are prevented in Success for All in many ways, including providing high-quality curriculum and instruction and involving parents in their children's education. Some of the most important program elements directed at preventing learning problems are those provided before students enter first grade—in prekindergarten and kindergarten.

One of the goals of Success for All and Roots and Wings is to see that all children attend prekindergarten, and if possible, full-day kindergarten. Research on prekindergarten has shown that for disadvantaged students, prekindergarten experience reduces the chances that students will be retained or assigned to special education in the early grades, and there is some evidence of long-term effects on high school completion and other important outcomes (see Berrueta-Clement, Schweinhart, Barnett, Epstein, & Weikart, 1984; Schweinhart, Barnes, & Weikart, 1993; Karweit, 1994a). Full-day kindergarten has been found to consistently increase end-of-kindergarten achievement more than half-day programs, although long-term outcomes are less well established (Karweit, 1994b). The philosophy of Success for All/Roots and Wings, however, is to build success one year at a time. Regardless of long-term outcomes, if prekindergarten and full-day kindergarten programs can deliver to first grade students who are better prepared to profit from a high-quality first grade experience, they are well worthwhile. We do not know if there are additive benefits of prekindergarten *and* full-day kindergarten, but we try to ensure that all children at least experience one or the other.

Prekindergarten and Kindergarten Curricula

It is not enough to ensure that students spend time in prekindergarten and kindergarten. The pre-k and kindergarten programs must be of high quality and must start students on the road to success. Success for All and Roots and Wings have developed programs for pre-k and kindergarten that are intended to see that all students enter first grade with the self-confident, positive attitude toward school, and orientation to reading they will need to succeed in the elementary grades. Also, a strong emphasis is placed on involving parents in their children's early learning experiences. Opportunities are created for the establishment of a strong school-home connection.

The prekindergarten and kindergarten programs in Success for All and Roots and Wings (Wasik, Bond, & Waclawiw, 1995) use a thematically based curriculum that is intended to develop oral language, literacy, listening skills, numeracy, creative expression, and positive self-esteem. The goal of the curriculum is to provide an experiential and child-centered curriculum that will provide children a needed foundation for success in the elementary school. The curriculum underscores the importance of a balance between child-initiated and teacher-directed instruction. It uses these integrated themes and focuses on the integration of language and communication skills in the context of literacy experiences. The curriculum underscores the importance of acquisition of such skills as the use of elaborated, descriptive language, recognition and production of the alphabet, understanding the conventions of print, and understanding the communicative function of language, as well as such specific skills as letter knowledge.

The key components of the prekindergarten and kindergarten curricula include thematic units; the Story Telling and Retelling program (STaR); Rhyme With Reason, a phonemic awareness program; emergent writing; shared book experience; the Peabody Language Development Kit; and learning centers.

Thematic Units

Children learn in wholes, not segmented parts. A thematic approach to learning helps children make sense of the world. The Success for All/Roots and Wings thematic units are an integrated curriculum organized around science and social studies topics. The program follows a model of expanding horizons of children, starting from the "known" and expanding outward. Thus, the thematic units are organized from units about "special me" to units about "my school" to units about the larger community and the world at large.

The thematic units consist of several components: an introduction that includes unit learning essentials, a letter to parents, and a dictionary of terms related to the units; theme learning lessons; literacy activities, which include the STaR program and shared book experiences, phonemic awareness, writing activities, learning center activities, math activities, science or social studies activities, music/creative movement/circle game activities, home learning activities; and a unit assessment.

The thematic units are organized as a resource guide to assist teachers in planning and implementing an integrated curriculum. The units are very comprehensive and contain a significant amount of information. Teachers are not expected to complete each activity in each unit; instead, they are expected to pick specific learning essentials and activities that fit the needs and developmental levels of their children and determine the time line they will follow. If the teacher plans, therefore, to spend 2 weeks on the *Plants in Our Lives* unit, she determines which learning essential best fits the needs and developmental levels of her children, selects the activities in each component that she wants to present, and maps out a plan for the intended time line.

The thematic units currently available for prekindergarten and kindergarten include Special Me and My Five Senses, Community Helpers, Plants in Our Lives, Space, Multicultural (which includes Kenya and Japan), Famous Black Americans, Dinosaurs, Recycling, Transportation, and Tools and Machines.

Story Telling and Retelling (STaR)

Children's literature and stories are read daily in Success for All/Roots and Wings prekindergarten and kindergarten classrooms. Children's stories are an important avenue for expanding children's experience and knowledge. On the most basic level, stories provide opportunities for exposure to the communicative function of language and the hands-on experience of seeing how print works. In discussing and retelling stories, children begin to learn that narratives have predictable elements (characters, settings, problems, and problem solutions), and this knowledge helps with reading comprehension later on. At another level, stories provide exposure to other worlds, other usages of language that provide models and metaphors for the child's developing communication abilities. The STaR program (Karweit, Coleman, Waclawiw, & Petza, 1990) is a literacy program that combines and exemplifies all these features of literacy learning.

STaR structures story telling activities to increase student involvement with and attention to children's literature. The goal of STaR is to enhance oral language, understanding of story structure, and comprehension skills. STaR combines techniques for structured retelling with strategies for telling stories that facilitate comprehension. Evaluations of the STaR program indicate positive effects on important prereading skills—receptive vocabulary, production of language, and story comprehension. STaR is used in prekindergarten, kindergarten, and early first grade. In the middle of first grade STaR is replaced by the Listening Comprehension program (see Chapter 2).

STaR is a set of procedures and materials to help structure story telling and retelling in preschool and kindergarten classes. The procedures include ways to organize the classroom space and storytelling time, ways to introduce the story and maintain student interest during the story, and techniques for reviewing and retelling the story. The materials are story kits, which are designed to accompany selected story books. A story kit consists of guide sheets (which include questions for introducing and reviewing the story) and story telling aids (story sequence cards and, in some cases, illustrations to cut out and make into flannel board figures or stick puppets). A list of the story book titles used in the STaR program is included at the end of this chapter.

STaR is designed for a whole-class format with a teacher and a teacher's assistant present. There are seven main activities in STaR:

1. Story introduction
2. Interactive story reading
3. Story structure review
4. Group story retelling
5. Individual story conference
6. Story critique
7. Story extension activities

The activities take a total of about 30 minutes per day in prekindergarten and kindergarten, 20 minutes per day in first grade (see Appendix 4.1 for a STaR 5-day schedule).

Story Telling (Day 1)

1. *Story Introduction.* The teacher selects a book to read to children that is appropriate to their developmental level. In selecting books teachers also try to link to the thematic unit currently being taught, to the time of year, and to other instruction. They set aside a special area (such as a carpet) for storytelling.

Storytelling is structured to increase the effectiveness of storytelling time. The introduction to the story takes about 5 minutes. It sets the stage and piques the curiosity of the students for the story they will hear. The story guide sheets include some suggested ways to introduce and prepare students for the stories they are about to hear. A typical strategy is to have children look at the front of the book and guess what the story might be about, suggest the characters in the story, or both. In addition, up to three unfamiliar vocabulary words may be introduced.

The last part of the introduction establishes the setting for the story. It is important to give the children some idea of when and where the story takes place to prepare them for what they are about to hear.

2. *Interactive Story Reading.* The next part of the storytelling is the actual reading of the story. The teacher reads the story with enthusiasm and expression, and frequently asks questions and summarizes what has happened so far to consolidate and extend the story. The story kits suggest critical points in the story to summarize the story and to ask predictive questions. Frequent summary questions during the storytelling help the children recall the events in the story. Predictive questions are also used to keep students involved and thinking about the story.

3. *Story Structure Review.* At the end of the actual reading teachers use summary questions to review the story with the students. They ask students to recall the title of the book, names and descriptions of the main characters, and major events. Sequence cards depicting the main events in the story may be used to help review the events and main ideas in the story.

Time	*Overview of Story Telling Sequence for Day 1* Activity	
5 minutes	**Story introduction**	Setting/theme
		Vocabulary
		Predictive questions
20 minutes	**Interactive story reading**	Summarize
		Predict
		Main idea
10 minutes	**Story structure review**	Title
		Characters
		Events

4. & 5. *Group Story Retelling and Individual Story Conference.* The purpose of story retelling is to give students an opportunity to make the story their own, to comprehend the nature of stories, to enhance vocabulary, and to improve oral language skills. The story kits include questions for story retell as well as sequence cards that can be used as aids for story retelling. There are two forms of story retelling: the group retell and the individual story conference. The individual retell allows a student to practice telling a story from beginning to end. The assistant carries out the individual story conference while the teacher is conducting a group retell with the rest of the class. In a 20-minute period, the assistant can usually listen to story retell from three to five children.

Time	*Overview of Story Retelling Sequence for Day 2* Activity	
5 minutes	**Story structure review**	Title Vocabulary Characters: Use sequence cards Events: Use sequence cards
20 minutes	**Interactive group retelling**	Sequence cards Dramatization Role play
20 minutes	**Individual story conference**	Conference with assistant Peer retell
5 minutes	**Story critique**	Sharing story opinions

For the interactive group retell, ideas for the retell found in the STaR guide sheets can be used. In addition to the sequence cards, story retell may be done using dramatization or role playing. Many of the STaR sheets contain ideas for story dramatization.

The individual story retell takes place at the same time as the group retell. Children are called up individually for the retell to the assistant. The retell takes about 5 to 8 minutes per child. (Note: It is not expected that every child will retell every story.) The assistant's job is to schedule the students for conferences and record the story retell. The assistant uses the individual retell questions provided for each story.

6. *Story Critique.* The story critique component of STaR is designed to give children the opportunity to share their opinions about the story in a risk-free setting. Not every child will enjoy every story read to them. It is important for children to understand that they can have a variety of opinions about stories that are read to them. Story critique allows the children to play the role of "critic" and learn to accept and respect their need to develop literacy attitudes. The children are taught a variety of techniques such as story rating and story frames to express their opinions about the stories.

7. *Story Extension Activities.* STaR story extension activities provide children with a variety of ways to further respond to literature in a meaningful way. Several extension activities can be motivating and effective: story rereading; story dramatization; art and cooking activities; story exchange, in which children tell their related experiences to the children; story group, in which children tell the STaR stories to their peers; and story journal.

Example of a STaR Story Guide Sheet

Appendix 4.2 is an example of a STaR sheet for the story *Nobody Listens to Andrew* by Elizabeth Guilfoile.

STaR for First Graders

First grade teachers use a 5-day version of STaR called Extended STaR. The weekly cycle for Extended STaR is as follows:

Day 1: Story preview and predictive writing activity
Day 2: Interactive story reading
Day 3: Review and retell the story
Day 4: Story elaboration
Day 5: Story-related writing

The schedule is presented in Appendix 4.3.

Day 1: *Story preview.* The purpose of the story preview is to engage the children in the story they are about to hear, to acquaint them with unfamiliar vocabulary words, and to get them to make story predictions about what they think the story will be about. This previewing strategy will enhance the children's comprehension abilities and can be used as a tool to help children select text they wish to read independently.

Visual cues: The teacher covers the title of the book and asks the children to predict what the story will be about. Showing several illustrations, the teacher asks the children to talk about what they think is going to happen in the story.

Verbal cues: The teacher may find it useful to present any unusual vocabulary that will keep children from comprehending the story or that are particularly central to the meaning of the story. The vocabulary is presented first as words and then in context and in sentences.

Predict: Students are asked to use the visual and verbal cues to predict what the story might be about. At this point, the children are asked to write a story that would incorporate what they have heard thus far. At the beginning of the year, for inexperienced writers, the story writing may be drawing a story and dictating the words that an assistant or the teacher writes down.

Day 2: *Interactive story reading.* Before reading the story, students engage in a discussion about what they currently know about the story. The teacher briefly discusses the story structure: title, characters, setting, possible problem or main idea, and solution or ending, reviewing any vocabulary that may be central to the understanding of the story. He or she then reads the story, stopping every few pages to ask summative and predictive questions that will motivate students to recall and comprehend story details and ideas.

Day 3: *Story structure review/retell.* On Day 3, activities begin with a brief review of story structures. Students then engage in a type of story retell activity. Suggested retell activities include the following:

Story circle: An activity in which students take turns elaborating on the details and ideas expressed by the last participant without repeating the sequence but always adding to the sequence of events to complete the story.

Sequence cards: Story sequencing material can often be used to foster the group retell of the story.

Story dramatization: Many stories lend themselves to dramatization. Students may engage in a story retell activity in which they share the sequence of the story through dramatization.

Story mapping: Another way to retell the story may be through a story mapping activity in which the children organize the story structures to convey the sequence of the story.

Day 4: *Story elaboration.* The activities on Day 4 extend the story for the children. For example, children may "interview" specific characters in the story to ask what they were thinking, or why they did a certain thing, or how they felt when a specific event occurred. Other activities might include comparison of characters in one story with characters in another story. The Day 4 activities are aimed at providing additional informa-tion and insights from the story that the children might use in their writing on Day 5.

Day 5: *Story-related writing.* The fifth day is used for story-related writing. This can include a variety of topics, such as what surprised the children most about the story, how the story was different from what they thought it was going to be, what they think happened next to a specific character in the story, and what they liked or didn't like about a character. Cooperative projects could be used in which students could contribute to a joint book making effort.

Emergent Writing

Oral language, reading, and writing are inherently connected. Typically, young children will begin exploring writing before they learn to read. In Success for All and Roots and Wings, children's writing and prewriting are stressed, not just because of their reading connection, but because of their definition of the "known" of children's lives. As soon as children begin to make marks with writing instruments, they are beginning to learn about language and how it works.

The emergent writing component in the curriculum begins with where the child is at the time and encourages the developmental progression of writing. Children are taught that print conveys meaning and that they are able to manipulate print to provide meaning to the reader and to show the purpose of their writing through multiple forms of text that relates to the writing situation.

Teacher training is an important component of emergent writing. Teachers are taught the developmental progression of writing, from scribbles, to linear repetition, to random-letter formation, and eventually letter-name writing. The teacher is instructed to provided numerous opportunities for the children to write and to be exposed to print. In the thematic units and in the STaR materials, there are suggestions for writing activities. Teachers are given strategies for making their classroom a print-rich environment and teaching the editing process to young children.

Phonemic Awareness

Phonemic awareness, the ability to recognize and manipulate sounds in words, is one of the most important building blocks of literacy. In a playful way, children understand how letter sounds are related to words. Phonemic awareness is not direct instruction of phonics. Instead, young children learn about sounds in words through exposure to poetry and rhymes.

The Rhyme With Reason program was developed to expose young children to the variety of sounds letters make in words and provide them the opportunities to manipulate these sounds in words. Rhyme With Reason is designed for a whole-class format. There are seven main developmental sequences in the program: exposure to ending rhymes, recognition of ending rhymes, production of ending rhymes, exposure to beginning sounds (alliteration), recognition of beginning sounds, production of beginning sounds, and simple syllable segmentation. Each sequence is presented in consecutive order. The phonemic awareness activities are done approximately three times a week in half-day prekindergarten and kindergarten programs, and every day in full-day kindergartens. The activities take approximately 10 to 15 minutes and can be integrated with movement and poetry activities as well as additional literature activities.

An extensive list of rhyming books, books that contain alliteration, and rhyming poetry is included in the Rhyme With Reason manual. Teachers are given strategies for selecting appropriate rhymes and teaching rhyme and alliteration.

Shared Book Experience

Shared book experience activities complement the STaR program. Whereas the STaR program emphasizes oral language and story comprehension and structure, shared book experience focuses children's attention on the mechanics of print.

Big Books used in the shared book experience contain short, predictable stories with illustrations. Teachers read the books to the children, pointing out where they start to read (front of the book, left side of the page), how the pictures illustrate the story, how each spoken word corresponds to a written one, and so on. Through several rereadings of predictable text, students began to isolate phrases on pages, words in phrases, and so on. The purpose of shared book experience is to reinforce not only that print carries meaning, but how books and print are related to reading for meaning.

The Big Books, which are chosen to feature rhythm, rhyme, and repetition, are used with suggested sequences of activities that teachers may use to focus children's attention on the mechanics of print. Specific strategies to fit into a 3-day or 5-day cycle are suggested in teacher's manuals. For example, in the 3-day cycle, on the first day the teacher simply reads the story through, pointing out words and pictures. On the second day, the teacher reads again and encourages the children to chime in. The 3rd day focuses on the details, such as cutting up sentence strips to convey the relations of words to phrases.

Peabody Language Development Kit

The Peabody Language Development Kit is also used in Success for All and Roots and Wings. The Peabody is used to provide additional models for language use and expression, as well as development of specific vocabulary skills. It contains lessons on such concepts as shapes, colors, classification, neighborhoods, foods, and clothing, and such language concepts as over/under and before/after.

The Peabody Language Development program is best used in small groups and is frequently taught by a trained paraprofessional. In the Peabody Language Development program, words and concepts are presented in a particular sequence so that the children are exposed to the same information in a particular order. The Peabody lesson typically takes about 15 minutes and is done while the classroom teacher is teaching concept development to a small group.

Learning Center Activities

Learning centers are an important aspect of the prekindergarten and kindergarten program in Success for All and Roots and Wings. Center areas recommended in the thematic units include the following: art, construction, dramatic play, water/sand, manipulative, science, writing, and listening/media. The activities in the center are related, and reinforce the theme that is being explored in class. The purpose of center activities is to allow young children to have the opportunity to play independently and learn in a "hands-on" fashion concepts that are presented in the thematic unit.

Concept development is emphasized in the prekindergarten and kindergarten center activities. Center time is not considered "free-play." Instead, center time is carefully planned to support the specific concepts that relate to the theme. For example, if the class is working on the Community Helpers unit, an art center activity presented in the unit suggests that the children make a fire fighter ladder. Such concepts as counting the number of rungs on the ladder, spacing the rungs of the ladder, and comparing and contrasting are also highlighted when doing this activity. Teachers incorporate higher-order concepts into the center activities and guide children to think about the many concepts that can be learned from the tasks as they circulate from center to center.

Alphabet Activities

Alphabet knowledge is built in Success for All and Roots and Wings using a wide variety of activities. Letters are introduced in various parts of the daily routine and are connected with the thematic unit, the story that is being presented, or both. Typically, the letter that is being worked on is presented during morning routine as a part of a morning message or the calendar activity. The letter activities are then woven throughout the daily theme. Children are given opportunities during writing or journal time to see the letter in print. During the STaR activity, the letter that is being worked on is presented again to the children. Often an alphabet book is used to reinforce the letters that have already been presented and to expose the children to new ones.

Scheduling

A typical day in a Success for All/Roots and Wings prekindergarten and kindergarten might follow the schedule presented here, assuming a half-day program. The half-day schedule contains the same elements as the full day, but less time is devoted to each activity. For example, STaR/Big Books follows a 3-day schedule in full-day kindergartens, but a 5-day schedule in half-day, and other activities may not appear every day.

Half-Day Early Learning Schedule

8:25- 8:30	Arrival (get together)
8:30- 8:45	Morning routines: Calendar, weather, morning message
8:45- 9:00	Theme learning
9:00- 9:25	STaR or shared book experience
	2 STaR stories per week
	5 shared book experiences per week (1 story)
	1 STaR story and 3 shared book experiences (1 story)
9:25- 9:35	Independent reading or journal writing
9:35-10:00	Center time activities: Art, construction, dramatic play, water/sand, manipulatives, science, listening/media
10:00-10:20	Small or total group learning (3 days per week) or shared writing (2 days per week)
	Teacher: Concept development
	Assistant: Peabody Language Development
10:20-10:30	Phonemic awareness: Music/movement/poetry
10:30-10:50	Math
10:50-11:00	Wrap up/sharing
11:00	Dismissal

Full-Day Early Learning Schedule

The content of the kindergarten curriculum depends in part on the objectives of the district. In districts that do not teach reading in kindergarten, Success for All focuses on prereading skills (including thematic units, STaR, Big Books, writing, and Peabody). If the district does typically teach reading in kindergarten, the Reading Roots program (see Chapter 2) is gradually introduced at midyear. The other activities are continued, but in a shorter form. A typical full-day kindergarten schedule in a school that does not expect full-scale reading instruction in kindergarten might be as follows:

8:25-8:30	Arrival	9:15-9:45	STaR
8:30-8:45	Morning routines: Calendar, weather, morning message	9:45-10:00	Journal writing (Entries can reflect either the theme learning objective or STaR story. In either case they need to relate to the theme.)
8:45-9:00	Theme learning		
9:00-9:15	Phonemic awareness: Music/movement/poetry		

10:00-10:45	Center time activities: Art, manipulatives, dramatic play, science, construction, water/ sand, writing, listening/media	11:45-12:15	Shared book experience
		12:15-12:30	Independent reading
		12:30-12:50	Recess
10:45-11:15	Small or total group learning	12:50- 1:20	Math
	Teacher: Concept development	1:20- 1:45	Writing
	Assistant: Peabody Language Development	1:45- 2:05	Music/movement/poetry
		2:05- 2:20	Sharing time
11:15-11:45	Lunch	2:20- 2:30	Preparation for dismissal

In Appendix 4.4, lesson plans from the Community Helpers unit for half- and full-day kindergarten are presented.

Appendix 4.1. STaR Weekly Schedule

Day 1
(Story 1)

1. **Story Introduction**
2. **Interactive Story Reading**
3. **Story Structure Review**

The activities take about 20 to 30 minutes per day. The interactive reading takes one day and the story retelling takes another day. That is, the 5 activities in STaR take 2 days to complete.

Day 2
(Story 1)

1. **Story Review and Interactive Retell**
2. **Individual Story Conference**
3. **Story Critique**

Day 3
(Story 2)

1. **Story Introduction**
2. **Interactive Story Reading**
3. **Story Structure Review**

In one week, 2 stories are covered. It is suggested that the 5th day be used for dramatic play, retelling of another story, or story-related writing.

Day 4
(Story 2)

1. **Story Review and Interactive Retell**
2. **Individual Story Conference**
3. **Story Critique**

Day 5

Story Extension Activities

Appendix 4.2. STaR Teacher's Guide

NOBODY LISTENS TO ANDREW

by
Elizabeth Guilfoile

STORY SUMMARY

One day, to his surprise, Andrew discovers a bear in his bedroom. When he tries to tell his family, no one will take the time to listen. Finally, Andrew creates such a scene that everyone is forced to listen and learns about the bear. The news of the bear sends panic through the neighborhood and soon everyone is involved in Andrew's predicament.

MATERIALS

- STaR Sheet
- Individual Conference Form
- Sequence Cards
- Book

Vocabulary

neighbor   listen   dog catcher

DAY 1

Story Introduction

Our story is called *Nobody Listens to Andrew.* It is about a little boy named Andrew who has something very important to say, but can't get anyone to listen to him. Why do you think no one will listen to Andrew? Have you ever had a problem like Andrew's in which no one would listens to you? How did that make you feel? How do you think Andrew will solve his problem? Let's read our story and listen to Andrew to find out what happens.

Interactive Story Reading

Begin reading the story, stopping when appropriate to ask predictive, summative, and inferential questions that will motivate children to interact with the story.

Page 5:   What do you think Andrew will say?

Who did Andrew ask to listen?

(*Mother*)

Page 7:   What did Mother say to Andrew?

(*"Wait Andrew. I must pay Mrs. Cleaner."*)

What did Andrew tell his father?

What did Father say to Andrew?

(*"Wait Andrew. I must cut the grass before dark."*)

Page 9:   What did Ruthy say to Andrew?

(*"Wait Andrew. I must put on my roller skates. I want to skate before dark."*)

Page 11:   What did Bobby say to Andrew?

(*"Don't bother me, Andrew. I must find my bat and ball. I want to play ball before dark."*)

What did Mr. Neighbor say to Andrew?

(*"Never mind Andrew. I must take my dog for a walk."*)

What do you think is in Andrew's bedroom?

Page 13:   Why was Andrew upset?

(*No one would listen to him.*)

What was Andrew trying to tell everyone?

(*There was a bear upstairs in his bed.*)

What did Andrew's family do after he showed them the bear?

(*They called the police, fire department, dog catcher, and zoo.*)

Page 23:   How did the bear get into Andrew's room?

(*The bear climbed the tree and came in through the window.*)

Page 25:   Where did they take the bear?

(*They took the bear to the zoo.*)

Page 26:   What did Andrew's father say?

(*"Next time we'll listen to Andrew."*)

Story Structure Review

Encourage children to recall the story title, characters, setting, story problem, and solution.

Story Review and Interactive Retell

Briefly review the elements of the story *Nobody Listens to Andrew*. Encourage children to recall the story title, characters, setting, problem, and solution. A story map could be used to record this information.

Provide a framework for children to interactively retell the story. The following are a list of activities that will foster communication about story details between teacher and children:

- Interactive Story Circle: In this activity students take turns elaborating on the details and ideas expressed by the last participant without repeating the sequence, but trying to add to the sequence of events to complete the story.
- Sequence Cards: There may be occasions when story sequencing materials can be used to foster the group retell of the story.

SC1—Andrew tried to tell his mother about the bear, but she was busy and wouldn't listen.	SC4—The police rushed to Andrew's home.
SC2—Andrew tried to tell his sister about the bear, but she would not listen.	SC5—The firefighters rushed to Andrew's home.
SC3—Andrew was upset because no one would listen. Finally his family listened to him.	SC6—Everyone went upstairs to see the bear.

- Story Dramatization: Students share the sequence of the story through dramatization. Many stories lend themselves to dramatization.
- Sharing: Teacher and children share their favorite story events with one another.
- Story Paths: Children organize the story structures to convey the sequence (or path) of the story and pattern of the story.
- Discussion Prompts: The answering of higher order questions lends itself to the understanding and retelling of story elements.

> What did Andrew find in his bedroom?
> Who did Andrew try to tell about the bear?
> Why didn't anyone listen to Andrew?
> How was Andrew able to get everyone to listen to him?
> How did the family and neighborhood react to Andrew's news?
> How did the bear get into Andrew's room?
> Why was the bear in Andrew's room?
> Who captured the bear?
> Why, from now on, will everyone listen to Andrew?
> What was your favorite part of the story? Why?

Story Critique Activities

Provide children with an opportunity to share their opinions about the story. Any of the following activities can be used to foster the story critique experience.

- Thumbs Up? or Thumbs Down?: Invite children to respond to a story by either giving it a thumbs-up for, "Yes, I liked the story" or a thumbs down for, " I didn't care for that story." Record children's responses on chart paper.
- Story Rating: Assist children in developing a story rating system. As a class, evaluate the story according to the rating criteria.

For example: 1 star = engaging title	1 star = enjoyable characters
1 star = eye-catching illustrations	1 star = interesting story

Story Critique Frames: Encourage children to tell what they either liked or disliked about the story.

    I liked the story _____ because _____.

    I disliked the story _____ because _____.

- Story Recommendations: Encourage children to think of reasons why they would or would not recommend a given story. As a class, write a story recommendation.

Story Extension Activities

- Discuss other ways Andrew could have informed his family about the bear.
- Write a story about a time when you had something important to say and no one would listen.
- As a class, write a story innovation using *Nobody Listens to Andrew* as a model. For example: *Nobody Listens to* _____.
- List reasons why it is important to listen to people.
- Role play Andrew telling his family about the bear.
- Record all of the information about the bear and continue to research project in the library to learn more about brown forest bears.
- Discuss ways in which the community helpers assisted Andrew with his problem.
- Write thank you letters to the community helpers from Andrew, which thank them for helping to capture the bear.
- Write a story about what happened to the bear when he was taken to the zoo.

Individual Story Conference Form

Name _____ Date _____

Teacher_____ School _____

Questions for Individual Story Retell

1. What was the title of the story? (*Nobody Listens to Andrew*)

   _____

2. Who were the story characters? (*Andrew, Mother, Mrs. Cleaner, Ruthy, Bobby, Daddy, Mr. Neighbor, police officer, firefighter, dog catcher, the zoo keeper, and the bear are the story characters.*)

   _____

   _____

3. What was Andrew's problem? (*There was a bear in his room and he tried to tell his family, but no one would listen.*)

   _____

   _____

4. How did Andrew finally get them to listen? (*He stomped his feet and said loudly, "There is a bear upstairs in my bed!"*)

   _____

   _____

5. Who came to help? (*The police, the firefighter, the dog catcher and the zoo keeper came to help.*)

   _____

   _____

6. What did Andrew's father promise would happen the next time? (*He promised that they would listen to Andrew.*)

   _____

   _____

7. What was your favorite part of the story? Why?

   _____

   _____

   _____

Appendix 4.3. Extended STaR Weekly Schedule

Extended STaR spans a week of and involves children in motivating and strategic learning activities that promote active participation in response to quality children's literature.

Day 1

1. Story Preview
2. Predictive Student Activity

Day 2

1. Story Introduction
2. Interactive Story Reading
3. Story Structure Review

Day 3

1. Story Review and Interactive Retell
2. Individual Story Conference
3. Story Critique

The daily Extended STaR lessons take about 20 minutes. Here is an outline for each of the 5 days.

Day 4

Group Story Elaboration: Prewriting Activities

Day 5

Story-Related Writing

Appendix 4.4. Community Helpers
Full-Day Sample Lesson

DAY 1

8:25-8:30	ARRIVAL

8:30-8:45   MORNING ROUTINES:
- Calendar
- Weather
- Morning Message

Today is Monday, September 18, 1995. We are going to learn about community helpers.

8:45-9:00   THEME LEARNING

People who work to take care of the people and property in a neighborhood are called community helpers.

9:00-9:15   PHONEMIC AWARENESS: MUSIC/MOVEMENT/POETRY
"Pretending"
"My Family and Their Jobs"

9:15-9:45   STaR
Day 1 *Nobody Listens to Andrew* by Elizabeth Guilfoile

9:45-10:00   JOURNAL WRITING
Draw and write about how the community helpers in the story helped to capture the bear.

10:00-10:45   CENTER TIME ACTIVITIES
Art: *Community Helpers Collage*
Dramatic Play: *Dramatize the story:* Nobody Listens to Andrew
Construction: *Construct a Community*
Manipulatives: *Tools of the Trade*

10:45-11:15   SMALL OR TOTAL GROUP LEARNING
Teacher: *Concept Development*
Assistant: *Peabody Language Development*

11:15-11:45   LUNCH

11:45-12:15   SHARED BOOK EXPERIENCE
Phase 1: *Off to Work* by Ron Bacon

12:15-12:30   INDEPENDENT READING

12:30-12:50   RECESS

12:50-1:20   MATH
               "Large, Medium, and Small"
               Display objects relating to community helpers. Children will order
               the objects from large to small.

1:20-1:45   WRITING
               Shared Writing: As a class, make a list of reasons why we need
               community helpers.

1:45-2:05   MUSIC/MOVEMENT/POETRY
               "Community Helpers' Song"
               "I Hear People"

2:05-2:20   SHARING
               *Have children share their journal entries, or any completed
               Center Time Project.*

2:20-2:30   PREPARATION FOR DISMISSAL

DAY 2

8:25-8:30   ARRIVAL

8:30-8:45   MORNING ROUTINES:
               ▨ Calendar
               ▨ Weather
               ▨ Morning Message
               *Today is Tuesday, September 19, 1995. We are going to learn
               about police officers.*

8:45-9:00   THEME LEARNING
               Police officers enforce the laws of the community to keep us safe.

9:00-9:15   PHONEMIC AWARENESS: MUSIC/MOVEMENT/POETRY
               "Traffic Policeman"
               "Mr. Policeman"

9:15-9:45   STaR
               Day 2 *Nobody Listens to Andrew* by Elizabeth Guilfoile

9:45-10:00   JOURNAL WRITING
               *Draw a picture of a police officer and tell how he or she helps to
               keep you safe.*

10:00-10:45   CENTER TIME ACTIVITIES
               Art: *Community helpers' paper bag puppets (police officer)*
               Dramatic Play: *Traffic Safety*
               Manipulatives: *Police Officer Puzzle*

10:45-11:15   SMALL OR TOTAL GROUP LEARNING
Teacher: *Concept Development*
Assistant: *Peabody Language Development*

11:15-11:45   LUNCH

11:45-12:15   SHARED BOOK EXPERIENCE
Phase 1 continued: *Off to Work* by Ron Bacon

12:15-12:30   INDEPENDENT READING

12:30-12:50   RECESS

12:50-1:20   MATH
"Address and Telephone Identification" Discuss the importance of knowing your address and telephone number, especially in an emergency situation. Talk about how police officers could better help someone if they knew their address and or telephone number. As a class, identify the numbers found in children's addresses and telephone numbers. Have individual children identify and recite their address and telephone number.

1:20-1:45   WRITING
Have children draw a picture of their house and include their address on the outside of the home.

1:45-2:05   MUSIC/MOVEMENT/POETRY
"The Lost Child and the Police Officer Game"
"Traffic Light Game"

2:05-2:20   SHARING
Have children share their journal entries, completed Center Time projects and house drawings.

2:20-2:30   PREPARATION FOR DISMISSAL

DAY 3

8:25 -8:30   ARRIVAL

8:30-8:45   MORNING ROUTINES:
- Calendar
- Weather
- Morning Message

Today is Wednesday, September 20, 1995. We are going to visit with Officer Friendly and learn about his or her job.

8:45-9:00   PHONEMIC AWARENESS: MUSIC/MOVEMENT/POETRY
Police officers enforce the laws of the community to keep us safe.

9:00-9:30	THEME LEARNING
	A visit from Officer Friendly.

9:30-10:00	SHARED WRITING
	As a class, write a thank you letter to Officer Friendly for visiting your classroom and telling you about his or her job.

10:00-10:45	CENTER TIME ACTIVITIES

10:45-11:15	STaR
	Day 1 *Curious George Visits the Police Station* by Marjorie and H. A. Rey

11:15-11:45	LUNCH

11:45-12:15	SMALL OR TOTAL GROUP LEARNING
	Teacher: *Concept Development*
	Assistant: *Peabody Language Development*

12:15-12:30	MUSIC/MOVEMENT/POETRY

12:30-1:00	SHARED BOOK EXPERIENCE
	Phase 2: *Off to Work* by Ron Bacon

1:00-1:15	INDEPENDENT READING

1:15-1:35	RECESS

1:35-2:05	MATH
	"Tell Us About It!" Present an object that could be used by a police officer, pass it around the circle and ask children to examine it (using all senses) carefully and silently. Then invite each child to tell something about the object.

2:05-2:20	SHARING
	Have children share their journal entries, or any completed Center Time projects.

2:20-2:30	PREPARATION FOR DISMISSAL

DAY 4

8:25-8:30	ARRIVAL

8:30-8:45	MORNING ROUTINES:
	▦ Calendar
	▦ Weather
	▦ Morning Message

Today is Thursday, September 21, 1995. We are going to talk about trash collectors and how they help to keep our neighborhoods clean.

8:45-9:00	THEME LEARNING *Trash Collectors work to keep our neighborhoods clean.*
9:00-9:15	PHONEMIC AWARENESS: MUSIC/MOVEMENT/POETRY *"Trash"* *"I Love Trash" Game*
9:15-9:45	STaR Day 2 *Curious George Visits the Police Station* by Marjorie and H. A. Rey
9:45-10:00	JOURNAL WRITING *Pretend you are George and write a letter of apology to the police chief and mayor for causing trouble at the Police Station.*
10:00-10:45	CENTER TIME ACTIVITIES Art: *Trash Truck Collage* Dramatic Play: *Recycling Center* Construction: *Recycled Box Buildings* Manipulatives: *Recycling Posters*
10:45-11:15	SMALL OR TOTAL GROUP LEARNING Teacher: *Concept Development* Assistant: *Peabody Language Development*
11:15-11:45	LUNCH
11:45-12:15	SHARED BOOK EXPERIENCE Phase 2: *Where Does All The Garbage Go?* by M. Berger
12:15-12:30	INDEPENDENT READING
12:30-12:50	RECESS
12:50-1:20	MATH **"Recyclable Trash: Yes or No?"**
1:20-1:50	WRITING **Shared Writing:** As a class, write an acrostic poem about trash collectors.
1:50-2:05	MUSIC/MOVEMENT/POETRY
2:05-2:20	SHARING TIME Have children share journal entries or any completed Center Time projects.
2:20-2:30	PREPARATION FOR DISMISSAL

DAY 5

8:25-8:30   ARRIVAL

8:30-8:45   MORNING ROUTINES:
- Calendar
- Weather
- Morning Message

Today is Friday, September 22, 1995. We are going to pick up trash around school.

8:45-9:00   THEME LEARNING
Trash Collectors work to keep our neighborhoods clean.

900-9:15   JOURNAL WRITING
Draw or write about the trash you picked up around the school.

9:15-9:30   PHONEMIC AWARENESS: MUSIC/MOVEMENT/POETRY

9:30-10:00   STaR
Day 3 *Curious George Visits the Police Station* by Marjorie and H. A. Rey

Story Extension Activity: Brainstorm good deeds George could do for the police chief, mayor, and police officers. For example, George could pick up trash or empty trash cans in and around the police station. Draw a picture of George helping out.

10:00-10:45 CENTER TIME ACTIVITIES

10:45-11:15 SMALL OR TOTAL GROUP LEARNING
Teacher: *Concept Development*
Assistant: *Peabody Language Development*

11:15-11:45 LUNCH

11:45-12:15 SHARED BOOK EXPERIENCE
Phase 2: *Where Does All The Garbage Go?* by M. Berger

12:15-12:30 INDEPENDENT READING

12:30-12:50 RECESS

12:50-1:20   MATH
"What Can It Be Used For?"
Select several common objects that are thrown away with out reusing. Pass the object around the circle and have children examine it silently. Encourage children to give suggestions for its use. Record suggestions on chart paper.

1:20-1:50	WRITING
	Shared Writing: Continue the acrostic poem about trash collectors.

1:50-2:05	MUSIC/MOVEMENT/POETRY

2:05-2:20	SHARING TIME
	Have children share journal entries, STaR story extension activity, or any completed Center Time projects.

2:20-2:30	PREPARATION FOR DISMISSAL

Community Helpers
Half-Day Sample Lesson

DAY 1

8:25-8:30	ARRIVAL

8:30-8:45	MORNING ROUTINES:
	▪ Calendar
	▪ Weather
	▪ Morning Message
	Today is Monday, September 18, 1995. We are going to learn about community helpers.

8:45-9:00	THEME LEARNING
	People who work to take care of the people and property in a neighborhood are called community helpers.

9:00-9:25	STaR OR SHARED BOOK EXPERIENCE
	STaR: Day 1
	Nobody Listens to Andrew by Elizabeth Guilfoile

9:25-9:35	JOURNAL WRITING
	Draw and write about how the community helpers in the story helped to capture the bear.

9:35-10:00	CENTER TIME ACTIVITIES
	Art: *Community Helpers Collage*
	Dramatic Play: *Dramatize the story:* Nobody Listens to Andrew
	Construction: *Construct a Community*
	Manipulatives: *Tools of the Trade*

10:00-10:20	SHARED WRITING
	As a class, make a list of reasons why we need Community Helpers.

10:20-10:30   PHONEMIC AWARENESS: MUSIC/MOVEMENT/POETRY
"Pretending"
"My Family and Their Jobs"

10:30-10:50   MATH
"Large, Medium, and Small"
Display objects relating to community helpers. Children will order
the objects from large to small.

10:50-11:00   WRAP-UP AND SHARING

11:00   DISMISSAL

DAY 2

8:25-8:30   ARRIVAL

8:30-8:45   MORNING ROUTINES:
- Calendar
- Weather
- Morning Message
*Today is Tuesday, September 19, 1995. We are going to talk about
police officers.*

8:45-9:00   THEME LEARNING
Police officers enforce the laws of the community to keep us safe.

9:00-9:30   STaR OR SHARED BOOK EXPERIENCE
STaR: Day 2
Nobody Listens to Andrew by Elizabeth Guilfoile

9:30-10:00   CENTER TIME ACTIVITIES
Art: *Community helpers paper bag puppets (police officer)*
Dramatic Play: *Traffic safety*
Manipulatives: *Police officer puzzle*

10:00-10:20   SMALL OR TOTAL GROUP LEARNING
Teacher: *Concept development*
Assistant: *Peabody Language Development*

10:20-10:30   PHONEMIC AWARENESS: MUSIC/MOVEMENT/POETRY
"Traffic Policeman"
"Mr. Policeman"

10:30-10:50   MATH
"Address and Telephone Identification" Discuss the importance
of knowing your address and telephone number, especially in an
emergency situation. Talk about how police officers could better

help someone if they knew their address and or telephone number. As a class, identify the numbers found in children's addresses and telephone numbers. Have individual children identify and recite their address and telephone number.

10:50-11:00   WRAP-UP AND SHARING

11:00   DISMISSAL

DAY 3

8:25-8:30   ARRIVAL

8:30-8:45   MORNING ROUTINES:
- Calendar
- Weather
- Morning Message

Today is Wednesday, September 20, 1995. We are going to visit with Officer Friendly and learn about his or her job.

8:45-9:15   THEME LEARNING
A visit from Officer Friendly.

9:15-9:30   SHARED WRITING
As a class, write a thank you letter to Officer Friendly for visiting your classroom and telling you about his or her job.

9:30-10:00   CENTER TIME ACTIVITIES

10:00-10:20   SMALL OR TOTAL GROUP LEARNING
Teacher: *Concept Development*
Assistant: *Peabody Language Development*

10:20-10:30   PHONEMIC AWARENESS: MUSIC/MOVEMENT/POETRY
"Traffic Policeman"
"Mr. Policeman"
"Traffic Light" Game

10:30-10:50   MATH
"Tell Us About It!" Present an object that could be used by a police officer, pass it around the circle and ask children to examine it (using all senses) carefully and silently. Then invite each child to tell something about the object.

10:50-11:00   WRAP-UP AND SHARING

11:00   DISMISSAL

DAY 4

8:25-8:30   ARRIVAL

8:30-8:45   MORNING ROUTINES:
- Calendar
- Weather
- Morning Message

Today is Thursday, September 21, 1995. We are going to talk about trash collectors and how they help to keep our neighborhoods clean.

8:45-9:00   THEME LEARNING
Trash collectors work to keep our neighborhood clean.

9:00-9:25   STaR OR SHARED BOOK EXPERIENCE
Phase 1

Shared Book Experience: *Where Does All The Garbage Go?* by M. Berger

9:25-9:35   INDEPENDENT READING

9:35-10:00   CENTER TIME ACTIVITIES
Art: *Trash Truck Collage*
Dramatic Play: *Recycling Center*
Construction: *Recycled Box Buildings*
Manipulatives: *Recycling Posters*

10:00-10:20   SMALL OR TOTAL GROUP LEARNING

DAY 5

8:25-8:30   ARRIVAL

8:30-8:45   MORNING ROUTINES:
- Calendar
- Weather
- Morning Message

Today is Friday, September 22, 1995. We are going to pick up trash around school.

8:45-9:00   THEME LEARNING
Trash collectors work to keep our neighborhoods clean.

9:00-9:25   STaR OR SHARED BOOK EXPERIENCE
Phase II
Shared Book Experience: *Where Does All The Garbage Go?* by M. Berger

9:25-9:35   INDEPENDENT READING

9:35-10:00   CENTER TIME ACTIVITIES

10:00-10:20   SHARED WRITING
                 As a class write an acrostic poem about trash collectors.

10:20-10:30   PHONEMIC AWARENESS: MUSIC/MOVEMENT/POETRY

10:30-10:50   MATH
                 "What Can It Be Used For?"
                 Select several common objects that are thrown away without
                 reusing. Pass the object around the circle and have children
                 examine it silently. Encourage children to give suggestions for its
                 use. Record suggestions on chart paper.

10:30-10:50   WRAP-UP AND SHARING

11:00   DISMISSAL

5

Roots and Wings

Adding Social Studies, Science,
and Mathematics to Success for All

At Lexington Park Elementary School, in a small town in southern Maryland, 10-year-old Jamal rises to speak. "The chair recognizes the delegate from Ridge School," says the chairwoman, a student from the local high school.

"I'd like to speak in favor of House Bill R130," he begins. "This bill would tell farmers they couldn't use fertilizer on land that is within 200 feet of the Chesapeake Bay. Fertilizer goes into the Bay and causes pollution and kills fish. Farmers can still grow a lot of crops even if they don't plant close to water, and we will all have a better life if we can stop pollution in the Bay. I yield to questions."

A hand goes up. The chairwoman recognizes a delegate from Carver School.

"How does fertilizer harm the Bay?" she asks.

Jamal explains how the fertilizer provides nutrition to algae in the Bay, and when too much algae grows, it deprives the other creatures of oxygen and sunlight. When he finishes, a delegate from Green Holly School is recognized.

"I'm a farmer," says 11-year-old Maria. "I can hardly pay all my bills as it is, and I've got three kids to feed. I'll go broke if I can't fertilize my whole field!"

The debate on the bill goes on for more than an hour. Student delegates who are playing the role of watermen speak about how their way of life is disappearing because of declining catches due to pollution. Business owners talk about how pollution ruins the local economy. Finally, the committee amends the bill to prohibit farmers from planting near waterways unless they are poor. The bill passes and later on is voted on by the whole House of Delegates.[1]

It is essential to ensure that every child can read, but this is not enough to fully restructure elementary schools. Students must also know mathematics, social studies, and science. They need to be able to creatively and flexibly solve problems, understand their own learning processes, and connect knowledge from many disciplines.

The vignette above illustrates one aspect of a program that builds on the base of success established by Success for All. This program, called Roots and Wings, is being developed, piloted, and disseminated under funding from the New American Schools Development Corporation (NASDC), a private foundation established to create school designs for the 21st century.

Roots and Wings schools use the prekindergarten, kindergarten, reading, tutoring, writing/language arts, and family support/integrated services programs of Success for All (although NASDC funding has enabled us to revise and improve these programs as well). What Roots and Wings adds to Success for All is two major elements. One is an integrated social studies/science program called WorldLab; the other is a new cooperative learning approach to mathematics instruction called Math Wings. These are described in the following sections.

WorldLab

The debate in the "House of Delegates" illustrates WorldLab, one of the most distinctive and innovative elements of Roots and Wings. In WorldLab, students take on roles as people in history, in other countries, or in various occupations. The students in the "House of Delegates" are participating in a 12-week unit called BayLab. They have been studying a local waterway, focusing on sources of pollution, watersheds, tides, the water cycle, and the ecology cycle of aquatic organisms. They have also been learning about government, economics, geography, and politics. Their work on these topics is done in preparation for a model state legislature, in which students write, propose, and debate many bills relating to cleaning up the waterway. In other WorldLab units, students take on roles as inventors, as delegates to the Constitutional Convention, as engineers designing efficient vehicles, as explorers in the 15th century, and as physicians seeking a cure for smallpox. In these simulations students work in small, cooperative groups to investigate topics of science and social studies. They read books and articles about their topics, write newspapers, broadsides, letters, and proposals, use mathematics skills to solve problems relating to their topics, and use fine arts, music, and computer, video, and other technology to prepare multimedia reports. Students ultimately learn all the usual content of elementary science and social studies (plus much more), but they do so as active participants in the scientific discoveries, historical events, and other political and economic systems they are studying.

The idea behind WorldLab is to make the contents of the entire elementary curriculum useful and relevant to children's daily lives by immersing them in simulations in which knowledge and skills are necessary. One key problem of traditional elementary schooling is that the content students are learning is not immediately useful to them. It is entirely possible to be a happy and successful 10-year-old with no knowledge whatsoever about the American revolution, or the rain cycle, or how to add fractions, or how to write a persuasive letter. Students may work to please their teachers or parents or to get a good grade, or they may be interested in some parts of the content they are studying, but motivation, curiosity, and insight are certain to be much greater when students need information or skills to solve problems that have meaning to them.

Simulations provide an ideal opportunity to make information immediately useful. In a well-designed simulation, students fully identify with the roles they take on. Maria, in the House of Delegates example, is a farmer with serious responsibilities: three children, a mortgage, bills, and taxes. She is also an elected representative to the Maryland House of Delegates. As a real-life kid and as a simulated farmer and delegate, Maria cares about the ecology of the Chesapeake Bay. She cares about it, however, from a particular perspective. She pays great attention to information about the effects of fertilizer runoff because this has direct relevance to her role. To participate intelligently in the debates, she has to have a deep understanding of watersheds, erosion, eutrophication, photosynthesis, the needs of sealife for oxygen, tides, economics and the economic impact of pollution on the Bay, government, laws, and many other topics. She has used math to solve real economic problems, has written impassioned letters to support her views, and has read books relating to the Bay to build her understanding of the issues she confronts in her simulated roles. The Bay unit is not only an interdisciplinary thematic unit. Because of its use of simulations, it is an opportunity to make knowledge and skills not only integrated but also useful.

Simulations can give students an emotional investment in the material they are studying. In a unit called Rebellion to Union, fifth graders received a distressing note from their principals. The note announced taxes (against the classes' simulated economies) on certain activities, such as using the pencil sharpeners, to help support the costs of WorldLab. The students in each class assembled their class governments, wrote back notes of protest, and decided to boycott the pencil sharpeners. After a while additional notes taxed the use of desks. Classes moved their desks into the hall and sat on the floor. Exasperated, the principals dissolved the class governments. At this, classes decided to "secede," and wrote a declaration of independence to explain and justify their actions.

Even though they knew it was a simulation, the students were deeply emotionally involved. They wrote letters, picketed the principal's office, and took great pleasure in defying her authority. When they then read the various drafts of the real Declaration of Independence, they could identify not only with the framers' words and logic but with their emotions. They were really there, not acting out a script but wrestling with similar questions, fears, and uncertainties. Later, the students became delegates to the Constitutional Convention and debated positions appropriate to the interests of their states and occupations. These children will never forget the American Revolution or Constitutional Convention. They were *there,* in their hearts and minds. They participated in the debates, stood up for their points of view, heard, saw, and felt what it was like. Everything they had learned in a 2-month unit was relevant and important to them.

The world outside the school is a crucial part of the WorldLab program, accessed by means of field studies, telecommunication, computer technology, and the involvement of community resource people. WorldLab units are designed to enhance student motivation and higher-order thinking processes by engaging students in the dynamic interdependence of economic, political, social, physical and biological systems. This "systems approach" to curriculum development represents a significant departure from traditional curricula because it requires integration rather than compartmentalization of information. In WorldLab, students are continually encouraged to ask questions, to collect data, to investigate, and to predict how elements of one system will impact on another system and on their own personal outcomes in the ongoing simulation. Yet students in WorldLab do more than merely study real-world problems; they take an active part in planning and implementing projects that contribute to the community, such as conducting a stream quality survey or participating in efforts to promote the health of a waterway.

The WorldLab process is structured to provide frequent use of scaffolds for scientific experiments and other information gathering investigations so that students' skills in thinking through the investigation process are continuously honed during their years in WorldLab. The questions that students formulate as they experience a unit become the basis for informational or scientific investigations.

1. *Problem:* Do different surfaces affect how far a battery will travel?

2. *Hypothesis:* I think that the battery will go the farthest on the cardboard.

3. *Procedure:* We made a track. Then put a book under the board. Then we put the cardboard at the end, then the cloth, then the towel.

4. *Results:* Our table found out the battery went the farthest on the cardboard.

Surface	*1*	*2*	*3*	*Average*
Cardboard	185 cm.	164 cm.	159 cm.	169.3 cm.
Cloth	158 cm.	150 cm.	134 cm.	147 cm.
Towel	119 cm.	11 cm.	118 cm.	116 cm.

5. *Conclusions:* Our hypothesis has been supported by the data we had on our experiment. It has been supported because the battery went the farthest on the cardboard.

—Clifford

Figure 5.1. Student Lab Report

As students conduct a scientific experiment, they learn how to develop a testable hypothesis, describe the procedure for experimentation, identify materials needed, record their data, and communicate their conclusions. Laboratory report formats used in all units assist them in understanding the experimentation process as a tool. Laboratory reporting requirements are simpler in the early grades and become more elaborate as students' skills grow. Figure 5.1 shows an example of a laboratory report filled out by fourth graders using the Inventors unit.

An information gathering investigation has a similar scaffold that is used in every WorldLab unit. Students first determine whether the question they are interested in can be investigated. When questions have been narrowed and focused, students learn how to use a variety of resources to find information related to their question. They use classroom books and texts, library books, encyclopedias, CD-ROM information bases, and community members, reached by phone or in classroom visits, to piece together the needed information.

Students work as members of a team in all WorldLab activities. Although each student is individually accountable for a product related to the topic being explored, the team works together to plan, assist, and provide feedback to each of its members as the work goes on. Team members are responsible for insuring that each members of the team understands the concepts being presented and is prepared with his or her portion of the work for the team's task. Weekly team scores provide feedback and goals that help the team work together. Scores on a weekly assessment, which use improvement points to allow every student to contribute equally to the team, are one component of the feedback.

Like the other components of Success for All and Roots and Wings, WorldLab units are structured. Units are organized into 5-day cycles of instruction, as well as a daily lesson sequence. This provides structure to support both teachers and students as they take on the many extraordinary opportunities that WorldLab provides. The daily cycle is made up of five parts, which are described here.

Setting the Stage. The agenda for the day is laid out, along with several key questions. Each student answers the key questions at the end of the day, so students know what they must focus on. Daily goals for cooperation are also established at this time.

Active Instruction. Basic information about the science or social studies content being studied is provided using a variety of presentation modes, including interactive discussion, videos, discovery opportunities, or presentations. Instructions for subsequent teamwork activities are provided.

Teamwork. Students work in their teams to carry out investigations, to gather information, or to conduct scientific experiments. Simulation activities are also carried out at this time. Each team member has an individual task that he or she is working on that contributes to the team product.

Time for Reflection. At the end of each day, students integrate the information they have gained with the goals for the day. Students review major concepts, discussing them with their teammates, and write in their journals to express their understandings of the work done.

Assessment. Assessment is done on a daily basis in daily conferences called "one-to-ones." These provide informal opportunities for the assessment of each student's product and allow for individual goal setting. In addition, a more formal assessment comes at the end of each 5-day cycle and takes a variety of forms. A letter taking a position supported by information gathered during the week, a completed lab report, a summary of information gathered, or a demonstration of mastery of content may be the basis for the end-of-cycle assessment.

A sample WorldLab lesson is provided in Appendix 5.1 at the end of the chapter.

WorldLab is a laboratory in which students can use and enhance the skills they are learning in other components of the Roots and Wings program, including reading, writing, and mathematics. Some of the materials included in WorldLab units are designed to be used during reading and language arts periods, and there is a close integration of reading and writing activities with WorldLab themes. Likewise, mathematics skills required in WorldLab investigations and simulations often become the subject of lessons in a mathematics class. Physical education, music, and the visual arts are integral components of WorldLab, used to enhance student investigations and participation in simulations.

The BayLab unit for Grades 4 through 5 is illustrative of the key components of the WorldLab model:

- A design that promotes an understanding of the interdependence of economic, political, biological, and physical systems
- Use of simulation, group investigation, experimentation, and cooperative learning
- Involvement of community resource people
- Encouragement of problem solving and other higher-order thinking processes
- Projects, completed by students, that help solve community problems

In the simulation component of the BayLab unit, students become citizens of a fictional place called Baytown, where they have a simulated family and occupation (such as farmer, builder, waterman, and so on). The unit was originally designed around the Chesapeake Bay, but has been adapted for use with any waterway. Students receive an income in their occupations but must pay taxes and bills for food, clothing, utilities, and shelter. In addition, students experience various "life events," which are pleasant and not-so-pleasant occurrences such as inheriting a sum of money or needing a washing machine repair. Other events occur that affect the income they earn in their occupation, such as a decrease or increase in the fish harvest or additional people moving into Baytown. Community resource people, such as watermen and farmers, are asked to share their knowledge about their occupations' impact on the bay with students. Students are engaged in activities that encourage them to think about different viewpoints on environmental issues. They quickly begin to realize that people in different occupations and family situations may have quite dissimilar perspectives about problems facing the Bay.

BayLab also engages students in a series of lessons designed to lead to investigations of important problems and topics that affect the Bay and how these may impact on their simulated lives in BayLab. Students try to identify "mystery objects" from the Bay, investigate plant and animal life in the waterways near the school, experience food webs and food chains, and learn about watersheds and the impact of oil spills on aquatic environments. They also carry out experiments to determine the effects of water salinity and dissolved oxygen levels on ecosystem relationships, using lab report forms designed to guide them in learning the steps in the scientific process. As BayLab lessons progress, student-generated questions about the Bay are continuously posted in the classroom. Using these questions, cooperative teams begin to investigate topics about the Bay, such as "What causes the yearly algae bloom in the Bay?" or "Why have sea grasses in the Bay been disappearing?" Students give presentations describing the outcomes of their research on specific BayLab topics. Students are continuously asked to estimate and predict outcomes, as well as analyze and interpret data about the Bay. Students also begin a project to enhance local waterways, such as participating in a Save Our Streams survey of stream quality in their area, or painting storm drains to warn people that pollutants should not be poured into storm drains.

Students are informed that they will next have an opportunity to run for election in a simulated State Legislature so that they can sponsor bills to help the Bay. In writing campaign speeches, students are asked to use the information they have learned about the Bay to propose bills they promise to introduce if elected. Students learn how to register to vote in the upcoming BayLab election and conduct extensive campaigns. Issues that arise in campaigns may require students to do additional research about particular Bay topics. Once the election has been held and the results announced, the class helps the elected Delegates and State Senators write bills to help enhance Bay life. Again, students use the information learned about the Bay in writing and revising these bills. Bills that are recommended by the classroom delegates and state senators are introduced at the culminating activity of the BayLab unit: A meeting of the BayLab Model State Legislature. Students from different classes (sometimes different schools) and their elected representatives come together to deliberate about bills to preserve and enhance the Bay. In committee meetings and on the floor of the House of Delegates and State Senate, students have an opportunity to bring to bear the knowledge they have learned in debating and revising submitted bills. A local notable may act as governor and will sign or veto the bills passed by the model legislature. Once the legislature session is completed, taxes are assessed for any programs that require new revenues (with accompanying groans from the taxpayers).

Other WorldLab units include the following:

- "From Rebellion to Union" (Grades 4 through 5) deals with the American Revolution. Students in this simulation take on the roles of patriots or loyalists with families and occupations of the period from 1763-1791 (including African Americans and Native Americans). They begin by being incited into a classroom mini-revolt over the issue of being taxed to pay for the WorldLab program. They then write their own classroom Declaration of Independence and Constitution. Students compare and contrast their own revolt with the revolt of the American patriots. Subsequently they act as a more broad-based Continental Congress and Constitutional Convention (including both African Americans and Native Americans) in deciding on the contents of a U.S. Declaration of Independence and Constitution. Science is incorporated through the need to understand and combat common diseases such as smallpox, which had such a devastating impact on revolutionary armies. Students create a slide-tape show or videotape with appropriate music of the time and art work to depict key events in the Revolutionary war and writing of the Constitution.

- "Encounters" (Grades 4 through 5) is a unit that helps students understand how the interactions between three major cultural groups, African, European, and Native

American, shaped the development of our nation. Students become historians and scientists in training. They explore the methods historians use by studying a local historic site. They become scientists as they investigate how scientific discoveries affected early American societies. Students recreate Ben Franklin's Traveling Electrical Show using Franklin's original experiments in static electricity. The unit includes authentic experiments to replicate and primary historical documents to investigate. Later in the unit, teams experiment with methods for growing crops typically grown during Colonial times. They collect data to help them decide how to produce the most bountiful harvest for their family. Ultimately, teams harvest and enjoy their crops. Students develop their roles as Africans, Europeans, or Native Americans during specific historical periods by composing "Day in the Life" stories about a typical day in the life of the character they are role playing. This personalizes learning and helps students appreciate what people were thinking and feeling as historic events unfolded. Students use computer software to research and publish their "Day in the Life" stories and assemble them into class books. At the conclusion of the unit, students plan and present an Encounters Fair to share their learning and insights with the local community.

▪ "Body Networks" (Grades 4 through 5) is an investigation of the nervous system that focuses on the role of the brain in controlling body functions. Students take the roles of consultants who develop public health announcements focused on safety procedures that prevent head injury and protect the brain. For example, students design, build, and test bicycle helmets and then produce commercials to persuade children to use them.

▪ "Inventors" (Grades 4 through 5) consists of four components: (a) reviewing inventions that have made an impact on modern society; (b) learning about the creative process and entrepreneurship by reading biographies of famous inventors; (c) engaging students in identifying a need for a product, designing a product to meet this need, and creating a campaign to sell the product; (d) using the World in Motion program developed by the Society of Automotive Engineers to assist students in taking on the roles of an engineering design team as they experiment with the laws of motion and apply what they have learned to create the most efficient vehicle in their class.

▪ "Adventures" and "Africa" (Grade 3) are units designed to be taught consecutively. They focus on geography, economics, and physical and earth sciences. "Adventures" prepares students for worldwide explorations by exploring their own school community first. As students prepare a visitor's center and guide to their school they apply newly mastered map making and research skills. They identify elements common to all communities. Next, students conduct experiments about buoyancy and navigation as they prepare to simulate a ship's crew on a voyage of discovery. They apply their findings as they make critical design decisions and build a clay ship that carries cargo and floats. They learn about the economic concepts of scarcity, opportunity cost, and supply and demand as they choose what to take along on their expeditions. Finally, they set sail for Africa, using the stars to plot their course. When they arrive, a simulation of life in an African community begins. They investigate the same aspects of community they identified earlier in their school. They compare and contrast government, communication, infrastructure, use of natural resources, foods, customs, and traditions, among other factors. Students find that communities exist to satisfy peoples' wants and needs. Students also discover a problem in this community. There has been a drought and water is scarce. Students work in teams to design a new irrigation system and apply water conservation methods to solve the problem. Students pack their bags and set sail for their next destination. Additional units will take students on adventures in Japan, Brazil, and finally a futuristic community in space.

▪ "Trees" (Grades 1 through 2) involves students in a study of the life cycle of trees throughout the year. Students become botanists as they identify what they already know about trees, and decide what they need to find out. The unit offers them a variety of opportunities to explore and investigate their questions with activities such as adopting a tree, observing it throughout the school year and writing about it in a journal, planting seeds and observing their growth, conducting experiments, and recording their findings in lab reports. Students "branch out" and investigate the role trees play in other parts of the world, such as South American rain forests. They build thinking, reading, and writing skills as they discover that trees are not only beautiful, but play an important role in providing food, shelter, recreation, and employment.

- "Harvests" (Grades 1 through 2) lets students take the trip of a lifetime in search of harvest celebrations around the world. In this multicultural, multidisciplinary unit, students compare and contrast different customs, traditions, and farming methods all related to the foods people eat in many diverse lands. The unit increases cultural awareness, respect for diversity, and an understanding of what we all have in common. Students receive passports, prepare itineraries, and take on the role of the international traveler to complete their investigation. The unit culminates with an international celebration of the harvest featuring student projects, cooking, and creative dramatics.

- "Eggs" (Grades 1 through 2) transforms young students into zoologists as they classify all phyla of living things that develop from eggs. Students learn how and why farmers candle and incubate quail and chicken eggs. When the eggs hatch, the students compare and contrast the chicks, observe their behavior, and chart their growth. Each team of zoologists investigates a different phylum of organisms to become experts on the subject. They conduct numerous experiments and record data. Teams observe tadpoles to learn about the life cycles of amphibians. They compare this to another wonder of nature as they wait and watch expectantly for the metamorphosis of a butterfly to occur. The unit culminates with each team teaching the class about their specialty.

MathWings

MathWings, the Roots and Wings mathematics program for Grades 1 through 5, is based on the standards of the National Council of Teachers of Mathematics (NCTM). A program to prepare students for mathematics in the 21st century needs to actively involve students in the conceptual development and practical application of their mathematics skills. The MathWings program reflects a balance of solid mathematical conceptual development, problem solving in real-world applications, and a maintenance of necessary mathematics skills.

Students enter school with a great deal of mathematical knowledge. They know about combining and separating, halves and wholes, and so on. What they need is a bridge between their preexisting knowledge and the formal representation of this knowledge in mathematical symbols. This requires the use of manipulatives, demonstrations, and discovery to help students build mathematical understanding. MathWings uses cooperative learning at all age levels while incorporating problem solving in real situations, skill practice and reinforcement for efficiency in application, calculator use, alternative assessments, writing, connections to literature and other disciplines, and application to the students' world and personal experiences. Although students help each other learn, they are always individually accountable for their own learning, and are frequently assessed on their progress in understanding and using math (see Slavin, 1995).

Critical Components of MathWings

The *NCTM Curriculum and Evaluation Standards* advocate emphasizing problem solving rather than rote calculation with algorithms. MathWings lessons involve the students in problem solving in "real" situations to give validity and purpose to their mathematics explorations, and in daily problem solving as part of the routine of math class. MathWings lessons also make connections to literature, science, art, and other subjects, as well as the students' world and personal experiences to provide this real-world problem-solving context.

Another strand of the Standards is mathematical reasoning. Students develop their ability to think through and solve mathematical problems when they use manipulatives to develop concepts and then represent what is actually happening with symbols. MathWings units are constructed to develop concepts from the concrete to the abstract so that each step of the reasoning is clarified. The Standards also promote the use of calculators for developing concepts and exploring advanced problem-solving situations rather than checking answers or replacing skills and mental math. MathWings students use calculators in this way to increase both their mathematical reasoning skills and the scope and complexity of the problems they can solve, and to focus their energy on mathematical reasoning rather than mere mechanical calculation.

The Standards emphasize communication, both oral and written, to clarify, extend, and refine the students' knowledge. MathWings students constantly explain and defend their solutions orally, and regularly write in their logbooks and other portions of their lessons. This emphasis on communication extends to the assessments as well. The Standards suggest the use of alternative assessments, which incorporate communication as well as calculation. MathWings units involve the students in many different types of assessment. The students complete Concept Checks in which they explain their thinking as they solve problems after every few lessons. They work on performance tasks at the end of each unit to use the skills they have learned to solve practical real-world situations and explain and communicate about their thinking. Teacher observations of students at work with manipulatives, collecting data, and so on, as well as their written and oral communications are also used to assess their understanding.

The use of cooperative learning in MathWings is based on years of research regarding effective strategies for classroom instruction. This research has shown that the cognitive rehearsal opportunities presented by cooperative learning, as well as the opportunities for clarification and reteaching for students who do not catch a concept immediately, have positive effects on academic achievement. Research has also shown that using cooperative learning in the classroom can have positive effects on interethnic relationships, acceptance of mainstreamed academically handicapped students, student self-esteem, liking of others, and attitudes toward school and teachers (Slavin, 1995). In cooperative learning, students work together to learn; the team's work is not done until all team members have learned the material being studied. This positive interdependence is an essential feature of cooperative learning.

Research has identified three key components that make cooperative learning strategies effective: team recognition, individual accountability, and equal opportunities for success. In MathWings, as in other Student Team Learning strategies (Slavin, 1994), students work in 4-member, mixed-ability teams. Teams may earn certificates and additional means of recognition if they achieve at or above a designated standard. All teams can succeed because they are working to reach a common standard rather than competing against one another. The team's success depends on the individual learning of all team members; students must make sure that everyone on the team has learned, because each team member must demonstrate his or her knowledge on an individual assessment. Students have an equal opportunity for success in MathWings because they contribute points to their teams by improving over their own individual performance, by bringing in their homework, and by meeting particular behavior goals set by the teacher. Students who are typically seen as lower achievers can contribute as many points to the team as high achievers.

The MathWings program is designed to use the calculator as a tool, not a crutch. Calculators enable the students to explore and demonstrate concepts in an appealing way. Students discover that they need to check their calculator answers for accuracy because the calculator is only as accurate as the information and process that is keyed into it. Thus, students develop their skills in estimating and predicting outcomes. Students also spend more time actually thinking about math and the processes that will most efficiently solve a given problem rather than focusing completely on tedious and lengthy calculations. Because of the speed of calculation with calculators, students are more willing to try several approaches to solving a problem situation or to reevaluate their answers and try a different method of solution. Finally, calculators build students' confidence in mathematics as they receive much positive reinforcement from correct solutions. This leads, in turn, to a greater willingness to tackle more challenging mathematical situations in the belief that they have the ability and the tools to solve them.

Manipulative use is a basic building block of the MathWings program at all levels. Students construct understanding and develop original methods for solving problems using manipulatives. As they work with manipulatives and discuss and defend their thinking, they gradually make the concepts their own. Once a problem can be solved with manipulatives, students draw a picture and then write a number sentence to represent what was happening with the manipulatives as they solved the problem. This gradual progression from concrete to pictorial to abstract provides a solid foundation of understanding on which the students can build. Every method or algorithm can be understood, and even reinvented, with manipulatives, thus replacing rote learning of algorithms with understanding of concepts and ways to efficiently apply them. Once the concepts have been firmly established and students understand how the algorithms work, they move away from using concrete manipulatives. Manipulatives, however, can be revisited at any time to remediate or extend a concept as needed.

Every MathWings Action Math unit has a literature connection that is an integral part of the concept development. Literature provides a wonderful vehicle for exploring mathematical concepts in meaningful contexts demonstrating that mathematics is an integral part of human experience. The use of literature incorporates the affective elements and demonstrates the aesthetic aspect of mathematics. Finally, the use of literature encourages students to pose problems from real and imaginary situations and to use language to communicate about mathematics.

MathWings involves the students in daily routines for skill practice and reinforcement to facilitate efficiency in calculation and application. Once the students have mastered the facts and basic algorithms, they become tools for the students to use as they develop concepts and problem solving. These daily routines include practice and weekly timed tests to encourage mastery of the basic facts, and then daily practice problems at varying difficulty levels to provide for fluency in the use of the essential algorithms.

MathWings is composed of two kinds of units: Action Math units, which are whole class units, and Power Math units, which are individualized units. Action Math units are 2 to 6 weeks in length and explore and develop concepts and their practical applications. One-week Power Math units are interspersed between whole class units and provide time for students to individually practice previous skills or explore more accelerated skills.

There is a frame around these units every day. This frame is provided by the Daily Routines, which are efficient ways to provide for team management, problem solving, and fluency of skills. Daily Routines are part of every Action Math or Power Math lesson.

Every day, students spend at least 60 minutes in their mathematics class. Daily lessons consist of three components, Check-In, Action Math or Power Math, and Reflection. Check-In and Reflection are the two routines that frame the lesson providing a warm-up at the beginning and closure at the end of class. These routines are important because the students know what to expect, and this builds confidence and feelings of ownership. The routines facilitate smooth and efficient class and materials management.

The first 15-minute segment is Check-In. Check-In is an efficient class start-up routine in which the teams regularly complete one challenging real-world problem as a team, learning problem strategies as a team. They also complete a facts study process twice a week, and check homework briefly every day.

The next 40 minutes in either Action Math or Power Math is the heart of the lesson. When the class is doing an Action Math unit, the lesson involves the students in Active Instruction, Team Work, and Assessment. During active instruction the teacher and students interact to explore a concept and its practical applications and skills. The teacher may present a challenging problem for students to explore with manipulatives to construct a solution, may challenge the teams to use prior knowledge to discover a solution, may ask the teams to find a pattern to develop a rule.

During team work the students come to consensus about their solutions to problems, their understanding of concepts and their thinking. A team member is chosen randomly to share his or her ideas with the class. Then students individually practice similar problems with teammates available for support. The team members check answers with each other and rehearse to be sure every team member can explain them.

At the end of the team work, there is a brief feedback opportunity. The teacher randomly chooses a team member to share the ideas or solutions of the team, and to explain their thinking. This enables the teacher to assess the understanding of the group as a whole and ensures that teammates are invested in making sure that all members of the team are mastering the concepts.

The final portion of an Action Math lesson is Assessment. One or more brief problems are used as a quick individual assessment of mastery of the concept or skill explored in the lesson.

When the class is doing a one-week Power Math unit, the 40-minute heart of the lesson involves each student in remediating, refining, or accelerating his or her skills. Students work at their own pace on the skill that they need to practice, completing check outs and mastery tests successfully to move to another skill they need to practice. Students who have mastered the basic skills explore accelerated units at their own pace. The teacher teaches minilessons to small groups of students (working on the same skills) gathered from various teams while the other students continue to work individually.

The last 5-minute segment of class is Reflection. This is an efficient routine to bring closure to the class time. During Action Math units Reflection involves a quick summary of the key concepts by the teacher. During both Action Math units and Power Math units, homework sheets are passed out, and a short entry is written in the MathWings Logbook in response to a writing prompt about the lesson.

A sample MathWings lesson is included in Appendix 5.2 at the end of this chapter.

All students should not only be given the opportunity to establish a solid foundation in mathematics, but also the opportunity to extend and stretch their knowledge and experience in mathematics. Thus, a program of mathematics should include a structure to accommodate a diversity of abilities and background mathematical knowledge, while ensuring that all students experience the depth, breadth, and beauty of mathematics. The MathWings curriculum incorporates this philosophy in its development.

Future of Roots and Wings

As of this writing, the additional components that make a Success for All school into a Roots and Wings school are just completing their piloting and are beginning to be disseminated. Existing Success for All schools in Maryland, Memphis, Miami, Cincinnati, Aldine (TX), and other locations are implementing the new curricula, and studies of the learning outcomes of these curricula are under way. Early evaluation evidence from our pilot districts are showing significant gains in students' reading, math, social studies, and science performance on Maryland state accountability assessments.

Roots and Wings is the future of Success for All. It is enormously important to ensure that every child succeeds in reading, but this is not enough. Every child must also become a thoughtful, strategic, and enthusiastic scientist, mathematician, historian, economist, and geographer. Children must know how to find and integrate information, to solve problems, to use their minds well. This is the goal of Roots and Wings.

There will always be schools that are only interested in the components that constitute Success for All, just as there will be schools that are only interested in MathWings or WorldLab. Each of these can stand on its own and make a contribution to student success. We hope and expect, however, that many schools will seek a broader, more coherent vision of what elementary schools could achieve with all students, a comprehensive approach encompassing curriculum, instruction, professional development, prevention, early intervention, and school organization, touching on all subjects and grade levels. These are the schools for which Roots and Wings was designed.

Note

1. Adapted from Slavin, Madden, Dolan, and Wasik (1994).

SKIMMER REGATTA 1—INVESTIGATE

Key Concepts

- A force is a push or a pull.
- Sir Isaac Newton's first law of motion is called the Law of Inertia. This is what it says: Still objects usually *stay* still unless a force makes them move. Moving objects usually *keep* moving unless a force stops them, slows them, or changes their direction.
- There are many forces pushing or pulling us all the time. For example, gravity is a force that pulls us toward the center of the earth, and all the air above us pushes down on us.
- Moving air or wind can push or pull things. It can make a windmill turn, a sailboat sail, or a skimmer move along a cardboard racecourse.
- Scientists repeat their experiments to see if they get similar results.
- Scientists always use a control in their experiments when they are comparing things; the control always stays the same, and the other things may vary.

LESSON OUTLINE

In this lesson, you will complete the following steps:

I. Setting the Stage Routines

II. Active Instruction
   A. Demonstrate the need for a control in an experiment
   B. Review directions to "Skimmer Regatta 1—Investigate"

III. Teamwork
   A. Teams complete "Skimmer Regatta 1—Investigate" steps 1 through 4
   B. Teach averaging to the whole class if necessary
   C. Teams complete "Investigate" steps 5 and 6
   D. Conduct One-To-One while teams are working
   E. Discuss how to make and record design decisions based on the results of their experimentation with their skimmer

IV. Time for Reflection
   A. Students write answers to the Concept Questions and review answers with teammates
   B. Review answers to the Concept Questions with the whole class
   C. Extend and Connect—Discuss familiar examples of how we deal with inertia
   D. Discuss how we can use what we learned about controls in experiments to be wise consumers

Advance Preparation

Clear an area in your room where the "race" demonstration described in Active Instruction can be held.

Materials

Per team:
*cardboard, about 2.5 m long and at least 30 cm wide
masking tape
skimmer
turkey baster, bulb removed
balloon
15-20 books
*NOTE: 2 cardboard fabric bolt holders taped end to end make a nice sturdy racecourse. These can usually be obtained for free from local fabric stores. Old window shades are another alternative and can be rolled up for easy storage.

Per student:
Discovery Log

OBJECTIVES	PRODUCTS OR ASSESSMENTS
STUDENTS WILL: • Make a team decision based on evaluation of collected data • Explain why they can only change one thing at a time every time they test their skimmer	• Completed design choice record (students must be able to defend their decisions) • Completed Data Record Sheet for "Investigate"

TEACHING THE LESSON

Setting the Stage

Post the Agenda on a chalkboard!

AGENDA.

Today we will:

1. Find out some things a scientist must be able to do well.
2. Experiment to find the best way to overcome inertia when we race our skimmers.
3. Make and record our first design decision.

CONCEPT QUESTIONS—PRESENT & PREDICT:

• Did your experiment with your skimmer support (agree with) Sir Isaac Newton's Law of Inertia? Explain.

• What was the control in your experiment? (What did you keep the same to make sure your test was fair?)

• Pretend you are reading the newspaper and you see this ad:

> DOUBLE DUPER SUPER BUBBLE GUM
> IS THE BEST GUM!
> IT MAKES BIGGER BUBBLES!
> IT HAS MORE YUM!
> BUY SOME SOON!

• Is anything missing from their claims? Explain.

Answers to the Concept Questions:

• Yes, Newton said that an object needs a force to act on it to make it start moving. Our skimmer did not move on its own, it only moved when we pushed or pulled it. Newton also said that things only stop moving when a force stops them. Our skimmer stopped when it bumped into the rails, or there wasn't enough force from the moving air left to keep it moving. It also stopped after it rubbed against the racecourse for a while. The forces of gravity, friction and air pressure became stronger than the force of air making it move along the racecourse. (Some students may say that friction slowed down their skimmer. Don't worry if most don't think of this idea yet. Friction will be introduced in the next cycle.)

• We made sure we used the same amount of air each time we blew the skimmer down the racecourse by measuring around the balloon with the same length of string.

• They do not tell you what this gum is better than. It makes bubbles bigger than what? What is it yummier than? You don't know what they are comparing it to.

AWARDING TEAM COOPERATION POINTS.
Award team cooperation points to teams that have all members participating and using their team roles correctly.

Active Instruction

1. Choose two students to help you with a short demonstration.

2. Tell the class that you are going to have these two students run a race to find out who is faster. Position the two students so that one will have a head start. Repeat that you think this is a good test to find out who is faster. Students may protest that this is not a fair way to run the race. If they don't, go ahead and run the race, and declare one student the fastest. Ask the class what they think of your test. Was it fair? Why or why not? Someone should point out that they were not tested the same way, that they both have to start from the same place to find out who is faster.

3. Tell the class that you are going to fix things, and run the race again. Line up the two students next to each other this time, but tell one they can only hop on one foot, not run. Run the race again. Students should once again protest that this was not a fair test! Ask them to explain why. You will have to "play dumb" to make this demonstration most effective. You may decide to run one more variation, maybe with one student running backwards and the other normally, to drive home the idea that the results of a test are not meaningful or usefull unless it is run fairly. Running a test fairly means that only one thing can be tested at a time, and that everything else should be as much the same as possible. For example, you can't find out who can run faster if the runners are not running the race under identical conditions.

4. Try one more example that you think your students can understand easily, and using **Think-Pair-Share,** have them tell you the right way to conduct the test involved. For example, ask what is wrong with this claim they might see in the newspaper:

Atlas tires are better! Get some for your car today!

(These tires are better than what, wooden wheels, old used tires, no tires at all? How are these tires better, do they last longer, grip the road better, or look nicer?)

Ask:

- **If you wanted to find out which brand of tire lasted the longest, how could you find out?** *(Accept any answer in which two or more brands are compared under the same conditions.)*

Summarize the answers by pointing out that you need to know what you are trying to find out, and you must compare only one factor at a time, keeping all other conditions the same.

Teamwork

1. Read the directions to "Skimmer Regatta I—Investigate" (Student Page #7) with the whole class.

Ask:

- **What are we trying to find out by doing this experiment?** *(The best way to push the skimmer to make it move the farthest.)*
- **What will act as the control in this experiment?** *(The same amount of air will be used each time we move the skimmer. This is done by always checking the balloon size with the same length of string. The nozzle of the air pump must always be kept behind the line marked A. The same racecourse and skimmer are used in each trial.)*

2. Teams complete steps 1 through 4 of "Investigate."

3. Conduct **One-to-One** while teams are working.

4. When most teams are finished, draw the attention of the whole class and **ask: Why do you think you do three trials each time you test your skimmer?** *(To see if you get similar results each time.)* **How do you know which number to use?** *(You need to find one number that's somewhere between the three, that gives a good picture of the three trials.)*

Ask:

- **Does anyone know a good way to do that with numbers?** *(Find the average of the three trials.)* If your students are not familiar with finding averages, tell them that you know an easy way to do it called "averaging." Demonstrate how to find an average of three numbers. Have each student practice finding averages using the data they just collected and recorded on their record sheets. Test Engineers should check their teammates for correct answers. Walk around and visit teams to make sure they understand the process.

5. Teams complete steps 5 and 6 of "Investigate." Continue to conduct **One-to-One.**

6. When teams are finished, **ask: How did you make your design decisions? On what did you base your opinion?** *(The data we collected, our observations.)*

• **Did your results agree or disagree with the way you thought things would turn out?** *(Answers will vary.)*

• **Why do you think it was harder to *get* your skimmer moving than it was to *keep* it moving?** *(We had to overcome inertia to get the skimmer moving, but once it was moving, inertia helped to keep it moving. Remember, things that are not moving stay still until a force makes them move, and things that are already moving keep moving unless a force stops them.)*

• **How could you be more certain that your data is painting a true picture of how your skimmer moves best?** *(Collect more data, look at the data of the whole class and see if there are any patterns.)*

Time   for   Reflection

1. Have each student write their answers to the Concept Questions in his/her Discovery Log.

2. Students share their answers in their teams and use **Discuss and Defend** to settle any disagreements.

3. Use **Numbered Heads** to sample student responses to the Concept Questions. Discuss the answers with the class if students still seem unsure of their answers.

EXTEND AND CONNECT.

4. **Ask: How can being good scientists help us be better consumers? What did we learn today that can help us make good decisions when we are shopping?** *(We must be careful when we read claims about a product. We must know what the makers are comparing the product to and how they carried out any tests they are using as evidence.)*

JOURNAL ENTRY.

Ask students to finish this sentence: "The thing I liked best about working on my skimmer was. . ."

HOMEWORK.

Assign Student Page #8, "Finding Averages."

Student Page 7

A WORLD IN MOTION
FORCE AND MOTION
CONTINUED

SKIMMER REGATTA

INVESTIGATE

Engineers usually work in teams to design new products. They must make many design choices. Engineers base their choices on what they learn in experiments. Choices are also based on what materials are available. Engineers experiment with different materials and different ways of using materials. You and the rest of your Engineering Design Team will design and build a skimmer during the next few days. Each day, you will investigate a science principle that will help you make wise design choices. At the end of the week, you will challenge the other teams' skimmers in the Skimmer Regatta. All skimmers must move by air power. A balloon attached to the turkey baster will supply the air power. Investigate each question and record your answers.

1. Make a record sheet like the one shown.

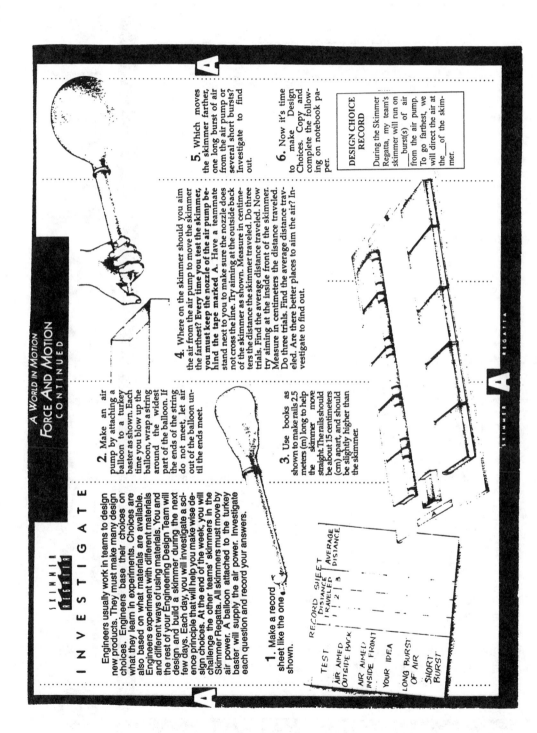

RECORD SHEET				
TEST	DISTANCE TRAVELED			AVERAGE DISTANCE
	1	2	3	
AIR AIMED OUTSIDE BACK				
AIR AIMED INSIDE FRONT				
YOUR IDEA				
LONG BURST OF AIR				
SHORT BURST				

2. Make an air pump by attaching a balloon to a turkey baster as shown. Each time you blow up the balloon, wrap a string around the widest part of the balloon. If the ends of the string do not meet, let air out of the balloon until the ends meet.

3. Use books as shown to make rails 2.5 meters (m) long to help the skimmer move straight. The rails should be about 15 centimeters (cm) apart, and should be slightly higher than the skimmer.

4. Where on the skimmer should you aim the air from the air pump to move the skimmer the farthest? Every time you test the skimmer, you must keep the nozzle of the air pump behind the tape marked A. Have a teammate stand next to you to make sure the nozzle does not cross the line. Try aiming at the outside back of the skimmer as shown. Measure in centimeters the distance the skimmer traveled. Do three trials. Find the average distance traveled. Now try aiming at the inside front of the skimmer. Measure in centimeters the distance traveled. Do three trials. Find the average distance traveled. Are there better places to aim the air? Investigate to find out.

5. Which moves the skimmer farther, one long burst of air from the air pump or several short bursts? Investigate to find out.

6. Now it's time to make Design Choices. Copy and complete the following on notebook paper.

> **DESIGN CHOICE RECORD**
>
> During the Skimmer Regatta, my team's skimmer will run on ___ burst(s) of air from the air pump. To go farthest, we will direct the air at the ___ of the skimmer.

SKIMMER A REGATTA

Name: _____   Date: _____

Finding Averages

1. Your skimmer traveled the following distances:

Trial	Distance Traveled
1	39 cm
2	41 cm
3	43 cm

Find the average distance your skimmer traveled. Show your work.

```
   39 cm
   41 cm            123 cm/3 = 41 cm
 + 43 cm
  123 cm
```

2. When you directed air at the back of your skimmer, you got these results:

Trial	Distance Traveled
1	42 cm
2	44 cm
3	46 cm

```
   42 cm
   44 cm            132 cm/3 = 44 cm
 + 46 cm
  132 cm
```

When you directed air at the inside of your skimmer, you got these results:

Trial	Distance Traveled
1	43 cm
2	38 cm
3	39 cm

```
   43 cm
   38 cm            120 cm/3 = 40 cm
 + 39 cm
  120 cm
```

Where should you direct air to make your skimmer go the farthest? Please show your work, and defend your answer.

Because the skimmer travelled ON THE AVERAGE 4 cm farther when I directed the air at the back of the skimmer, that is where I should direct the air.

Student Page 8

Appendix 5.2. Sample MathWings Lesson

Number Sense Level C
Lesson 8

GOAL: Students will be able to determine whether numbers in written material, calculator answers, and answers to math problems are reasonable.

Outline

I. Check-In

II. Active Instruction

    Analyze the numbers in written material to see if they are reasonable.

    Demonstrate the need for using estimates to check calculator answers.

III. Teamwork

    Team consensus

    Have students use number sense to estimate answers and explain their reasoning.

    Team mastery

    Have each student use number sense to estimate answers and explain his or her reasoning.

IV. Assessment

    Have each student use number sense to estimate 539 + 192 and explain his or her reasoning.

V. Reflection

Introduction for Teacher

Estimation is the math we use most often in daily life. We estimate while shopping at the store, doing projects, and evaluating written material to see if it makes sense. Your students need to be able to *estimate* (make a good guess at) answers to determine if the actual answers they find are reasonable. You need to help your students analyze problems, written material, or other data to determine if the numbers used are reasonable. You want them to become thoughtful citizens and critical consumers. It is important for your students to estimate answers when solving written problems and also when using the calculator. It is easy to make a careless mistake or hit the wrong key on the calculator. If they have no idea what the answer should be, they might not realize if their answer or the calculator answer is a mistake.

Key Concepts

An estimate is a good guess or an educated guess at an answer, *not* a wild guess.
Estimates are used to **decide** whether numbers in written material, answers to math problems, and calculator answers are **reasonable.**

Prepare

Transparencies
- Reasonable Numbers Paragraph, master included (page 150)

Teaching materials
- Markers

Team materials
- Student
  Calculator

CHECK-IN

Team set-up

Problem solving/facts

Homework

ACTIVE INSTRUCTION

Reasonable Numbers in Written Material

Explain:

Key concept: An estimate is a good guess or an educated guess at an answer, *not* a wild guess.

Point out:

Key concept: We use **estimates** to **determine** whether numbers in written material, calculator answers, and answers to math problems are **reasonable.**

Show the transparency of the Reasonable Numbers Paragraph and read it through with the class, underlining the numbers as you read. Explain that some of the numbers in the paragraph make sense and are reasonable and some of them don't make sense.

Have team members discuss each number in the paragraph and decide if it makes sense and is reasonable in the context. Ask them to be sure every member of the team can explain which numbers are reasonable, which aren't, and how they know.

Randomly choose team members or spokespersons to share their ideas with the class and come to a consensus.

(Four friends might easily have a party, so that is reasonable.

9:00 a.m. is in the morning not in the afternoon.

600 minutes is 10 hours, which is not a reasonable amount of time to play games.

180 raisin cookies, 120 mystery cookies, and 140 chocolate cookies is 440 cookies not 340 cookies.

440 cookies means that each person would eat 110 cookies, which is too much to eat at one sitting.

6:00 p.m. is a reasonable time for supper.)

Point out:

It is a good idea to always analyze numbers in things you read to see if they make sense.

Explain:

It is a good idea to think about the numbers in advertising, because advertisers often use numbers to get you to buy something. For example, a car will be advertised for $9,995 because the advertisers know that people will think $9,000, because they see the 9 first, rather than $10,000, even though $9,995 is almost $10,000.

Reasonable Calculator Answers

Point out:

It is specially important to estimate the answer when using a calculator because it is easy to hit the wrong key, and if you have no idea what the answer should be, you might not realize it if the answer on the calculator is a mistake.

Write "8 + 11" on the chalkboard, ask the students to use their number sense to estimate the answer, and randomly choose a student to share the estimate (8 is about 10 and 11 is about 10, so the answer is about 20).

Now have the students use their calculators to solve the problem. Tell them that they looked too quickly and accidentally hit the × key instead of the + key because they are very similar and to see what answer they get (88).

Have team members compare their actual answers and their estimates and discuss whether they think their answer is reasonable. Randomly choose a team member to share their idea with the class. (No—it is way too big. We must have done something wrong, so let's try again.)

Now have them *very carefully* use their calculators to solve the problem and compare their new answers with their estimates to see their answers are reasonable. Randomly choose a student to share his or her answer and whether or not it is reasonable. (Yes, 19 is close to 20, so it is reasonable.)

TEAMWORK

Team Consensus

Tell the class that they can also use their number sense to decide on a reasonable answer for a number problem. Write 123 + 589 on the chalkboard. Explain, **I might think 123 is about 120 and 589 is about 600, so the answer is about 720. Or I might think 123 is about 100 and 589 is about 600, so the answer is about 700. Since estimates are not exact, people can have different estimates that are all reasonable.**

Quickly find the answer on the calculator and note that 712 is close to both 700 and 720, so it is a reasonable answer.

Write the following problems on the chalkboard:

$$117 + 479$$
$$896 - 148$$

Ask the teams to use their number sense to estimate answers to these problems without actually solving the problems. Have the team members take turns sharing their thinking out loud so that everyone on the team can think about it and see if it makes sense. Have them be sure that everyone on the team rehearses how to find estimates. (117 is about 100 and 479 is about 500, so 117 + 479 is about 600. 896 is about 900 and 148 is about 150, so 896 − 146 is about 750.)

Have the team members quickly find the answers with their calculators, compare their answers and their estimates, and come to a consensus about whether the answers are reasonable. Randomly choose a student to share the estimates, how he or she got the estimates, the answers, and whether the answers are reasonable. (117 is about 100 and 479 is about 500, so 117 + 479 is about 600. 596 is about 600, so it is reasonable. 896 is about 900 and 148 is about 150, so 896 − 148 is about 750. 748 is about 750, so it is reasonable.)

Team Mastery

Write the following problems on the chalkboard:

93 + 12

89 − 48

214 + 898

896 − 108

1,394 + 978

1,505 − 387

541 + 713

862 − 247

456 + 149

795 − 508

Have the students use their number sense to estimate answers to these problems.

Ask every student to work four problems. Then have them check in with their team members to come to consensus on their answers. If a team member has incorrect answers or can't explain how he or she got them, have other team members explain the process and then have the student do four more problems. If a team member has the correct answers and can explain how he or she got them, have that student help other team members who need more practice.

Ask students to find the answer with their calculators and decide whether their answers are reasonable. *Have every member of the team rehearse how to estimate to decide if the answers are reasonable and how to explain their thinking.*

Circulate as students work to observe their understanding of number sense estimation. When teams have demonstrated understanding, move on to Numbered Heads Together.

Possible answers:

93 + 12: 93 is about 100 and 12 is about 10, so the answer is about 110. 105 is about 110, so the answer is reasonable.

89 − 48: 89 is about 100 and 48 is about 50, so the answer is about 50. 41 is about 50, so the answer is reasonable.

214 + 898: 214 is about 200 and 898 is about 900, so the answer is about 1,100. 1,112 is about 1,100, so the answer is reasonable.

896 − 108: 896 is about 900 and 108 is about 100, so the answer is about 800. 788 is about 800, so the answer is reasonable.

1,394 + 978: 1,394 is about 1,400 and 978 is about 1,000, so the answer is about 2,400. 2,372 is about 2,400, so the answer is reasonable.

1,505 − 387: 1,505 is about 1,500 and 387 is about 400, so the answer is about 1,100. 1,118 is about 1,100, so the answer is reasonable.

541 + 713: 541 is about 550 and 713 is about 700, so the answer is about 1,250. 1,254 is about 1,250, so the answer is reasonable.

862 − 247: 862 is about 850 and 247 is about 250, so the answer is about 600. 615 is about 600, so the answer is reasonable.

456 + 149: 456 is about 450 and 149 is about 150, so the answer is about 600. 605 is about 600, so the answer is reasonable.

795 − 508: 795 is about 800 and 508 is about 500, so the answer is about 300. 287 is about 300, so the answer is reasonable.

Numbered Heads Together

Use Numbered Heads Together, or another strategy, to randomly choose a team member to explain how the team got the estimate and give the answer explaining whether it is reasonable for 214 + 898. (214 is about 200 and 898 is about 900, so the answer is about 1,100. 1,112 is about 1,100, so the answer is reasonable.)

ASSESSMENT

Write the following problem on the chalkboard:

$$539 + 192$$

Ask each student to use number sense to estimate the answer, find the answer with the calculator, decide whether it is reasonable, and write a sentence to explain his or her thinking.

Collect the assessments as you point out that 539 is about 550 and 192 is about 200, so the answer is about 750. Explain that 731 is about 750, so the answer is reasonable. Remind the students that they may have estimated differently, but their estimate should be somewhere in that ballpark.

REFLECTION

Key Concepts Summary

An *estimate* is a good guess or an educated guess at an answer, *not* a wild guess. *Estimates* are used to *decide* whether numbers in written material, answers to math problems, and calculator answers are *reasonable.*

Homework

Lesson 8 Homework Sheet (p. 152)

Logbook

Write about whether you think you can count to 1,000 by 1s in 1 minute and how you know whether or not you can.

Team Wrap-Up

Reasonable Numbers
Paragraph

Four friends were having a party at 9:00 a.m. on Friday afternoon after school. After they had played games for 600 minutes, they were hungry. They decided to have their snack of 180 raisin cookies, 120 mystery cookies, and 140 chocolate cookies. They ate all 340 cookies and were still hungry, so they decided to go home for supper at 6:00 p.m.

Parent Peek

Your child will be exploring estimation in Lessons 8, 9, and 10. *Estimation is one of the most important math skills.* In fact, we use estimation far more often in real life than we use paper and pencil to do problems for exact answers.

We often estimate almost unconsciously without thinking of the strategies we are using to get approximate answers in real-life situations. *We use different estimation strategies,* depending on the problem and which strategies we are most comfortable using.

Remember, an *estimate* is a good guess, or an *educated guess,* at an answer, not a *wild guess.* Answers in estimation will vary depending on the strategy and thinking used, and *any answer that is in the right ballpark is acceptable.*

One of the estimation strategies is number sense. In this lesson, your child used number sense to estimate answers. We use our number sense to decide whether numbers in written material, answers to math problems, and calculator answers are *reasonable.* Your child can use number sense to estimate an answer for a number problem or to check whether an exact answer makes sense.

$\approx$ *is the symbol* that means one amount "is about as much as" another amount. For example, $97 \approx 100$ means 97 is about 100.

Try using your number sense to estimate $123 + 589$. You might think $123 \approx 120$ and $589 \approx 600$, and $120 + 600 = 720$, so the answer ≈ 720. Or you might think $123 \approx 100$ and $580 \approx 600$, and $100 + 600 = 700$, so the answer ≈ 700. *Remember, since estimates are not exact, people can have different estimates that are all reasonable.* The exact answer is 712, which is close to both 700 and 720, so it is a reasonable answer.

LESSON 8 HOMEWORK: ANSWERS   Name _____
NUMBER SENSE C: Date _____

Show Your Work When Needed

Skill Problems	Mixed Practice

1. Estimate the answer to 345 + 126. Show your work. **345 is about 350, 126 is about 125, 350 + 125 = 475, so the answer is about 475.**	1. 75
	        + 25
	        ——
	         100

2. 568 + 125 = 443. Is the answer reasonable and how do you know? **No, because 5 + 1 = 6, so the hundreds place is definitely too small.**	2. 75
	        − 25
	        ——
	          50

3. Estimate the answer to 527 − 216. Show your work. **527 is about 500, 216 is about 200, 500 − 200 = 300,** so the answer is about 300.	3. 77
	        + 15
	        ——
	          92

4. 672 − 431 = 241. Is the answer reasonable and how do you know? **Yes, because there is no regrouping and 6 − 4 = 2.**	4. 77
	        − 15
	        ——
	          62

5. Five dozen doughnuts is 15 doughnuts. Is this answer reasonable and how do you know? **No, because one 12 is almost 15, so 5 12s is much more than 15.**	5. 34
	        + 56
	        ——
	          90

Please turn the page and do the problems on the back.

Real-World	Problems
1. Tom gave his friend half his collection of 100 baseball cards and kept 50 for himself. Is this reasonable and why?	**1/2 of 100 = 50 cards, so each of them would have 50 cards. It is reasonable.**
2. Nancy ate half of a candy bar and gave her sister half of the candy bar and her cousin the last half of the candy bar. Is this reasonable and why?	**No, because 3/2 is more than one candy bar.**
3. Samantha baby-sat for 2 hours at $2 an hour and earned $4. Is this amount reasonable and why?	**Yes, because 2 × 2 is 4.**

PROBLEM SOLVING

Barry had three baseball hats (Orioles, Blue Jays, Angels) and two team T-shirts (Tigers and Giants). How many different outfits could he make out of them?

He could make six different outfits:
Orioles/Tigers, Orioles/Giants
Blue Jays/Tigers, Blue Jays/Giants
Angels/Tigers, and Angels/Giants

6

Family Support and Integrated Services

Tavon Jones lives in a Baltimore housing project and attends a Success for All (SFA) school in which virtually all children are in poverty.[1] He had completed kindergarten the year before Success for All began at his school. According to his teachers' reports, Tavon was already headed for serious trouble. He was angry and aggressive, dealing with both teachers and other students as if they were out to get him. Tavon had to be removed from class frequently because of his disruptive behavior. He had little energy to put into learning when he was in school, and he was not in school very consistently. Even when he did come to school, he usually arrived late, closer to 10:30 than 8:30.

Tavon was born when his mother was a young teenager. His mother felt helpless. She loved her son and wanted him to succeed in school but had few resources to help him, being hardly more than a child herself. Her son's response to the school was just like his mother's. The only way she knew how to react to Tavon's problems in school was to become angry and aggressive. In the first weeks of first grade, when the school contacted her about problems that Tavon was having, her response was to stomp into school cursing, threatening to take him out of the school because it couldn't deal with him.

Coordinated efforts by teachers, the facilitator, family support team members, and Tavon's mother worked to turn things around for Tavon. After the social worker made the mother feel respected and welcome, she was able to encourage his mother to participate in parenting classes held at the school. She became more confident in her ability to handle her son. With assistance from the attendance monitor, Tavon's attendance started to improve. At

155

first, the school called his mother early every morning to get her started early enough to get her son to school. For a while, the attendance monitor met the mother halfway to school. Everyone made a concerted effort to make Tavon's mother feel welcome at the school by showing her respect and treating her as a partner. Tavon's teacher sent good news notes home with Tavon when he met the behavioral goals jointly set by Tavon and his teacher. Even as his behavior improved, Tavon still had very serious academic problems; on all tests given at the beginning of first grade, he showed no evidence of having any prereading skills. Tavon was given an instructional program in which he could be successful and was given one-to-one tutoring, which provided not only the academic support that he needed but also gave him emotional support. His tutor was a special person with whom he could share his struggles and successes. The tutor and Tavon's classroom teacher met frequently with the family support team to coordinate plans and activities around his needs and strengths.

As Tavon's mother began to work cooperatively with the school, Tavon's attitude toward school improved. He still has a strong temper, but he is learning how to deal with angry feelings in a constructive way. Tavon is in school on time every day. Learning still does not come easily for him, but he knows that if he works hard, he can learn, and he is proud of the steady progress he is making. His mother has developed a good deal of self-confidence as well and is now employed in a store in the neighborhood.

Tavon's experience, which is like that of many students in Success for All, shows the importance of a relentless, coordinated approach to meeting all students' individual needs. Ensuring high-quality instruction, tutoring, and other academic supports is not enough for a child like Tavon who may be failing for reasons that have little or nothing to do with academics. Some children fail because of erratic attendance or poor behavior. Some have serious health problems, or need eyeglasses or hearing aids. Some lack adequate nutrition or heat at home. Some are homeless or are threatened with losing their homes. If a school is serious about ensuring success for *every* child, then it must have the capacity to recognize and solve all of the nonacademic problems that are barriers to a child's success in school.

The Success for All program places a strong emphasis on increasing the school's capacity to relate to parents and to involve parents, as well as health and social service agencies, in solutions to any nonacademic problems students may have. Each Success for All school establishes a Family Support Team for this purpose. The composition of the Family Support Team varies from school to school depending on the personnel available and the school's needs. The school's Title I parent liaison, counselor, social worker, nurse, and other resource staff usually make up the Family Support Team, along with building administrators (principal or vice principals) and the facilitator. In schools with serious attendance problems, an attendance aide may be added.

The focus of the Family Support Team is to identify and build on the strengths of parents, communities, and individual children. All parents want their children to succeed in school, but some have such difficult lives that they need help to create home environments conducive to school success. Family Support Teams begin with a fundamental respect for parents. They see parents as partners in achieving success for their children, a goal shared by parents and school staffs alike. They enlist parents in a cooperative quest to do whatever it takes both at home and at school, and to engage whatever community resources may be available to ensure that each child succeeds in school.

Family Support Teams usually meet weekly. They discuss two types of issues. One type of issue is planning schoolwide programs to increase parent involvement, programs to improve the school's ability to monitor and respond to truancy, and so on. For example, the team may plan a program for parents on helping children with homework, or plan a session with teachers on dealing with behavior problems. The second type of issue discussed by the Family Support Team involves problems with individual children. Teachers and other staff often refer a child to Family Support because they believe he or she is having problems in school that the teacher cannot solve on his or her own. Examples of such problems might include truancy, behavior problems, health problems, and psychological problems. In addition,

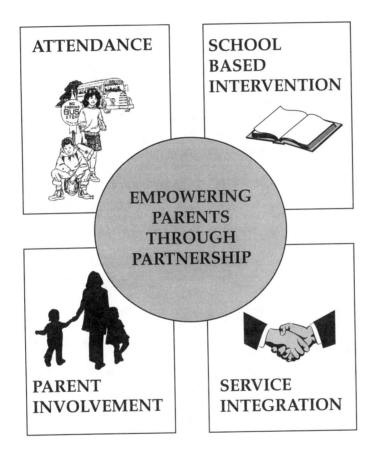

Figure 6.1. Family Support

students who are not making adequate academic progress despite classroom and tutorial assistance are referred to the Family Support Team even if there are no obvious family problems; the team's goal is to investigate to find out if family interventions may help get the child on track.

The main activities of the Family Support Team are described in the following sections (see Haxby, Lasaga-Flister, Madden, Slavin & Dolan, 1995, for more details).

Parent Involvement

Parent involvement is a key component for student success in Success for All. Research indicates that parental involvement is correlated with increases in attendance, increases in achievement, and decreases in behavioral problems (see Epstein, 1989). In addition, parent involvement can be an effective way to meet the needs of a culturally diverse population. Success for All stresses the need for a strong parent involvement program that is linked to improvements in curriculum and instruction.

Traditionally, schools and families have seen themselves as separate institutions that interact with the child. This separation, however, can be detrimental for many children. In particular, it is clear to all schools working with children from poor families that problems from the community and the family impinge daily on the academic life of students. Students arrive at school hungry, homeless, angry or depressed about family problems, and unable to concentrate on educational tasks. Schools have become increasingly aware that they cannot address the needs of these children alone. The needs of poor children demand the involvement of the family and the community for schools to be most effective. It is a school's job to recognize the family as an integral part of the school system and to work with families in devising ways to increase parent participation and encourage community support of schools.

Parental involvement is recognized as a valuable component of a school system, but there is no one type of parental participation that is "right." Because the goal of any parental involvement strategy is to involve as many parents as possible, a range of parent involvement is necessary to suit the needs and preferences of a variety of parents, from participation in the governance of the school, to helping a child with homework, to helping a teacher by preparing materials.

Some specific ways in which parents are involved in Success for All schools are discussed next.

Parent Involvement in School Governance

It is an old adage for most community organizers that for people to be very involved in an activity they need to "own" it. Ownership is fostered by being involved in the development and implementation of any project. All too often poor parents stay away from schools because they do not see the school as "theirs." More often the school is viewed as yet another institution that is trying to do something *to* them. For effective parent involvement to occur, there needs to be a critical shift in thinking of the school as an institution that does things *to* parents to thinking of it as an institution that does things *for and with* parents. Ownership is greatly fostered if parents see themselves in the role of decision makers in the school.

One key way to have parents be decision makers is to ensure that they have a role in school governance. The creation of a Building Advisory Team is often particularly effective. This team is composed of teachers, administrators, and parents. They have the mandate to advise the principal on general school direction and planning. Some key tasks for the Building Advisory Team may be

- to review or develop a schoolwide discipline policy
- to set direction for parent involvement projects
- to evaluate the need for community services on site
- to review and implement homework guidelines
- to evaluate school climate

Typically, the team evaluates the entire school climate and advises on general direction and goals. This team can meet between four and six times per year. When the team has made recommendations, they often work closely with the Family Support Team to ensure that programs are implemented.

In-School Parent Volunteer Support

Parental involvement has traditionally been defined by participation as a volunteer in the school. This is an important, rewarding activity and can make a tremendous difference for financially strapped schools. Parents can participate in a wide range of activities that enhance school effectiveness.

The following are examples of these activities.

Volunteer Listener Program. The best way to learn to read is to read. Students in Success for All are encouraged to read at home every night. Some schools encourage reading by having an incentive program in which students can earn a small prize or privilege by collecting certificates from parents or other adults that indicate the child has read to them for 20 minutes each evening. Some children may have parents who work at night or are unavailable for after-school reading time. Parent volunteers at these schools act as volunteer listeners for these students during lunch or free time. Students can read to these parents and obtain extra certificates. The job of the volunteer listeners is to listen and to let the child know that he or she is doing a great job. Volunteer listeners are not tutors—they are there to encourage students to read and take pride in their reading. Both parents and students enjoy the additional one-to-one interaction during the school day. Students who just need extra practice can use the volunteer listeners in the building.

Some schools have used their volunteer listeners to celebrate "improvement" in reading. Any child who has made any progress can receive a reading award. Volunteer listeners collect the reading awards from a central location (often a box in the office) and listen to several children read. In one school, the parents bought and decorated special chairs that the children sit in when they read to the parents.

Homework Room. Other schools have used parents and teachers to man an after school homework room. Staff were aware that some children find it difficult to complete home assignments or do not have a quiet place to work. Parents can elect to have their child attend the after school homework room one or more days per week. Generally one parent and one teacher supervise and provide homework help when needed.

Other In-School Parent Volunteer Activities. Parents in most schools are encouraged and trained to participate in a wide variety of school activities. Parents help in the classroom, media center, cafeteria, and on the playground. Often schools provide training in these areas and certificates for participation. Parents can and do provide invaluable service in all areas of the school.

Teacher and School Communication to Parents

A vital component of fostering the link between parents and schools is to make consistent efforts to increase teacher and school communication to the parent. This increase in communication by the school does several things. Initially, it models for everyone the perception that parents are an integral part of the school community. This modeling helps to cement the mind-set for staff as well as parents that families need to be respected, valued, and involved in the daily activities of the school. Parents who perceive the school as working to involve them say that the school is a good one (see Epstein, 1989). In addition, parents give teachers who frequently contact them high ratings. Fostering this sense of a positive school community is crucial to effective parent/school partnerships.

In many schools, most parents hear only from teachers and schools at the yearly parent-teacher conference or when their child is in trouble. Frequent communication between teacher and parent is "a bad sign," something to be avoided. This sets a negative tone for all interaction. All too often parents feel that "no news is good news" and cringe when the phone rings or school personnel stop by. Particularly for parents whose children are having difficulty, there is a temptation to avoid the school. Of course, this reinforces only the school's belief that "the parents who most need to be here never come."

The more respectfully the school approaches parents—the more frequently parents are contacted, are involved in the daily functioning of the school, and are given good news about their child—the more likely they are to be more involved in the school. In Success for All, school personnel routinely do welcome visits for new students, and conduct fall information visits. Teachers send home success cards, newsletters, and good news notes. Informational meetings, often called "Second Cup of Coffee" occur on a regular basis in most schools. In some schools, Second Cup of Coffee consists of coffee and pastries in the lobby to encourage parents to stop by and chat informally with Family Support personnel. In other schools, Second Cup of Coffee has evolved into regular meetings with presentations on topics of concern to families. In all cases, the purpose is to create positive connections with families. Everyone shuns aversive experiences and there is nothing more aversive than hearing a barrage of negative things about one's own children. The goal of teacher and school communication is to alter the negative cycle and build a more positive connection.

Parent Involvement in Curriculum

Success for All schools place a strong emphasis on involving parents in supporting the curriculum at home. All students are urged to read to someone at home for 20 minutes each night. Students are given share sheets and paperback books to take home. Parents are often asked to sign a form indicating that students have done their reading. In the fall most schools have a Success for All Kick-Off Demonstration Night. This is designed to keep parents informed about the program of instruction that their child is receiving and to give them tips on how to support the program at home. Students and teachers demonstrate the reading program.

Raising Readers. As parents become more aware of the reading program and are given specific tips on how to support the program at home, they have responded positively and actively. One way that parents have become more aware of the curriculum is through the Raising Readers program. Raising Readers consists of a series of workshops in prekindergarten (pre-k) through second grade designed to familiarize families with the SFA reading program and provide training so parents can support identified reading skills at home. In the upper grades, Raising Readers concentrates on providing incentive programs for reading. In addition to the workshop series, take-home libraries are provided with guides and extension questions to facilitate interactive reading at home.

The goal of the workshop series is not only to familiarize parents with SFA curriculum, but also to provide parents with both the skills and materials needed to promote parent/child interaction around literacy. The content of each series or workshop is based on the curriculum for each grade level. At all grade levels, the key components of the structure include the following:

- Parents attend with their children.
- Grade-level teachers explain and model a key component of the reading curriculum with the children.
- Teachers discuss how to help children at home with the identified skills.
- Parents and children practice with each other the skill modeled by the teacher.
- Parent and child create a "make and take" activity together to facilitate home practice of literacy skills.

A typical Raising Readers workshop would occur first thing in the morning. Family Support personnel would have been involved in publicizing the workshop. Families receive several flyers, banners are posted outside the school, and sometimes personal calls are made to key classes or families to encourage participation. Generally, families arrive with their children and the school provides a continental breakfast. The teacher may be modeling reading with the children and strategies to encourage listening comprehension. The parents use the same materials and practice the identified skills with their own child. Parents and children then are able to take home the lending library books to use at home. Parents have been very enthusiastic about the program. Turnouts have consistently been high. Most schools report between 50% to 75% of parents participate in the workshops. In addition, parents report enjoying the take home libraries. Typically, even the most high-risk families want to help their children at home, and they report that this program has given them the information and support to do it.

Training nights for parents are held throughout the school year to keep parents involved in curriculum support. Schools have experimented with teaching pre-k parents the Story Telling and Retelling (STaR) program and having parents make "big books" with their child. In addition, parents have been trained in cooperative learning and have formed teams in which to participate in designing school programs. The more parents can participate in the curriculum, the more enthusiastic parents become.

Attendance

Family Support Teams also work to improve school attendance. Children need to attend school consistently to learn. Successful attendance strategies require a schoolwide approach. Success for All schools have instituted a successful attendance program that addresses three fundamental areas: (a) monitoring, (b) intervention, and (c) prevention.

A monitoring system is necessary to ensure that all children arrive safely at school and are accounted for early in the day. A comprehensive monitoring system does three things: it increases the safety of students because all students are accounted for early, it creates a school norm that all absences are important, and it provides the necessary information for quick intervention on attendance problems. Effective monitoring systems allow school personnel to try to get the targeted child to school the same day. Attendance monitors use a record-keeping system that identifies students having attendance problems at a glance, enabling the school to follow up with at-risk absent children immediately.

Intervention also aims for quick response. We recommend hiring an attendance monitor who will be able to go into the community and meet with families. Through the use of this monitor, timely and strenuous outreach efforts are possible. This is particularly important for areas in which many families may not have phone service. If the monitor finds that an attendance problem does not improve or that a family has a variety of needs, the Family Support Team will provide case planning, further intervention, or referral. If the behavior causing attendance problems is to be changed, knowledge is not enough—action is vital.

Prevention programs involve setting a schoolwide norm for attendance and putting into place programs that are proactive. Prevention programs include a wide range of incentive programs designed to reward individuals, classrooms, and families whose children consistently attend school. The best solution to any problem is to prevent it from occurring.

School-Based Intervention

The goal of Success for All's innovative curriculum, teaching strategies, and tutoring is to have every child achieve. Some students, however, cannot benefit as much as we hope from improved instruction because they have serious family, behavioral, or attendance problems. The school-based intervention component of the Family Support Team is designed to ensure that these children do not fall "through the cracks." It is here that success for *most* must be translated into success for *all*.

Faculty, administration, or parents may refer a child to the Family Support Team. Referral forms are distributed early in the school year at parent and faculty meetings, and are always available in the school office. Referrals are sent to the facilitator, who initially screens students to ensure that standard Success for All classroom strategies and tutoring are already in place; the Family Support Team is not a substitute for good classroom management.

Once a referral has been reviewed, the facilitator brings the case to the Family Support Team. Each case is assessed, a case manager assigned, and an action plan developed. The classroom teacher and the parent must be involved in the development of an action plan. If necessary, the case manager can schedule a meeting with a parent after the initial team assessment. To develop effective action plans the team uses materials that are designed to promote solution-oriented thinking. All too often, teams become stymied by the endless assessments of problems possible in tough cases with multiproblem families. Family Support Teams use solution sheets designed to focus the team on the most important problems that are most likely to be solvable by the school, and to move the team forward on small-step solutions that involve school, family, and community. This approach necessitates that teams become adept at finding strengths and resources. Family Support is committed to the notion that people change from their strengths, not from their weaknesses. Solutions, therefore, are often found if teams are adept at identifying strengths and resources as well as problems.

After an action plan has been developed, the referral source is given a copy of the plan and encouraged to notify the team if any progress or deterioration is noticed. The team regularly reviews all cases to ensure that progress is being made, or to adjust the action plan so it is more effective.

The process of school-based intervention is diagrammed in Figure 6.2.

Composition of the Family Support Team

Funding levels and needs determine the composition of a school's Family Support Team personnel, so each school's team will vary. For the Family Support Team to function well, it is vital that each member has the time to meet and implement decisions. This may involve changing people's schedules or responsibilities. For example, if a school cannot hire a clinical social worker, other school personnel will need to implement the classroom and family-based behavior modification programs. Other personnel may also need to make occasional home visits to families who are hard to reach. These interventions are time consuming but necessary; Success for All is predicated on the belief that *every* student can succeed, and there are always some children who would fail without the services Family Support Teams provide.

Service Integration Between Community and School

Many students and families in Success for All schools have problems that require services from a range of community agencies. Often, families are unable or unwilling to access these services. Schools and community agencies have found that families are more likely to make use of needed services if the service is provided in a familiar location. Schools have often

SCHOOL BASED INTERVENTION

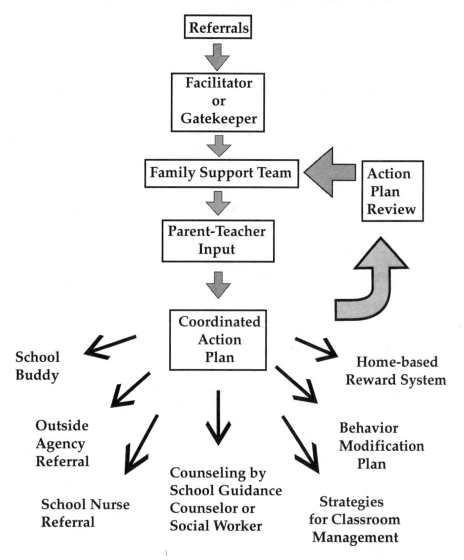

Figure 6.2. School-Based Intervention

been particularly successful locations. On-site services are also helpful for the schools. Quicker intervention with better follow-through and feedback are possible when agencies are available on site.

Family Support Teams try to be aware of local services and make referrals, whether the services are on or off site. If a family is without heat or shelter, for example, it is the job of the Family Support Team to provide information and help families obtain needed services. This assistance may involve more than just providing a referral. Families often do not obtain community services because of problems with transportation, or because of their inability to negotiate the labyrinth of large bureaucratic institutions. The team may help families with these problems and provides as much assistance as possible to make sure that the family is able to follow through on the referral. The Family Support Team members can also check to make sure that referrals led to services and that these services solved the problem.

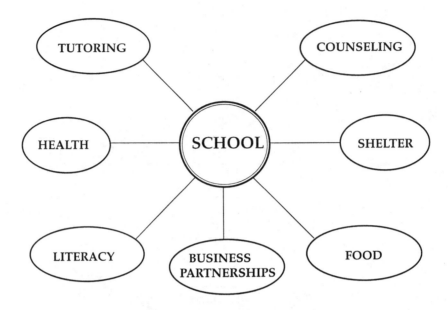

Figure 6.3. Service Integration

Teams assess community services that are most often needed by the students and families in their community. Special attention is paid to services that may strongly affect student performance. Once a team has assessed these needs, the team becomes aware of how to obtain those services in the community and investigates if it is possible to provide some of those services on site. A few common examples are shown in Figure 6.3.

Health: Some schools have obtained an on-site nurse practitioner from the local health department to help with sick or injured children and to do injections and physicals. All teams, however, know how to obtain needed medical care for students. In particular, it is important to know how to quickly obtain required shots, glasses, and eye and hearing exams. Family Support Teams try to ensure that these services are provided to students in a timely manner.

Counseling: Some Success for All schools have linked with community family counseling agencies to provide on-site family counseling. One school has linked with a drug and alcohol prevention program to provide support for children of substance abusers. Community mental health programs are increasingly trying to provide some satellite services at schools and may have programs in the school area. Family Support Teams usually know about counseling programs in the community, particularly programs with no fee or sliding fee scales.

Food: If a child is hungry he can't learn. One school has linked with a local agency to be a food distribution site for its community. Parents who have rarely been in the school building come regularly to pick up food and thereby become acquainted with the school.

Shelter: Providing housing to needy families is problematic in most cities. Family Support Teams usually know the emergency shelters in town and try to work with the family to support the child while the family is homeless or in temporary living situations. It is better for a student to be supported at his old school while the family is trying to obtain permanent housing. The fewer upheavals the better for the student during this time. Family Support Teams have been instrumental in helping to plan transportation and additional supports for homeless students.

Tutoring: Many schools have worked with local universities, high schools, retirement groups, or churches to obtain additional tutoring for their students. Particularly for marginal students, or older students who do not qualify for Success for All tutoring, this is an invaluable service. Tutoring is most effective if it is on site, and often these groups are happy to provide tutoring at the school. If a team is going to begin to make community linkages, this is often a good place to start.

Literacy: Parent literacy affects the academic success of students. Several Success for All schools have begun to work with local literacy groups to provide parent literacy programs on site. In general, parents involved in these school-based sites also participate in volunteer activities during the school day. Some schools also offer after school computer programs for parents and children.

Business linkages: Local businesses have become more involved in supporting education over the last few years. Business leaders are increasingly aware that schools produce the workers of tomorrow, and that the effectiveness of their own enterprises depends on the ability of schools to deliver quality employees. Consequently, both small and large businesses have made real commitments to local schools. Success for All schools have found that effective partnerships have occurred when schools energetically approach local business and structure some specific ways in which the business partner can help. Sometimes effective linkages fail to develop because the partner is unclear about how much of a commitment they are making and what sort of help is needed. Just asking a business to be a partner and to help the school may be too vague. A clearly organized presentation of needs, some suggestions by the school about projects that the business partner could participate in, and ways to highlight the partnership to the community have generally been more successful approaches. Some examples of activities of local business involvement in Success for All schools include the following:

- Providing incentives for attendance or reading. Fast-food restaurants, local movie rental stores, and convenience stores have often been large providers of small incentives for school programs.
- Providing additional tutoring for students.
- Donating furniture for parent rooms or reading corners.
- Providing mentorship programs or after-school club activities.
- Providing public relations material for parents and the community for special school projects. For example, local photographers have taken pictures of students involved in Success for All activities. Partners have provided T-shirts or buttons to families to publicize special projects as part of outreach education about Success for All.

Obviously, the activities of Family Support Teams vary depending on available staff, student and family needs, and community investment in the school. All teams must make sure that the needs of children who are having difficulty are being met, that school attendance programs are working, and that parents are encouraged to participate in school. Other activities will depend on the time and resource constraints of the team.

The multifaceted role of the Family Support Team is crucial in addressing the needs of students who are at the highest risk of school failure. An effective team not only attempts to meet the needs of at-risk students but also creates a schoolwide climate that fosters respect for parents, high parent involvement, and a proactive approach to the complex problems faced by many students and families in Success for All schools.[2]

Notes

    1. This vignette, a composite of experiences with many children and families involved in Success for All schools, is adapted from Slavin, Madden, Karweit, Dolan, and Wasik (1992).

    2. For more on family support and integrated services in Success for All and Roots and Wings, see Haxby et al. (1995).

7

Facilitators, Professional Development, School Restructuring, and Networking

The implementation of Success for All or Roots and Wings requires substantial change in school organization and practices. It affects curriculum, instruction, assessment, early childhood programs, Title I, special education, promotion/retention policies, parent involvement, relations with health and social service agencies, and internal school governance. It requires the active participation of every staff member in an existing staff; no Success for All or Roots and Wings school has ever been able to select staff specifically for the program. It requires dramatic changes in daily teaching methods for teachers who may have decades of experience doing something else. It requires a change in beliefs about the school's ability and responsibility to ensure the success of every child, no matter what.

How does all this change come about? How do Success for All and Roots and Wings enter a school, solicit the enthusiastic participation of school staffs, train staff in program procedures, monitor and improve implementation over time, assess progress toward desired goals, and maintain coordination among the many pieces of the program? These are extremely important questions that we have had to address as we "scale up" Success for All from a pilot program to become a replicable, reliably effective model for school change. This chapter discusses our practices and experiences with implementation of change in a wide variety of schools.

Establishing Success for All in New Sites

As of fall 1995, there were a total of more than 300 schools in 70 districts in 24 states implementing Success for All or Roots and Wings in collaboration with our group at Johns Hopkins. In addition, adaptations of Success for All are being implemented in Canada, Australia, the Netherlands, and Israel for a total of about 50 non-U.S. schools. The majority of U.S. schools are inner-city schools serving very disadvantaged African American populations; however, many are rural, many have white majorities, and many have significant numbers of Hispanic or Asian students, some of whom have limited English proficiency. All of the districts involved in Success for All and Roots and Wings have approached us, usually after reading about and/or visiting schools already implementing the program.

Our procedures for negotiating with districts vary according to the district's characteristics and needs, but there are several procedures we insist on. One is the clear support of the district's administration. This involves a number of financial conditions (see Chapter 9), as well as a commitment to allow the Success for All or Roots and Wings schools to deviate from district policies (if necessary) on such matters as curriculum, Title I, special education, and promotion/retention.

We require that schools submit an application that commits them to provide the support necessary for successful implementation. A copy of this form appears in Appendix 7.1.

Another requirement is a process by which principals are given a free choice to participate or not, and then in schools with strongly committed principals, teachers must have an opportunity to vote (by secret ballot) on whether or not to participate. We require that at least 80% of teachers buy in. In practice, most votes are more typically 90% to 95% positive. We insist on the exercise, however, because we think it is essential that teachers know they had a free choice, and that any disgruntled individuals know that their colleagues were overwhelmingly in favor of the program. Most often, project staff make a presentation to the interested schools (who have already done some investigation about Success for All) in the winter or spring before the program is to begin, and then give the staffs about a week to discuss, debate, read, and (if possible) send a delegation to visit existing schools. We do everything we can to see that teachers are fully informed, have all of their questions answered, and are not pressured into voting for the program.

When Success for All or Roots and Wings enter a district for the first time, we recommend starting with no more than five schools, and then expanding in future years. For the pilot schools we try to avoid any conditions (such as substantial additional funding) that could not be replicated elsewhere in the district. We have found that if pilot schools operate with extraordinary funding or other special circumstances, the conditions are difficult to maintain over time. Some schools receive as much as $25,000 to cover first-year costs, but more than this can be counterproductive in the long run.

At the end of the school selection process we have typically one to five schools in districts in which the central administration is unambiguously supportive with principals and staffs who have freely chosen to participate. We have learned that this buy-in process is essential. When rough times come (and they always do), everyone involved in an innovation needs to remember that they chose the path they are on.

Professional Development

The philosophy of professional development behind Success for All and Roots and Wings is that although initial training is important, real change in teachers' practices takes place in the classroom, not the workshop. We consider professional development to be a process that never ends. Teachers in Success for All and Roots and Wings schools are constantly refining their instructional methods, learning new strategies, discussing their methods with other teachers, visiting each others' classes, and using assessments of student progress to guide changes in their teaching methods.

Most professional development is provided by a corps of trainers at Johns Hopkins University in Baltimore, or by Johns Hopkins trainers in other locations. At present, there are full-time Johns Hopkins trainers located in New York, Alabama, Texas, Florida, and California, and part-time trainers (typically facilitators in Success for All or Roots and Wings schools) in many locations. The New York, Texas, and California trainers have particular expertise in applications of Success for All in bilingual and ESL contexts, and they work throughout the country in schools with many English language learners. In addition, there are regional training programs that take full responsibility for all aspects of training and follow-up. These are located at the Southwest Regional Educational Laboratory (SWRL) in Southern California, and at the University of Memphis. Facilitators and teachers in existing Success for All schools often participate in training and mentoring of new schools in their regions.

Initial training for a staff new to cooperative learning is ordinarily provided in August for a September start-up. This training is typically scheduled for 3 days. Some schools, however, phase in the program in some or all grades starting midyear.

Many schools begin implementing Success for All in the younger grades (such as preschool to Grade 3 or kindergarten to Grade 3) and then move on to the upper elementary grades in the 2nd year. Beyond an orientation to the program and some team building among the school staff members, the main focus of initial training is on the changes in curriculum and instruction teachers will be making right away, as soon as school starts. Roots and Wings schools start with the reading components, and are therefore identical to Success for All schools in their first year. This means that almost all schools start with STaR, Peabody, and thematic units for preschool and kindergarten, Reading Roots for first grade, and Beyond the Basics for teachers of Grades 2 and above. Tutors (who also teach a reading class) also participate in the Reading Roots training. They later receive their own 2 days of training on strategies for assessment and tutoring of at-risk students.

Around midyear, writing/language arts is usually introduced for teachers of Grades 1 to 3, and Reading Roots for kindergarten teachers. In the 2nd year of implementation, reading and writing may be introduced to the upper grades. Roots and Wings schools would typically introduce WorldLab and Math Wings in the 2nd implementation year (see Chapter 5). Along the way, training sessions are held on classroom management, cooperative learning, family support, pacing, assessment, special education, and other topics, and to refine and extend topics presented earlier.

The training makes extensive use of simulations and demonstrations. For example, in learning how to use cooperative teams in Reading Wings, teachers work in teams themselves. In training STaR and Reading Roots, the teachers pretend to be students. In addition, videotapes depicting each of the program elements are shown to the teachers. Teachers are always told the theories behind what they are learning, but the main emphasis is on giving them active, hands-on, pragmatic experience with strategies that will work.

After initial training, trainers return for additional major professional development sessions, such as introduction of the writing/language arts programs, extension of Reading Roots to kindergarten and Beyond the Basics to the upper grades, and so on. After initial training, however, the main responsibility for staff development passes to the facilitator, and the role of Johns Hopkins and regional training program staff focuses more on enhancing the facilitator's skills than on direct teacher training. The facilitator's function in Success for All and Roots and Wings and the role of our staff in maintaining quality implementations are described in the following sections.

The Facilitator

The first and most important decision a school makes after it has been designated as a Success for All or Roots and Wings school is to select a facilitator (see Madden, Livingston, & Cummings, 1995). The facilitator is the linchpin of the entire program; the effectiveness of the program depends to a substantial degree on his or her skills as an agent of change. Facilitators are typically very experienced teachers, usually with backgrounds in reading, early childhood, or Title I. A good facilitator is one who has the respect of his or her colleagues, has enormous energy and interpersonal skills, and has a deeply felt certainty that every child can learn. Most Success for All and Roots and Wings schools have full-time facilitators, but some (especially in less disadvantaged communities) have half-time facilitators who do some tutoring in the afternoon.

A 5-day training session for new facilitators is held in Baltimore each spring, and overlaps with an annual national conference for facilitators and principals of experienced schools. In this way, new facilitators can meet experienced ones from their own regions, and mentoring and local support network relationships can begin. We strongly encourage new facilitators to spend as much time as possible visiting experienced schools and shadowing their facilitators, so that they can learn first hand what facilitators do.

In some cases, new facilitators attend teacher training in districts other than their own so that they can knowledgeably participate as "experts" in the training provided to their home schools. Whenever possible, we try to give new facilitators a formal role in initial training to help strengthen their credentials as friendly local experts.

Defining the precise place of the facilitator within the school's organizational structure is a delicate process. The facilitator must be seen as a friend and supporter to the teachers, and therefore should not have a formal or informal role in teacher evaluation. Teachers should always be glad to see the facilitator in their classroom and should feel free to share problems as well as successes. The facilitator must resist principals' natural temptations to put them in a role like that of a vice principal. Facilitators need to be observing classes and organizing meetings of key staff, not collecting lunch money or monitoring the playground. They need to spend their time working as change agents, not facilitating the school's routine day-to-day operations.

The overarching responsibility of every facilitator is to ensure that the program achieves its goals—that it delivers *success,* not just services. This means that the facilitator is constantly checking on the operation of the program and its outcomes. Is every teacher proficient in implementing the curriculum? Is every teacher moving rapidly enough to bring all students to grade level? Is every teacher using effective classroom management techniques? Are the tutors supporting students' success in the regular classroom? Is the Family Support Team succeeding in reaching out to parents, and are they on top of any recurring attendance problems? Most important, is every child on a path to success, and if not, are all involved staff members working in a coordinated way to get the student on track? The facilitator operates to make sure that no child is being forgotten and that all staff are working together effectively.

The facilitator has three main responsibilities. One is to provide coaching and follow-up to help teachers and tutors implement changes in curriculum and instruction. Another is to help make sure that the teachers, tutors, family support staff, and principal are all coordinating their activities around the success of all children, and that they are talking and planning together. Finally, the facilitator manages the 8-week assessment program (see Chapter 2), using assessment information to help make grouping decisions, to decide who needs tutoring, and to identify individual children who are not making adequate progress and help staff explore options for serving these children.

Coaching

Perhaps the most important role the facilitator plays within a Success for All or Roots and Wings school is as a coach or change agent to help teachers and tutors effectively implement changes in curriculum and instruction. They carry out this role in a variety of ways.

The most common way facilitators coach teachers is through classroom visits. Some facilitators schedule their visits in advance, whereas others simply tell teachers they may be dropping by in a given week, which allows for more flexibility. Sometimes, facilitators may just stop in for a few minutes, give teachers a "thumbs up" sign or other indication of approval, and then move on; at other times, facilitators may observe teachers for a longer time and then schedule a time to sit down with the teacher to discuss the teacher's needs.

Classroom visits are extremely important in monitoring change. Regardless of the amount or quality of professional development, teachers need feedback on how they are doing in their own classes, and they need suggestions and help targeted to their own personal classroom problems.

Facilitators often teach demonstration lessons. They may arrange coverage so that they can assemble a few teachers at the same time for a lesson in one teacher's class, or they may do a short demonstration for one teacher. Alternatively, many facilitators identify a teacher who is doing an excellent job with a particular part of an instructional program and cover other teachers' classes while they watch the expert teacher's lesson. A facilitator may videotape outstanding lessons to show to the teachers later on. In doing this, a facilitator tries to find something outstanding in the work of every teacher. For example, Ms. Smith may demonstrate her STaR lesson, Ms. Jones her partner reading, and Mr. Williams his writing lesson. Seeing other teachers' solutions to the same problems they are confronting is enormously useful to teachers, and the process of using teachers within the same building as "experts" for each other helps build professionalism and cohesiveness among the staff.

In all of their coaching work, facilitators try to communicate respect and approval for teachers, and try to avoid coming across as a supervisor or evaluator. This is why we insist that facilitators not be asked to provide principals with information that could be used in formal evaluations. That is also why we train facilitators to accentuate the positive, to recognize good teaching rather than dwell on deficits or errors, and to involve teachers in solving each other's problems rather than pretending to be the only expert in the building.

Although the facilitator's main role in professional development is to follow up on training by coaching teachers, facilitators also provide more formal training sessions. For example, following the main training sessions conducted by Johns Hopkins or regional training program staff, school-based facilitators may conduct staff development sessions on classroom management, cooperative learning, or other topics, depending on their expertise and the school's needs. Facilitators have a particularly important training role with teachers who are new to the school or are new to teaching.

Maintaining Coordination

In programs as complex as Success for All or Roots and Wings, there is a need to be sure that all of the program components and services are working together toward the same objectives. One of the facilitator's major tasks is to see that classroom teachers, tutors, family support staff, and other school staff are communicating with each other and are supporting each other's efforts rather than simply providing services and hoping that others will fill in gaps. The facilitator monitors the flow of information between tutors and reading teachers and between family support staff and teachers, and tries to find ways to overcome any barriers to open communication.

The facilitator also helps teachers help each other by scheduling meetings at which teachers and tutors can discuss what they are doing. Schools schedule common planning times or regular after-school meeting times for teachers at each grade level. In these meetings, the facilitator draws out the teachers, asking them to share successes and problems and to make supportive and useful suggestions to each other. Facilitators may show videotapes of excellent lessons or describe from their notes an outstanding lesson to illustrate some point.

Managing Eight-Week Assessments and Exploring Options for Children Having Difficulties

As noted in Chapter 2, 8-week assessments play a crucial role in the Success for All/Roots and Wings reading program. An important (and time-consuming) part of the facilitator's role is to manage the 8-week assessment program. This involves making sure that teachers have the tests they need, collecting tests after they are given, organizing the test data, and using it to suggest alternative placements or services for individual children.

For example, the facilitator looks for children who could be accelerated to a higher reading group, for children who appear to be in need of tutoring, and for children who are currently receiving tutoring but may be able to exit from tutoring. Decisions about group placements and tutoring are made collaboratively between the facilitator, the teacher, the tutor involved, or all three. Facilitators may set aside time to observe a struggling student during reading class or tutoring time to suggest alternative teaching strategies or materials. The 8-week assessments provide a regular opportunity to examine and adjust the reading program for all students. It is the facilitator's job to see that the data are collected and then used to help ensure the success of every child.

A key goal of the Success for All/Roots and Wings program is to keep students with learning problems out of special education and to keep them from being retained. This does not, however, simply mean throwing problems back on the teachers or "socially promoting" failing students. Instead, a Success for All or Roots and Wings school tries every strategy possible to meet students' needs so they can keep up with their age mates.

The facilitator leads the effort to intervene before a student is assigned to special education. Teacher referrals go to the facilitator before they go to a child study team. The facilitator then meets with the teacher and others to try to understand what the child's problem is and how it can be solved without involving the special education system. For example, if a child is exhibiting serious behavior problems, the facilitator, teachers, and Family Support Team may design a home-based reinforcement program. A child having a problem with one teacher may be transferred to another. The same approach is taken with children in danger of being retained.

A Day in the Life of a Success for All Facilitator[1]

It is 7:45 a.m. on an October Monday at Baltimore's Brighton-Early Elementary School, a Success for All school in its 2nd year of implementation. Most of the school is still dark and deserted, but in the library there is a spirited discussion going on. The first grade teachers and tutors are having a grade-level meeting to discuss problems they are having with the Reading Roots program. Quietly managing the meeting is Alice Lyle, the Success for All facilitator.

Various teachers bring up problems of pacing and classroom management, and discuss individual children who are having particular problems. Ms. Lyle tries to get the teachers and tutors themselves to suggest solutions to their own and each others' problems. She volunteers to cover one teacher's class later in the week so the teacher can observe a colleague who has worked out an effective way to get students organized for partner reading, and sets up a time to coteach a demonstration lesson with a new teacher who is having trouble with Listening Comprehension lessons. She encourages the tutors to discuss the strategies they are using successfully with children, and the classroom teachers think of ways they can support those strategies in reading class. At 8:15 the meeting ends and teachers go to their classrooms to prepare for the students' arrival.

The building principal, Mr. Walker, is supervising the free breakfast program in the cafeteria. Ms. Lyle joins him there to catch up with him "on the fly" on several issues, including those she discussed with the first grade team. During the brief homeroom and announcement period, Ms. Lyle brings boxes of softcover trade books to two of the third grade teachers who have requested them for their home reading program.

At 8:45, reading period begins. To the sounds of "Reading Jogs Your Mind" played over the loudspeaker, children change classes for reading. Ms. Lyle is pleased to see that the changing of classes is going very smoothly, and she smiles and gives a "thumbs up" sign to several teachers who are monitoring the process in the hall.

When the children are settled, Ms. Lyle starts her "Monday stroll" through the building. She visits all the classes briefly, just long enough to see what lesson each teacher is on and to get a flavor of what is happening. She keeps notes on a clip board, identifying issues to bring up with teachers later on. After the "stroll," Ms. Lyle spends time with two fourth grade teachers who are using Reading Wings for the first time this year. During her class visits, Ms. Lyle listens to children read, models how to monitor partner reading, praises students who are working well in their cooperative groups, models preventive classroom management strategies by moving close to a pair of students who are giggling to each other, and signals to the teacher that she likes what she's seeing.

In her "Monday stroll" and other brief classroom visits, Ms. Lyle is identifying teachers who need more intensive help. Later in the week she will meet with these teachers, discuss any problems, and collaboratively work out a plan. The plan could include having Ms. Lyle teach a demonstration lesson, covering a class so the teacher could observe another teacher, or a series of observation sessions followed by feedback and additional observations.

At 10:15 the reading lesson ends and students return to their homerooms. Ms. Lyle checks in with a preschool teacher who had asked for help with her STaR program, and then looks in briefly on two kindergarten classes that are doing thematic units on African American history. At 10:45 Ms. Lyle visits a tutor who is experiencing a great deal of trouble with one child. In the observation she notices that the child is squinting at the page. After he leaves, she suggests to the tutor that the child may need glasses, and she makes a note to mention this to the Family Support Team.

At 11:00 the Family Support Team meets. It is attended by the principal, the school's social worker, and the parent liaison and a second grade teacher, as well as Ms. Lyle. The teacher is there to discuss a problem she is having with two children. One has inconsistent attendance, frequently coming to school late or not at all. Another is constantly getting into fights. The team first discusses the truant child. After trying out several ideas, they decide to have the social worker meet with the child's mother and to arrange to call her at 9:00 each day the child is absent. In addition, they propose to ask a neighbor who walks her child to school every day to stop by and pick up the child each morning. The teacher suggests a behavior contract system for the child who gets into fights. The parent liaison agrees to meet with the child's parents and to set up a system in which the teacher will send home a note each day the child stays out of fights. The parents will be given ideas for fun things to do with the child when he brings home a "good day" note.

After the teacher returns to her class, Ms. Lyle brings up the child who seems to need glasses, and the group discusses how to get vision screening for all children and how to get glasses from the local Lion's Club for those who cannot afford them. They also discuss upcoming "parent evenings," additional ways to involve parents in the school, and other topics.

It is now 11:45—lunch time. As usual, it's a working lunch for Ms. Lyle. Today she meets with the school's special education resource teacher to plan a workshop on strategies teachers can use in the classroom to help students with learning disabilities. The special education teacher teaches a reading class composed of students with and without individual education plans (IEPs) and she tutors identified special education students in the afternoon. Much of her job, however, is preventing students from being referred to special education by helping classroom teachers and tutors meet students' needs. Ms. Lyle and the special education teacher discuss several children who are having serious learning problems and brainstorm strategies to adapt to their needs without entering the formal special education referral system.

After lunch, Ms. Lyle videotapes two tutoring sessions. The videos will be sent to Johns Hopkins for feedback and suggestions, and used in telephone conferences with Hopkins staff to help Ms. Lyle build her own skills in noticing and responding to effective and ineffective tutoring strategies. Afterwards she meets with a third grade teacher to plan an observation the next day. She drops in on a "Read-In" going on for first graders, where parent volunteers and some students from the middle school across the street are listening to first graders read. At 1:45, she meets a student who is new to the school and gives him an informal reading inventory to place him in a reading group. She then briefly visits all of the fourth grades, which are beginning to use MathWings.

Immediately after school, Ms. Lyle has a brief meeting with the fifth grade teachers to discuss their writing program. They are preparing class "mystery books" to be read to the school at a Halloween assembly. They discuss some problems they are having with the peer editing process, and Ms. Lyle promises to visit their classes to see if she can make some suggestions.

At 3:30 Ms. Lyle has a cup of coffee with the principal, Mr. Walker, who has had an equally exhausting day. She tells him all the good things she's seen that day, and discusses vision screening, an upcoming workshop on classroom management, and some issues around special education and Title I. At last, Ms. Lyle goes home, where she will spend part of the evening going over the results of the first 8-week reading assessments to identify children who need to be in a different reading group, need tutoring, or are not making adequate progress.

Is every facilitator's day as full as this one? Most facilitators would say that Ms. Lyle's day is, if anything, an easy one, because there were no crises in it. What our experience with facilitators tells us is how much it takes to bring about systemic change throughout high-poverty elementary schools. Nothing less than the extraordinary efforts of talented facilitators, whose entire job it is to bring about change, will ensure the full implementation of a program as comprehensive as Success for All.

For more on facilitators, see Madden et al., 1995.

Maintaining Program Integrity: The Johns Hopkins Role

When Success for All began in Baltimore, the role of our staff was much like that of school-based facilitators. We conducted training, monitored implementation, attended Building Advisory Committee and Family Support Team meetings, and so on. As we have expanded beyond Baltimore, our role has had to change substantially (Slavin, 1994). We now have full-time trainers located in various parts of the United States, and we make use of many talented staff from existing Success for All schools to help us. In addition, our focus is now on enabling schools to manage Success for All on their own. We still conduct the initial training of teachers and facilitators, but our function after the initial training is directed toward empowering the school's staff to solve its own problems as much as possible.

Trainers from Johns Hopkins and regional training programs are responsible for the initial training provided to new Success for All and Roots and Wings schools. They then work with the new schools to help them implement the program over time. Two trainers visit new schools for about 6 days each year to conduct additional training and to monitor implementation.

After the initial training, our efforts in new Success for All schools focus on enhancing the skills of the school-based facilitators to manage the program on their own. For example, in visits to the schools, our trainers spend time in classes and tutoring sessions with the school-based facilitators. The main purpose of these visits is to help the school-based facilitators see what our trainers see. They share observations and insights to come to a common understanding of what portions of each teacher's lessons are good, what portions are in need of improvement, and what strategies the school-based facilitators might try to improve the teachers' skills.

These visits are supplemented by frequent telephone contacts between our staff and the school-based facilitators. In addition, we have increasingly been using speaker phones at the schools to enable our facilitators to have "meetings" with several school staff members, and we are beginning to have school-based facilitators videotape teachers' lessons and send them to us so that our staff can offer feedback and suggestions. In addition, school-based facilitators send us monthly reports to keep our staff informed of the program's progress and problems.

Maintaining the integrity of the program while allowing it to meet the different needs of different schools and communities is a constant, dynamic process. Part of this process takes place in the early negotiations, when our staff works with district and building administrators to adapt the model to district resources, needs, and interests. When the program is under way, there are frequent questions about adaptations and alterations to meet the needs of specific groups of children or local circumstances.

In addition to training and supporting implementation of Success for All/Roots and Wings, our staff has several other roles. We are continually working to develop and improve our curriculum materials, teachers' manuals, and training materials and procedures. Our research staff leads the development activities, but many of our trainers have one or more areas of curricular expertise in which they do some development.

We are very conscious of the problems of "scaling up" a program from pilot to national dissemination without watering down the program or losing the features that made it effective in its early sites. We are trying at every stage to maintain the quality and integrity of the model by building on our strengths and insisting on systems that ensure top-quality implementation at every participating school without being so rigid or prescriptive that the program cannot adapt to meet local needs.

Schools Helping Schools

Perhaps the most important way Success for All and Roots and Wings are extending their reach to a larger number of schools without sacrificing quality is by increasingly engaging staffs of successful, experienced schools in the training and follow-up in new schools. School staffs rarely take full responsibility for training and follow-up without the active involvement of trainers from Johns Hopkins or regional training sites, but they can take over some of the training and most of the follow-up. The advantages of this are significant. Local schools that have successfully implemented Success for All or Roots and Wings have staffs that know every detail of the model and how to make it work in an environment very similar to that of the new school. Experienced and new schools can establish "mentoring" relationships in which staff exchange visits, materials, and ideas. When the new school runs into troubles large or small, the mentor school is nearby and ready to help. Schools often establish local support networks to help each other implement Success for All or Roots and Wings over the long run.

School-to-school mentoring lets the real experts—the teachers, facilitators, and principals in successful Success for All schools—share their wisdom of practice and hard-won experience. It gives new schools an attainable vision of what Success for All or Roots and Wings should be like. It gives staffs of new schools support when they run into problems or opposition. Mentor schools know the local situation, so they can help new schools adapt to local realities more readily than our Hopkins trainers can.

Mentoring. Staffs of mentor schools can play a critical role in providing local models of effective implementation that others can visit, in participating in training and follow-up, and in giving advice and support to new schools. Mentoring arrangements can significantly reduce the amount of time Johns Hopkins or regional training center facilitators need to spend at a school, and can therefore reduce the costs of implementing Success for All or Roots and Wings. The ideal arrangement for bringing new schools into the Success for All/Roots and Wings family is a combination of initial training from Johns Hopkins or regional training program staff in collaboration with local mentor schools followed up by the mentor school staff, with occasional visits from Johns Hopkins to add additional elements and check on the schools' progress.

Apprenticeship. Just as one-to-one tutoring is the most effective form of instruction for children, one-to-one apprenticeship is the most effective way to learn a complex task. One of the best services a mentor school can provide to a new Success for All school is to provide an opportunity for key staff from the new school to work side by side with their experienced counterparts.

Apprenticeship opportunities often involve individuals designated to be facilitators in new schools working with experienced facilitators. This is a particularly effective use of apprenticeship. The facilitator's role is extremely complex and demanding; no training program or manual could begin to describe in adequate detail the thousand tasks every facilitator must do well.

The more time a new facilitator can spend in an experienced school, the better. The new facilitator can be of concrete value to the experienced one in helping with 8-week assessments and regrouping, organizing materials and supplies, and so on, while gaining concrete information about the facilitator's role. The new facilitator may attend all the meetings the experienced facilitator attends, including those of Grade-Level Teams, Family Support Teams, and Building Advisory Teams. The new facilitator may also visit classrooms and tutoring sessions with the experienced facilitator so that they can compare notes afterward on strengths and weaknesses of lessons and constructive strategies for helping teachers improve their lessons, classroom management strategies, and other practices. The new facilitator might spend time with family support staff, going on home visits with them or participating in programs for parents. After the new school is up and running, the facilitator from the mentor school may arrange to spend a day or two with the new facilitator to "shadow" him or her and provide feedback and ideas.

Apprenticeships can be equally useful for other key staff, such as principals, family support staff, tutors, and teachers.

Networking

Building a national network of Success for All and Roots and Wings schools is one of the most important things we're trying to do at Johns Hopkins. An isolated school out on the frontier of innovation can sometimes hang on for a few years, but systemic and lasting change is far more likely when schools work together as part of a network in which school staff share a common vision and a common language, share ideas and technical assistance, and create an emotional connection and support system. This is the main reason we have an annual conference for experienced and new sites. At the annual conference we provide valuable information on new developments and new ideas (most of which we have gotten directly from the schools we work with). We are also trying to build connections between the experienced schools, so that they can share ideas on issues of common interest and build significant relationships with other schools pursuing similar objectives, and we are also trying to create an esprit de corps, a pride in what we are all trying to do together, an understanding and acceptance of the struggle needed to achieve the goal of success for every child.

In addition to national conferences, there are many other things we do to build an effective support network. We publish a newsletter, *Success Story,* which focuses on new ideas and outstanding accomplishments of our schools. In our conversations with schools we are constantly putting schools in touch with other schools to help them with specific issues, such as bilingual education, year-round schedules, use of Title I funds in nonschool-wide circumstances, use of special education funds to support tutoring, and so on.

One of the most common activities of local support networks for Success for All and Roots and Wings is regular meetings among key staff. Most often it is facilitators or facilitators and principals together who meet about once a month to discuss common problems and explore ways to help each other. Sometimes principals or Family Support Teams meet separately from time to time to discuss issues of particular concern to them.

For more on "scaling up" of Success for All and Roots and Wings, see Slavin, Dolan, and Madden, 1994.

Note

1. This vignette is a composite of the experiences of several facilitators in several Success for All schools. It is primarily the work of Alta Shaw and Lynne Mainzer, both of whom have been building facilitators and Hopkins trainers. All names, including that of the school, are fictitious.

Appendix 7.1. Success for an Application

To Whom It May Concern:

We appreciate your interest in Success for All. The enclosed application is designed to ensure that sites that are considering SFA adoption plan with Johns Hopkins early in the process so implementation can be as easy as possible. Success for All is a schoolwide restructuring project, so many areas of a school's program are affected. A successful implementation requires careful planning and decision making. This application form should help you work through many decisions that must be made for successful implementation at your school.

A facilitator job description is enclosed in this packet. The facilitator, a key position in SFA, is often chosen early in the process. The description should clarify the skills needed for this important person.

Finally, adoption of Success for All can occur only after a school has gone through several steps.

Success for All Adoption Process

1. Send for information packet on SFA.
2. Distribute information to staff. Meet to decide whether there is interest in the project.
3. Visit with nearby SFA schools to see the program in action and to talk with teachers and administrators. (If you are unsure of what sites might be easiest to visit, call Chris Kane at Johns Hopkins 410-516-8816.)
4. Meet with the district to make sure that funding options are being pursued.
5. Have Johns Hopkins come to the school and present an overview for the district and school staff.
6. **Conduct a vote for teachers (80% of faculty must vote for the program).**
7. Meet with parents and community to review the program and adoption process.
8. Complete the application form and return it to JHU accompanied by completed teacher ballots.
9. Send application to Johns Hopkins for review and confer with JHU on site application.
10. The application is approved by district, site, and JHU. The program is ready to start.

To schools interested in adopting the Success for All program:

At this stage, you should know quite a bit about the Success for All program. You have probably read awareness materials as well as the Success for All monograph and viewed one or more video tapes; some of your staff members should have visited at least one Success for All school. In addition, you should have been visited by a Hopkins Success for All staff member who has given you this application.

This document is designed to provide you with an opportunity to look at the requirements for an effective Success for All program and the resources available at your site to make sure that the two match. When we receive this document, we will be able to determine whether your school has the commitment and resources to implement Success for All and whether we have the training resources available to meet your needs. Unfortunately, because our training resources are limited, we cannot work with all schools that apply.

To help you fill out this application, the following materials are included:

- Description of three start-up options
- An estimate of materials costs
- SFA facilitator job description
- SFA site application
- SFA sample ballot

Adoption of Success for All requires a vote in favor by 80% of the staff on a secret ballot. The vote is conducted after the awareness process is complete and prior to the completion of the application. Please remember to enclose the completed ballots (which are anonymous) and a list of the names and positions of the staff members voting with this application.

Please include letters from parents of students in your school and from community members to document their knowledge about Success for All and their support of your application. It is crucial to the effectiveness of the program that parents and community members be fully informed and supportive.

A job description for the school-based Success for All facilitator is also included in this packet since the facilitator is usually chosen early in the implementation process. This description should clarify the skills needed for this important position.

Mail the completed application and supporting materials to:

Success for All
CSOS
Johns Hopkins University
3505 North Charles Street
Baltimore, MD 21218

If you need assistance in completing this application, contact the Hopkins facilitator below:

_____
Hopkins Facilitator

_____
Phone Number

Application Checklist:

_____ Application completed and signed by principal
_____ Application signed by district
_____ Ballots and list of teacher voting enclosed
_____ Letter(s) from parent group indicating support
_____ Letter or letters from community members indicating support

Beginning Success for All

DISCOVERY STAGE

All staff members should read the Success for All monograph published by the Educational Research Service, and the contents should be discussed as a staff at a staff meeting.

If possible, a selected group of staff members should visit a Success for All site near them and discuss their observations with the rest of the staff members.

VOTING STAGE

A Hopkins staff member or a staff member from a regional training site visits the school, presents the video, and gives an overview of Success for All. Additional introductory materials and articles about Success for All are made available.

Vote: In a secret ballot, 80% of the staff must vote in favor of making a commitment to SFA. The ballots should be passed out at the awareness session and collected and sent to Hopkins or the regional training site following the vote. An authentic vote by secret ballot is essential to the success of the program. The amount of change required by the program cannot be achieved without the complete cooperation of the staff.

Meetings should be conducted by school staff members with parents and community members to be certain that they are fully informed at every stage and to ensure their interest and commitment to the program.

APPLICATION STAGE

After a positive vote for Success for All, the application must be completed by the school, signed by a district superintendent and submitted to the Success for All program staff at Johns Hopkins for approval. The application must include the ballots from the vote regarding adoption of Success for All, the list of staff members voting, and supporting letters from parents and community members. Success for All staff members will review the application and notify the school of the result of the review within 30 days.

CONTRACTING STAGE

After the application is approved by Success for All, training is negotiated. In this contract, a Hopkins facilitator is assigned, the basic sequence of training activities for **three** years is planned, and the number of days needed for training, follow-up, and monitoring of the project for the first year are specified. At the end of each year, implementation is reviewed and contracts are renegotiated.

START-UP

Midyear start-up involves implementing Family Support, STaR and other elements of the pre-K and K program, and Beyond the Basics in the first year and achieving full implementation when Beginning Reading begins in September of the second year. Writing training would occur in the spring of the first year. Gradual start-up is appropriate for schools making a commitment to the program in the middle of a year or for those who wish to have ample planning time and a gradual pace of phase-in to ensure that all staff are comfortable with all elements of the program.

Pre-K through first grade start-up involves implementing Family Support, STaR, and other elements of the kindergarten program, as well as Beginning Reading, in September of the first year. Beyond the Basics and writing would be trained late in the first year. All elements of the program would be in place by September of the second year. Pre-K through first grade start-up is appropriate for schools making a commitment to the program by April (for the following September) who wish to have ample planning time and a gradual pace of phase-in to ensure that all staff are comfortable with all the elements of the program.

Full program involves implementing all of the program elements at once and can occur only in August/September. Schools should have voted to make a commitment to SFA before April if they plan to start the full program in September. Writing training will occur in the second half of the first year if staff members are comfortable with the reading program implementation. Full start-up requires the school to initiate many new things at once, but it is appropriate for schools who feel they have the commitment and resources to do this.

Schools Beginning Success for all and Roots and Wings (Year 1): Materials Cost Estimation

This form provides schools beginning Success for All and Roots and Wings (Year 1) with an itemized estimation of the materials costs involved with the program. Totals for individual schools will vary. The figures will be given for two hypothetical schools: School A and School B. (Items without an item number are indicated by an asterisk (*) and must be ordered from a publishing company or book distributor, not Johns Hopkins.)

Hypothetical School Parameters

School A: 5 tutors • 3 classes per grade level • 30 students per class • 1 PK
School B: 8 tutors • 6 classes per grade level • 30 students per class

			School A		School B	
Item #	Description	Unit Cost	Quantity	Total Cost	Quantity	Total Cost
FS-P	Family Support Parent Postcard (pack of 100)	$7.00	1	$7.00	1	$7.00
FS-AC	Family Support Attendance Cards (pack of 500)	$30.00	1	$30.00	1	$30.00
FS-N	Family Support Meeting Notice (pack of 100)	$5.00	1	$5.00	1	$5.00
FS-M	Family Support Manual	$20.00	3	$60.00	3	$60.00
FS-BB	Books and Breakfast Kit	$40.00	1	$40.00	1	$40.00
S1	Thematic Units	$35.00	3	$105.00	6	$210.00
S2	Alphabet Big Book with Teacher Instructions	$80.00	3	$240.00	6	$480.00
S3	Big Print Book Fairy Tales with Teacher Instructions	$40.00	1	$40.00	1	$40.00
S4	Big Print African Folk Tales	$30.00	1	$30.00	1	$30.00
S5	STaR Teacher Manual	$3.00	7	$21.00	12	$36.00
S6	STaR Guide Sheets	$30.00	3	$90.00	3	$90.00
S7	STaR Sequence Cards	$180.00	2	$360.00	3	$540.00
*	STaR Books (88 books per lot)	$293.64	3	$880.92	3	$880.92
*	Peabody Language Development Kit Level (P)	$515.00	3	$1,545.00	6	$3,090.00
RR1-S	Reading Roots Teacher Material Set	$71.00	12	$480.00	11	$440.00
Duplication	Duplication Costs of RR	@3¢ per page		$288.00		$573.00

Item #	Description	Unit Cost	School A Quantity	School A Total Cost	School B Quantity	School B Total Cost
RR4-S	Set of Shared Stories—48 Stories (set of 50)	$1,000.00	1	$1,000.00	2	$2,000.00
*	Peabody Language Development Kit (Level 1)	$295.00	3	$885.00	6	$1,770.00

Item #	Description	Unit Cost	School A Quantity	School A Total Cost	School B Quantity	School B Total Cost
BB1	Beyond the Basics Teacher Manual	$35.00	14	$490.00	27	$945.00
BB2	Listening Comprehension Manual	$10.00	17	$170.00	30	$300.00
	Treasure Hunt Masters for a basal series					
	Grade 1.2	$25.00	1	$25.00	1	$25.00
	Grade 2.1	$25.00	1	$25.00	1	$25.00
	Grade 2.2	$25.00	1	$25.00	1	$25.00
	Grade 3.1	$25.00	1	$25.00	1	$25.00
	Grade 3.2	$25.00	1	$25.00	1	$25.00
	Grade 4	$50.00	1	$50.00	1	$50.00
	Grade 5	$50.00	1	$50.00	1	$50.00
	Grade 6	$50.00	1	$50.00	1	$50.00
THO-1	How to Write a Treasure Hunt	$4.00	1	$4.00	1	$4.00
Duplication	Estimated Duplication Costs of Treasure Hunts	@3¢ per page		$2,820.00		$5,628.00
BB-RC1	RC A1 to A29	$45.00	1	$45.00	1	$45.00
BB-RC2	RC 1 to 44	$45.00	1	$45.00	1	$45.00
BB-RC3	RC 101 to 134	$45.00	1	$45.00	1	$45.00
BB-RC4	RC 201 to 222	$45.00	1	$45.00	1	$45.00
Duplication	Duplication Costs of BB-RC1-BB-RC4	@3¢ per page		$3,595.00		$7,042.00
BR5-M	Tutoring Manual	$20.00	5	$100.00	8	$160.00
TOTAL				**$13,698.92**		**$24,855.92**
	Optional Classroom Libraries (50 books per classroom for independent reading. Needed if library resources at the school are not adequate).	$4.00	750	$3,000.00	1,500	$6,000.00
TOTAL				**$16,698.92**		**$30,855.92**
	Optional use of novels for class instruction. SFA recommends that novels be used as frequently as possible to enrich the reading material available for students. This estimate provides for the purchase of 25 novels and support materials.					
*	Novels (25 class sets of 25)	$4.00	750	$3,000.00	750	$3,000.00
	Novel Treasure Hunts[a] (1 master set per novel)	$6.00	25	$150.00	25	$150.00
Duplication	Estimated duplication	@3¢ per page		$1,875.00		$1875.00
TOTAL				**$21,723.92**		**$35,880.92**

a. There may be cost savings on basal Treasure Hunt purchase and duplication if novels are used.

SCHOOLS BEGINNING SUCCESS FOR ALL OR
ROOTS AND WINGS IN SPANISH:
MATERIALS COST ESTIMATION

This form is to give schools beginning the Success For All program with Spanish materials an itemized estimation of the materials costs involved with the program. Figures are given per class.

Item #	Description	Unit Cost	
FS-NS	Spanish Family Meeting Notice (pack of 100)	$10.00	
FS-SP-S	Spanish Flourescent Success Postcards (pack of 250)	$15.00	
FS-BB-S	Family Raising Readers—*Creando Lectures*	$25.00	
S2-s	Spanish Alphabet Big Book	$90.00	
*	STaR Books (100 books per lot)	$333.68	
S6-S	Spanish STaR Guide Sheets (2 sets of 50)	$30.00	
	TOTAL for Family Support and STaR	**$503.68**	
BR1-S	*Lee Conmigo*—Spanish Manual	$30.00	
BR2-S	Spanish Components (Set)	$10.00	
BR-SA1	Spanish Initial Assessment—*Lee Conmigo*	$1.00	
BR-SA2	Spanish Eight Week Assessment— *Lee Conmigo*	$5.00	
BR3-S	Spanish Share Sheets to *Lee Conmigo*— Master Set	$15.00	
Duplication	Estimated duplication cost @3¢ per page	$99.00	
*	Syllabic Picture Cards, Macmillan		
SS-RR-SS	Lee Conmigo Shared Stories	$325.00	
	TOTAL for Lee Conmigo	**$485.00**	

Treasure Hunts

(Treasure Hunts for Harcourt Brace Jovanovich 1993 available in Spring 1997)

	Macmillan Campanitas de Oros 1987		
MCO P	*Tara, Tara, la Guitarra*	$25.00	Grade Level 1
MCO 1	*El Sol y la Luna* (1)	$25.00	
MCO 2.1	*A Ver, a Ver, a Ver* (2.1)	$25.00	Grade Level 2
MCO 2.2	*Pluma, Tintero y Papel* (2.2)	$25.00	
MCO 3.1	*La Pájara Pinta* (3.1)	$25.00	Grade Level 3
MCO 3.2	*Lima, Naranja y Limon* (3.2)	$25.00	
MCO 4	*Las Mañanitas* (4)	$50.00	Grade Level 4
MCO 5	*Érase que se Era* (5)	$50.00	Grade Level 5
	(The above books must be ordered directly from Macmillan)		
Duplication	Estimated duplication cost for eash grade level @3¢ per page	$151.20c	
	TOTAL for *each* grade level using Macmillan Campanitas	**$201.20**	

Item #	Description	Unit Cost
	MacMillan McGraw-Hill 1993	
MC Hill 1.4	*Luna Lunera*	$100.00
MC HILL 2.1	*Naranja Dulce*	$100.00
MC HILL 2.2	*Puerta el Sol*	$100.00
MC HILL 3.1	*¡A Girar, Girasol!*	$100.00
MC HILL 3.2	*¡A Navegar!*	$100.00
MC HILL 4.1	*Caracola*	$200.00
MC HILL 5.1	*Donde Digo Digo*	$200.00
	(The above books must be ordered directly from Macmillan)	
Duplication	Estimated duplication cost for each grade level @3¢ per page	$151.20
	TOTAL for each grade level of using Macmillan McGraw-Hill	**$351.20**

FACILITATOR
JOB DESCRIPTION

A key component of Success for All is the facilitator position. The facilitator is a school-based, full-time person who provides support to teachers to ensure the successful functioning and accurate implementation of the SFA program. The job involves support of faculty, in-class modeling, and materials organization and distribution. Johns Hopkins has found that strong senior teachers are best able to perform this job well. Senior teachers have often been more comfortable with the hands-on nature of this position and have already earned a level of credibility and respect.

JOB RESPONSIBILITIES

- Monitor program implementation
- Ensure fidelity of all aspects of Success for All
- Organize and distribute Success for All materials
- Organize 8-week assessments, reading groups, tutoring assignments
- Model curriculum for teachers and tutors
- Mentor classroom teachers and tutors in reading curriculum
- Co-chair family support team
- Facilitate communication between tutors and reading teachers
- Communicate and coordinate program with Hopkins facilitators
- Inform and publicize the SFA program to community and school
- Conduct regular grade-level meetings

NECESSARY SKILLS

The facilitator must possess a strong understanding of the reading process, particularly early reading. In addition, the facilitator should have a strong background in the fundamentals of cooperative learning. Good organizational and interpersonal skills are crucial for this position.

SUCCESS FOR ALL SITE APPLICATION

School: _____

Address: _____

Phone: _____ Fax: _____

Principal: _____

Facilitator (if selected): _____

District: _____

Contact person: _____ Position: _____

Phone: _____ Fax: _____

Current School Description

How many students are there in the school? ____

What is the percentage of students eligible for free or reduced lunch? _____

Is this a schoolwide Chapter 1 program? ____ Yes ____ No

What grade levels are there in the school? _____

What is the approximate number of students per grade level? _____

What is the number of self-contained special education classes? _____

# of students? _____

What is the number of resource classrooms? ____ # of students? ____

How many students were referred to special education in past year? ____

What percentage of students have as their primary language a language other than

English? ____ Please list primary languages. _____

_____

In what languages do you have bilingual programs? _____

How many separate bilingual classes? _____ Number of students/class _____

At what grade level are students transitioned into English reading? _____

How many separate ESL classes? _____

Number of students/class? _____

What ESL program/materials are used? _____

Please describe any other staff development or districtwide programs being

implemented at this time. _____

_____

_____

Attendance Information

What was the school's attendance during past year? _____%

How many retentions have there been during past year? _____

How many suspensions during past year? _____

What is the yearly transiency rate of your school? (Transiency = % of students

moving in and out) _____

Commitment

To participate in SFA, 80% of school staff must vote to participate in the program. Please enclose completed anonymous ballots when submitting this application.

Has staff voted to participate in program? _____ Yes _____ No

Number voting _____ Yes   Number voting _____ No

Facilitators

For full school implementation, Success for All requires a full-time facilitator to ensure adequate teacher support and program integrity

Will the facilitator be full-time next year? _____ Yes _____ No

Arrangements have been made with another SFA school for your facilitator to spend 1 week observing and job shadowing the facilitator at an experienced site.

_____ Yes _____ No

Start-Up Plan

In Success for All, there are three ways to begin. A school can elect to do full implementation in the fall of the first year, start up midyear, or begin just Pre-K through Grade 1 in fall of the first year. Please look at the more complete description of these methods enclosed in this packet to select the start-up that works the best for your site.

For Year 1, this site is selecting (check one)

_____ Full Implementation

_____ Midyear Start-up

_____ Pre-K through 1

Training Commitment

The following are the recommended training days for SFA. Please indicate whether this site is proposing any changes in standard training design. It is important for special education teachers and assistants to attend training so that they will be knowledgeable about the program, whether or not they will be directly teaching the components. When asked to list number of participants, please list total number of staff members—including assistants, special education teachers, central office staff, and soon—that you plan to have trained.

In trainings involving more than 40 people, additional trainers will be required.

Please indicate if initial training ($700 per day plus travel costs) has been approved for the following:

Overview of SFA and Family Support (full staff, 1 day)   _____ Yes _____ No

Number of participants _____

Pre-K-K (2 days) . . . . _____ Yes _____ No

Number of participants _____

Beginning Reading (Reading Roots) (2 days). . . . . _____ Yes _____ No

Number of participants _____

Beyond the Basics (2 days) . . . . _____ Yes _____ No

Number of participants _____

Family Support (Team only, 2 days) . . . . _____ Yes _____ No

Number of participants _____

Tutor Training (1 day) . . . . _____ Yes _____ No

Number of participants _____

Additional training days may be necessary if schools have a large number of Spanish bilingual students using the SFA reading program. A plan may need to be developed with JHU.

Implementation checks and additional training days (at $800 per day plus travel costs) have been approved for the following:

Year 1

Curriculum (8 days)   _____Yes _____ No

Family Support (1 day)   _____ Yes _____ No

What is the number of in-service days available for ongoing training needs? _____

Will the school or district provide substitutes

or release days for contracted training?   _____ Yes _____ No

Have adequate training days and implementation visits been approved for Year 2?

Curriculum (10 days)   _____ Yes _____ No

Family Support (2 days)   _____ Yes _____ No

Have adequate training days and implementation visits been approved for Year 3?

Curriculum (5 days)   _____ Yes _____ No

Family Support (1 day)   _____ Yes _____ No

Are you planning to coordinate training with other SFA schools? _____ Yes _____ No

If yes, which schools: _____

Are any existing SFA schools planning to help

your school implement the program?   _____ Yes _____ No

If yes, which schools? _____

Previous Training

Has staff had previous cooperative learning training? _____ Yes _____ No

If so, please indicate which:

_____ Kagan   _____ Slavin   _____ Johnson & Johnson

_____ Other (please describe) _____

What percentage of staff members are currently using cooperative learning? _____%

Please describe the kinds of activities currently in use and the number of teachers involved.

_____

_____

_____

Continuing Staff Development

It is very important that staff members have opportunities to meet with others using the same program components and facing the same issues to share and problem solve. The facilitator is responsible for organizing these meetings and ensuring that they are productive.

Are monthly grade-level team meetings scheduled currently?_____ Yes _____ No

If not, will they be scheduled after start-up? _____ Yes _____ No

Schedule and Reading Groups

SFA requires a 90-minute uninterrupted block for reading. Time for additional language arts instruction will need to be scheduled for another time during the day. If this site is requesting any change from the standard SFA schedule, please submit the plan.

The 90-minute uninterrupted reading block will exist. ____ Yes ____ No

(If not, attach proposed schedule.)

SFA requests heterogeneous grouping for homerooms. It is crucial that homerooms be heterogeneously grouped so that all students have equal opportunity for success.

Homerooms will be heterogeneously grouped. _____ Yes _____ No

The school intends to use cross-grade reading grouping. _____ Yes _____ No

Reading will be scheduled at the same time for what grades? _____

What grades will be working together in cross-grade grouping? _____

What grade levels will be involved in SFA in the

First year? _____

Second year? _____

Third year? _____

Please list how many classes you expect to have at each grade level listed.

Number of 1st grades _____

Number of 2nd grades _____

Number of 3rd grades _____

Number of 4th grades _____

Number of 5th grades _____

Number of 6th grades _____

Please list any combination classes you will have. _____

Will all of your Chapter I teachers become teacher/tutors? _____ Yes _____ No

If not, why not? _____

List teaching staff besides grade-level teachers and tutors who will be teaching

a reading class (e.g., librarians, special education teachers, art, music,

PE teachers, etc.) _____

_____

_____

Calculate the number of reading groups you will have (homeroom teachers,

teacher/tutors, and other reading teachers). Total _____

Is adequate space available for the additional reading groups?_____ Yes_____ No

Tutoring

One-to-one tutoring is a core component of Success for All and a key resource for students who are at risk of failure. Organizing school resources to ensure maximum one-to-one tutoring is crucial. Nine tutoring slots per tutor can usually be arranged.

How many full-time certified teacher/tutors are expected when SFA implementation is begun? _____

How many tutoring slots will each teacher/tutor have available each day? _____

How many full-time assistant-level tutors are expected? _____

How many tutoring slots will each assistant-level tutor have available each day? _____

How many total one-to-one tutoring slots will be available per day? _____

Is there adequate space for tutors? _____ Yes _____ No

Describe space: _____

In addition to certified teachers, schools often supplement tutor support by providing after-school tutoring, tutoring by volunteers and business partners, or peer tutoring. Please list resources that will be available in your building.

Will after school one-to-one tutoring be available? _____ Yes _____ No

How many students will be served? _____

Will you organize cross-age tutoring opportunities? _____ Yes _____ No

Will there be tutoring provided by volunteers from businesses? _____ Yes _____ No

Please list any other tutoring resources you anticipate._____

_____

_____

Pre-Kindergarten and Kindergarten

Success for All recommends that schools have a half-day Pre-K program and/or a full-day kindergarten program. Please indicate what will be available at the beginning of program implementation.

How many Pre-K classes will there be? _____

Will assistants be available for each Pre-K class? _____ Yes _____ No

How many kindergarten classes will there be? _____

Will kindergarten be full day _____ or half day _____?

Will assistants be available all day for each kindergarten class? _____ Yes _____ No

Bilingual

Success for All has a Spanish beginning reading program titled Lee Conmigo for schools that have bilingual Spanish classes. For Grades 2 through 5, make sure to check the order form to ensure that Treasure Hunts are available for you.

Will SFA instructional materials in Spanish be used? _____ Yes _____ No

In what grades do you plan to use instructional materials in Spanish? _____

What basal series is in use for Spanish instruction? _____

Approximately how many classes will use Spanish materials?

_____ K _____ G1 _____ G2 _____ G3 _____ G4 _____ G5 _____ G6 _____

How many students per class? _____

Special Education

Whenever possible, SFA prefers that special education students be mainstreamed for reading and that special education teachers teach a standard reading block. Please indicate the plan for your school.

Will special education students be mainstreamed for reading?

_____ All _____ Some _____ None

Will special education teachers teach a reading block?

_____ All _____ Some _____ None

Will nonmainstreamed special education classes use SFA materials?

_____ All _____ Some _____ None

Please describe your school's approach to mainstreaming. _____

_____

Family Support

If current attendance is below 95%, the formal attendance-monitoring component of SFA must be used. This component requires a full-time or part-time attendance monitor.

Will you have an attendance monitor next year? _____ Yes _____ No

Will your attendance monitor be _____ Full-time _____ Part-time?

Is there a prereferral team already in place? _____ Yes _____ No

Is there weekly meeting time available for the team? _____ Yes _____ No

How long will teams meet? _____

If a school has a team that develops plans for regular education children who are experiencing difficulty, this team should form the basis of a school's Family Support Team. In addition, the facilitator, administrator, teacher representative, nurse, and any local service providers who conduct on-site services are usually invited to become members of the Family Support Team.

Please list members of projected Family Support Team by job title.

_____   _____

_____   _____

_____   _____

Teachers need to be able to attend meeting of the Family Support Team when a student of theirs is being discussed.

How will this school address class coverage for teachers? _____

_____

_____

What outside agencies provide services at the school? _____

_____

_____

_____

Is there after-school programming in place at your school? _____ Yes _____ No

If yes, please check after school activities. ____ Homework room ____ Recreation

____ After-school tutoring ____ Other _____

List three examples of parent involvement programs currently in place. _____

_____

_____

_____

_____

List home-school connections currently in place (PTA, newsletter, home visits).

_____

_____

_____

_____

List community business partnerships. _____

Materials

In this program, beginning readers through first-level readers must use materials developed by Success for All. Beyond this level, the SFA reading process can be used with a variety of trade books and basals. SFA provides materials to be used in conjunction with novels and various basal series. If your basal series is not listed on the current JHU order form, arrangements for development or use of novels must be made with JHU before approval of the application can be given.

What basal series is currently in use? _____

Copyright?_____

Is that basal now available on the order form? _____ Yes _____ No

Does the district project changes in the basal series? _____ Yes _____ No

The next adoption date is _____

Will novels be available?_____

How many novel sets of at least 15 are available? _____

How many of these novels are on the order form list? _____

Will teacher manuals be provided for all teachers and tutors? _____ Yes _____ No

Will a Peabody Kit be available for each Pre-K, kindergarten,

and first-grade teacher? _____ Yes _____ No

Are there adequate storage facilities for materials? _____ Yes _____ No

Districts usually purchase a master set of materials for Grades 2-6+. It is the school's or district's responsibility to duplicate individual student copies and test copies.

Will the school or district be in charge of copying/collating materials?

_____ School _____ District

Budget

Enclosed in this packet is a brief guide to help schools and districts estimate cost of the program.

What is the source of funding for the development fees? ($7,000 for the first school in the district, $2,000 for each additional school). _____

_____

How do you plan to fund training costs? _____

_____

Amount available _____

Training materials for participants cost approximately $4 per participant or can be duplicated at the district. What resources are available to cover these costs?_____

_____

What is the source of funding for materials? _____

_____

Amount available _____

How will you fund the costs for necessary staff?

Facilitator? _____

Tutor(s)? _____

Additional Family Support staff salaries?_____

_____

I have reviewed the initial application for **SFA** and approve beginning implementation.

_____
Principal

I have reviewed the initial application for **SFA** and approve beginning implementation.

_____
District Manager

I have reviewed the initial application for **SFA** and approve beginning implementation.

_____
SFA Co-Director

Success for All Ballot

To participate in Success for All, faculty members must decide by an 80% vote whether or not to implement the program. Please vote by checking your responses below.

Yes   No

☐   ☐   I have listened to an awareness talk by JHU staff.

☐   ☐   I have read the monograph on Success for All.

☐   ☐   We have discussed adoption of Success for All as a staff.

☐   ☐   I have visited a Success for All school.

Circle one:

I would like our school to adopt Success for All.

I am not interested in adopting Success for All.

(cut ballots here)

Success for All Ballot

To participate in Success for All, faculty members must decide by an 80% vote whether or not to implement the program. Please vote by checking your responses below.

Yes   No

☐   ☐   I have listened to an awareness talk by JHU staff.

☐   ☐   I have read the monograph on Success for All.

☐   ☐   We have discussed adoption of Success for All as a staff.

☐   ☐   I have visited a Success for All school.

Circle one:

I would like our school to adopt Success for All.

I am not interested in adopting Success for All.

8

Research on Success for All

One of the guiding principles in the development of Success for All has been an emphasis on rigorous research.[1] The elements of the program are themselves derived from research on reading, writing, early childhood education, school organization, parent involvement, integrated services, professional development, and school change. The outcomes of the program have been extensively studied in longitudinal evaluations in 19 schools, which have been compared to 19 matched control schools in 9 districts in different parts of the United States. In each evaluation, experimental and control students have been given individually administered reading assessments, in which they must, among other things, read stories and respond to questions about them. These assessments, administered by testers who are unconnected to the project, get to the essence of what reading is about, and avoid the problems of using test scores that are involved in district or school accountability. These scores are thus objective, broadly based, and fair indicators of children's abilities to read and comprehend text. The use of well-matched control groups makes it likely that scores in Success for All schools are being compared to those of schools that are good representations of what the Success for All schools would have been like without the program. The schools and districts being studied over time are those that were the earliest to implement the program, and all schools are being followed over many years to the determine long-term effects of the program. With individually administered test data on thousands of children in many schools in many districts, Success for All is without any doubt the most extensively evaluated schoolwide restructuring program ever developed (see Madden, Slavin, Karweit, Dolan, & Wasik, 1993; Slavin et al., 1994; Slavin et al., 1996; Slavin, Madden, Karweit, Dolan, & Wasik, 1992; Slavin, Madden, Karweit, Livermon, & Dolan, 1990).

We began longitudinal evaluations of the program in its earliest sites, six schools in Baltimore and Philadelphia and one in Charleston, South Carolina. Later, third-party evaluators at the University of Memphis, Steve Ross, Lana Smith, and their colleagues, added evaluations in Memphis, Montgomery (AL), Ft. Wayne (IN), and Caldwell (ID). Most recently, studies focusing on English language learners in Modesto and Riverside, California, have been conducted by Marcella Dianda and John Flaherty of the Southwest Regional Laboratory. Each of these evaluations has compared Success for All schools to matched comparison schools on measures of reading performance, starting with cohorts in kindergarten or in first grade and continuing to follow these students as long as possible (details of the evaluation design appear later). Vagaries of funding and other local problems have ended some evaluations prematurely, but most have been able to follow Success for All schools for many years. As of this writing, there are 7 years of continuous data from the 6 original schools in Baltimore and Philadelphia, and varying numbers of years of data from 7 other districts, for a total of 23 schools (and their matched control schools). Table 8.1 lists the districts and characteristics of the schools.

Evaluation Design

A common evaluation design, with variations due to local circumstances, has been used in all Success for All evaluations. Every Success for All school involved in a formal evaluation is matched with a control school that is similar in poverty level (percentage of students qualifying for free lunch), historical achievement level, ethnicity, and other factors. Children in the Success for All schools are then matched either on district-administered standardized test scores given in kindergarten (in Baltimore and Philadelphia) or on Peabody Picture Vocabulary Test (PPVT) scores given by the project in the fall of kindergarten or first grade. In some cases, analyses of covariance rather than individual child matches were used, and at Key School in Philadelphia (P1 in Table 8.1) schools were matched but individual children could not be (because the school serves many limited-English proficient students who were not tested by the district in kindergarten).

The measures used in the evaluations were as follows:

1. *Woodcock Reading Mastery Test.* Three Woodcock scales, Word Identification, Word Attack, and Passage Comprehension, were individually administered to students by trained testers. Word Identification assesses recognition of common sight words, Word Attack assesses phonetic synthesis skills, and Passage Comprehension assesses comprehension in context. Students in Spanish bilingual programs were given the Spanish versions of these scales.

2. *Durrell Analysis of Reading Difficulty.* The Durrell Oral Reading scale was also individually administered to students in Grades 1 through 3. It presents a series of graded reading passages that students read aloud, followed by comprehension questions.

3. *Gray Oral Reading Test.* Comprehension and passage scores from the Gray Oral Reading Test were obtained from students in Grades 4 through 5.

Except at Key, analyses of covariance with pretests as covariates were used to compare raw scores in all evaluations, and separate analyses were conducted for students in general and for students in the lowest 25% of their grades. At Key, analyses of variance were used and results were reported separately for Asian (mostly Cambodian) students and for non-Asian students.

The tables and figures presented in this chapter summarize student performance in grade equivalents (adjusted for covariates) and effect size (ES; proportion of a standard deviation

TABLE 8.1 Characteristics of Success for All Schools in the Longitudinal Study

District/School	Enrollment	Free Lunch (%)	Ethnicity (%)	Date Began SFA	Data Collected	Preschool?	Full-Day K?	Comments
Baltimore								
B1	500	83	B-96, W-4	1987	88-94	Yes	Yes	First SFA school; had additional funds first 2 years.
B2	500	96	B-100	1988	89-94	Some	Yes	Had additional funds first 4 years.
B3	400	96	B-100	1988	89-94	Some	Yes	
B4	500	85	B-100	1988	89-94	Some	Yes	
B5	650	96	B-100	1988	89-94	Some	Yes	
Philadelphia								
P1	620	96	A-60, W-20, B-20	1988	89-94	No	Yes	Large ESL program for Cambodian children.
P2	600	97	B-100	1991	92-93	Some	Yes	
P3	570	96	B-100	1991	92-93	No	Yes	
P4	840	98	B-100	1991	93	No	Yes	
P5	700	98	L-100	1992	93-94	No	Yes	Study involves only students in Spanish bilingual program.
Charleston, SC								
CS1	500	40	B-60, W-40	1990	91-92	No	No	
Memphis, TN								
MT1	350	90	B-95, W-5	1990	91-94	Yes	No	Program implemented only in grades K-2.
MT2	530	90	B-100	1993	94	Yes	Yes	
MT3	290	86	B-100	1993	94	Yes	Yes	
MT4	370	90	B-100	1993	94	Yes	Yes	
Ft. Wayne, IN								
F1	330	65	B-56, W-44	1991	92-94	No	Yes	SFA schools (and controls) are part of desegregation plan.
F2	250	55	B-55, W-45	1991	92-94	No	Yes	SFA schools (and controls) are part of desegregation plan.
Montgomery, AL								
MA1	450	95	B-100	1991	93-94	No	Yes	
MA2	460	97	B-100	1991	93-94	No	Yes	
Caldwell, ID								
CI1	400	20	W-80, L-20	1991	93-94	No	No	Study compares two SFA schools to Reading Recovery school.
Modesto, CA								
MC1	640	70	W-54, L-25, A-17, B-4	1992	94	Yes	No	Large ESL program for students speaking 17 languages.
MC2	560	98	L-66, W-24, A-10	1992	94	Yes	No	Large Spanish bilingual program.
Riverside, CA								
R1	930	73	L-54, W-33, B-10, A-3	1992	94	Yes	No	Large Spanish bilingual and ESL programs. Year-round school.

Key: B = African American; L = Latino; A = Asian American; W = White.

197

separating the experimental and control groups), averaging across individual measures. Neither grade equivalents nor averaged scores were used in the analyses, but they are presented here as a useful summary. Outcomes are presented for all students in the relevant grades in Success for All and control schools, and also those for the students in the lowest 25% of their grades, who are most at risk. In most cases the low 25% was determined based on Peabody Picture Vocabulary Test scores given as pretests. In Baltimore, Philadelphia, and Charleston, South Carolina, however, Peabody pretests were not given and low 25% analyses involve the lowest-performing students at posttest.

Each of the evaluations summarized in this chapter follows children who began in Success for All in first grade or earlier, in comparison to children who had attended the control school over the same period. Because Success for All is a prevention and early intervention program, students who start in it after first grade are not considered to have received the full treatment (although they are, of course, served within the schools).

To summarize the outcomes from all schools and all years involved in experimental control comparisons, this chapter uses a method of analysis called a multisite replicated experiment (Slavin & Madden, 1993), in which each grade level cohort (students in all classes in that grade in a given year) in each school is considered a replication. In other words, if three Success for All first grades have proceeded through school X over a 3-year period, this would produce three effect sizes, as each first grade cohort (compared to its control group) produces an effect size representing the experimental-control difference in student achievement that year. For example, across 23 schools ever involved in Success for All evaluations, there are a total of 55 first grade cohorts from which experimental and control achievement data have been collected. This procedure is a direct application of a procedure common in medical research called multicenter clinical trials (Horwitz, 1987). In such studies, small-scale experiments located in different sites over extended time periods are combined into one large-scale experiment. For example, patients entering any of several hospitals with a given disease might be given an experimental drug or a placebo at random. If the disease is relatively rare, no one hospital's experiment would have an adequate sample size to assess the drug's effects, but combining results over many hospitals over time does provide an adequate sample. In schoolwide reform, the "patient" is an entire grade level in a school, perhaps 100 children. Obtaining an adequate sample of schools at any point in time would require involving thousands of children and hundreds of teachers.

The idea of combining results across experiments is not, of course, foreign to educational research. This is the essence of meta-analysis (Glass, McGaw, & Smith, 1981). Meta-analyses, however, combine effect sizes (proportions of a standard deviation separating experimental and control groups) across studies with different designs, measures, samples, and other features, leading to such charges as that they may mislead readers by "combining apples and oranges" or by missing unwritten or unpublished studies in which effects were zero or negative (Matt & Cook, 1994; Slavin, 1986).

Combining results across geographically separated experiments into one study is also not unheard of in educational research. For example, Pinnell, Lyons, DeFord, Bryk, and Seltzer (1994) studied the Reading Recovery tutoring model in 10 Ohio districts. Three variations of Reading Recovery and another tutoring program were compared to control groups in each district, and results were then aggregated using the cohort of tutored first graders as the unit of analysis. A multisite replicated experiment only adds to this design the accumulation of experimental-control differences over time.

Reading Outcomes

The results of the multisite replicated experiment evaluating Success for All are summarized in Figure 8.1 and Tables 8.2 through 8.6 for each grade level, 1 through 5. Each table shows

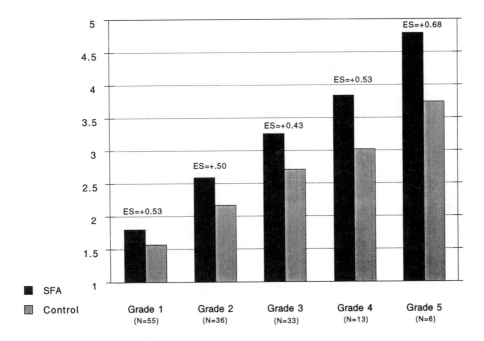

Figure 8.1. Composition of Success for All and Control Schools in Mean Reading Grade Equivalents and Effect Sizes, 1988-1994

means in raw scores, grade equivalents, and effect sizes. The analyses compare cohort means for experimental and control schools; for example, the t statistics presented in Table 8.2 compare 55 experimental to 55 control cohorts, with cohort (50 to 150 students) as the unit of analysis. Each mean in Table 8.2 represents about 4,000 students. The standard deviations show variation among school means, but effect sizes are means of all experimental/control comparisons, which are computed using individual student data. Grade equivalents are based on the means, and are only presented for their information value. No analyses were done using grade equivalents.

The results summarized in Tables 8.2 through 8.6 show statistically significantly (p = .05 or better) positive effects of Success for All (compared to controls) on every measure at every grade level, 1 through 5. For students in general, effect sizes averaged around a half standard deviation at all grade levels. Effects were somewhat higher than this for the Woodcock Word Attack scale in first and second grades, but in Grades 3 through 5 effect sizes were more or less equivalent on all aspects of reading. Consistently, effect sizes for students in the lowest 25% of their grades were particularly positive, ranging from ES = +1.03 in first grade to ES = +1.68 in fourth grade. Again, cohort-level analyses found statistically significant differences favoring low achievers in Success for All on every measure at every grade level.

Changes in Effect Sizes
Over Years of Implementation

One interesting trend in outcomes from comparisons of Success for All and control schools relates to changes in effects sizes according to the number of years a school has been implementing the program. Figure 8.2, which summarizes these data, was created by pooling effect sizes for all cohorts in their first year of implementation, all in their 2nd year, and so on, regardless of calendar year.

TABLE 8.2 Cohort Means for Success for All and Control Schools: Grade 1
($N = 55$ Experimental and Control School/Cohorts)[a]

	All Students		Lowest 25%	
	SFA	*Control*	*SFA*	*Control*
Durrell Oral Reading				
Mean	6.28	4.75	3.27	2.07
(*SD*)	(1.83)	(1.49)	(2.61)	(2.05)
GE	1.98	1.73	1.48	1.27
t	6.73***		5.41***	
ES	+0.43		+0.65	
Woodcock Passage Comprehension				
Mean	15.15	12.48	8.76	6.18
(*SD*)	(2.65)	(3.26)	(3.96)	(3.84)
GE	1.61	1.47	1.29	1.16
t	6.24***		6.32***	
ES	+0.42		+0.86	
Woodcock Word Attack				
Mean	13.60	8.08	8.58	3.59
(*SD*)	(3.60)	(3.43)	(5.33)	(3.32)
GE	1.82	1.50	1.53	1.16
t	16.32***		9.78***	
ES	+0.79		+1.70	
Woodcock Word Identification				
Mean	29.05	23.23	18.31	13.22
(*SD*)	(6.78)	(6.22)	(8.18)	(6.40)
GE	1.79	1.60	1.45	1.28
t	9.58***		7.27***	
ES	+0.49		+0.80	
Mean *GE*	1.80	1.57	1.44	1.22
Mean *ES*	+0.53		+1.03	

a. Numbers in this table represent averages of means, standard deviations, and effect sizes from 55 cohorts
of first graders in 23 schools, a total of about 4,000 students in Success for All schools and 4,000 control
schools.
*$p < .05$; **$p < .01$; ***$p < .001$.

Figure 8.2 shows that mean reading effect sizes progressively increase with each year
of implementation. For example, Success for All first graders score substantially better than
control first graders at the end of the first year of implementation (ES = +0.49). The
experimental-control difference is even higher for first graders attending schools in the 2nd
year of program implementation (ES = +0.53), increasing to an effect size of +0.73 for
schools in their 4th implementation year. A similar pattern is apparent for second and third
grade cohorts.

There are two likely explanations for this gain in experimental-control differences. One
is that as schools get better at implementing Success for All, outcomes improve. This is a
logical outcome, which gives evidence of the degree to which ongoing professional development, coaching, and reflection enable school staffs to progressively improve student
achievement over time. It is also important to note, however, that although 1st-year first
grade cohorts started the program in first grade, 2nd-year cohorts started in kindergarten and

TABLE 8.3 Cohort Means for Success for All and Control Schools: Grade 2
($N = 36$ Experimental and Control School/Cohorts)[a]

	All Students		Lowest 25%	
	SFA	*Control*	*SFA*	*Control*
Durrell Oral Reading				
Mean	12.39	10.10	7.08	4.47
(*SD*)	(2.27)	(2.22)	(3.36)	(2.60)
GE	3.00	2.61	2.11	1.68
t	4.97***		7.04***	
ES	+0.38		+1.01	
Woodcock Passage Comprehension				
Mean	25.30	21.52	17.12	12.54
(*SD*)	(2.48)	(3.71)	(7.22)	(4.90)
GE	2.43	2.05	1.71	1.48
t	4.61***		3.70**	
ES	+0.41		+0.96	
Woodcock Word Attack				
Mean	20.15	14.28	12.46	5.91
(*SD*)	(3.87)	(3.94)	(6.94)	(4.41)
GE	2.42	1.86	1.74	1.34
t	8.52***		8.68***	
ES	+0.71		+1.75	
Woodcock Word Identification				
Mean	46.29	39.08	33.84	23.92
(*SD*)	(5.79)	(6.80)	(11.11)	(9.07)
GE	2.52	2.15	1.93	1.63
t	7.27***		6.13***	
ES	+0.48		+0.87	
Mean *GE*	2.59	2.17	1.87	1.53
Mean *ES*	+0.50		+1.15	

a. Numbers in this table represent averages of means, standard deviations, and effect sizes from 36 cohorts of second graders in 15 schools, a total of about 2,500 students in Success for All schools and 2,500 control schools.
*$p < .05$; **$p < .01$; ***$p < .001$.

most 3rd- and 4th-year cohorts started in prekindergarten. Some or all of the gain in effect sizes could be due to a lasting effect of participation in the Success for All prekindergarten and kindergarten program.

Whatever the explanation, the data summarized in Figure 8.2 show that although Success for All has an immediate impact on student reading achievement, this impact grows over successive years of implementation. Over time, schools may become increasingly able to provide effective instruction to all of their students, to approach the goal of success for *all*.

Do Success for All Effects Last?

In many ways, the effects of any prevention and early intervention can only be determined in the long run, especially after children are no longer receiving direct intervention. As of this writing, the first two Baltimore cohorts (students who started in the program

TABLE 8.4   Cohort Means for Success for All and Control Schools: Grade 3
(*N* = 33 Experimental and Control School/Cohorts)[a]

	All Students		Lowest 25%	
	SFA	Control	SFA	Control
Durrell Oral Reading				
Mean	17.65	14.85	10.56	7.23
(SD)	(2.50)	(2.56)	(2.97)	(3.31)
GE	3.87	3.41	2.69	(2.14)
t		5.42***		6.76***
ES		+0.36		+0.96
Woodcock Passage Comprehension				
Mean	30.98	25.78	21.56	14.20
(SD)	(3.69)	(2.87)	(4.68)	(5.47)
GE	3.03	2.48	2.06	1.56
t		5.63***		6.10***
ES		+0.51		+1.78
Woodcock Word Attack				
Mean	24.06	19.21	14.35	9.40
(SD)	(4.03)	(4.37)	(7.06)	(6.62)
GE	2.91	2.32	1.87	1.57
t		6.07***		6.43***
ES		+0.45		+1.18
Woodcock Word Identification				
Mean	55.38	48.13	41.90	32.05
(SD)	(5.87)	(5.03)	(7.37)	(7.39)
GE	3.24	2.64	2.30	1.88
t		6.87***		7.24***
ES		+0.39		+0.85
Mean GE	3.26	2.71	2.23	1.79
Mean ES		+0.43		+1.19

a. Numbers in this table represent averages of means, standard deviations, and effect sizes from 33 cohorts of third graders in 10 schools, a total of about 2,000 students in Success for All schools and 2,000 control schools.
*$p < .05$; **$p < .01$; ***$p < .001$.

in kindergarten or first grade) have now completed sixth and seventh grades, respectively. This provides a first opportunity to assess the lasting impact of Success for All beyond the elementary grades.

The comparison of Success for All and control students from the five Baltimore Success for All and control schools show that there is a lasting effect of the program into middle school. Success for All students scored significantly higher than control on every reading measure at each grade level ($p < .05$ or better). The mean effect size across the five measures was +0.48 in sixth grade (a difference of 1.3 grade equivalents) and +.41 in seventh (1.0 grade equivalents), only slightly less than the effect sizes for Baltimore Success for All schools in the fourth and fifth grades when students are still in the program. Mean effect sizes for children in the lowest 25% of their grades were +.68 for sixth graders and +.92 for seventh graders. The disturbing news, however, is that neither Success for All or control

TABLE 8.5 Cohort Means for Success for All and Control Schools: Grade 4
(N = 13 Experimental and Control School/Cohorts)[a]

	All Students		Lowest 25%	
	SFA	Control	SFA	Control
Gray Comprehension				
Mean	22.38	18.01	14.17	5.42
(SD)	(3.33)	(2.74)	(4.04)	(2.63)
GE	3.78	3.10	2.43	1.44
t		3.67**		4.19**
ES		+0.44		+2.21
Gray Passage				
Mean	32.78	24.37	13.20	2.97
(SD)	(7.40)	(4.90)	(5.11)	(2.87)
GE	4.48	3.64	2.44	1.20
t		3.79**		4.68**
ES		+0.51		+1.64
Woodcock Passage Comprehension				
Mean	34.31	28.80	24.60	13.18
(SD)	(2.84)	(1.93)	(2.97)	(4.03)
GE	3.46	2.78	2.36	1.54
t		6.11***		15.27***
ES		+0.62		+1.61
Woodcock Word Attack				
Mean	26.27	19.51	11.60	4.87
(SD)	(4.97)	(2.28)	(3.93)	(3.21)
GE	3.35	2.35	1.68	1.27
t		4.46***		2.41**
ES		+0.47		+2.26
Woodcock Word Identification				
Mean	63.65	55.11	47.89	31.53
(SD)	(4.64)	(4.01)	(5.16)	(6.17)
GE	4.13	3.21	2.62	1.87
t		5.77***		4.67**
ES		+0.61		+2.87
Mean GE	3.84	3.02	2.31	1.46
Mean ES		+0.53		+1.68

a. Numbers in this table represent averages of means, standard deviations, and effect sizes from 13 cohorts of fourth graders in 7 schools, a total of about 700 students in Success for All schools and 700 control schools.
*$p < .05$; **$p < .01$; ***$p < .001$.

students are growing much in reading in the middle grades. This is an indictment of the middle schools in inner-city Baltimore rather than an indictment of Success for All elementary schools, but it is nevertheless distressing. These findings increase our commitment to expand Success for All into middle schools, so that children can continue to grow in reading and other skills during their critical early adolescent years.

TABLE 8.6   Cohort Means for Success for All and Control Schools: Grade 5 ($N = 6$ Experimental and Control School/Cohorts)[a]

	All Students		Lowest 25%	
	SFA	Control	SFA	Control
Gray Comprehension				
Mean	27.36	21.65	17.79	8.98
(SD)	(3.21)	(3.66)	(4.62)	(2.31)
GE	5.27	3.63	3.06	1.80
t		3.55**		3.66*
ES		+0.59		+1.35
Gray Passage				
Mean	43.32	31.37	17.20	8.36
(SD)	(7.72)	(6.17)	(4.80)	(3.52)
GE	5.43	4.37	2.92	1.74
t		6.61***		6.20**
ES		+0.67		+1.36
Woodcock Passage Comprehension				
Mean	37.48	32.60	28.76	22.81
(SD)	(2.43)	(1.42)	(2.45)	(2.99)
GE	4.10	3.23	2.78	2.18
t		7.51***		3.50*
ES		+0.69		+0.79
Woodcock Word Attack				
Mean	29.60	21.73	17.49	8.23
(SD)	(3.25)	(1.07)	(3.00)	(1.37)
GE	4.50	2.61	2.15	1.51
t		6.22**		8.27***
ES		+0.74		+1.83
Woodcock Word Identification				
Mean	69.94	60.35	54.20	40.78
(SD)	(4.63)	(2.76)	(5.25)	(3.72)
GE	4.79	3.74	3.12	2.24
t		5.36**		5.23**
ES		+0.71		+1.15
Mean GE	4.82	3.52	2.81	1.89
Mean ES		+0.68		+1.29

a. Numbers in this table represent averages of means, standard deviations, and effect sizes from 6 cohorts of fifth graders in 6 schools, a total of about 250 students in Success for All schools and 250 control schools. *$p < .05$; **$p < .01$; ***$p < .001$.

Does Success for All Ensure Success for *All?*

In a study of Baltimore third graders, Madden et al. (1993) examined the performance of Success for All and control students on the Durrell Oral Reading Test to see how close the program comes to ensuring the success of every child by third grade, a key program goal. Clearly, this goal has not yet been achieved. A total of 15.7% of Success for All third graders were performing at least one year below grade level, and 3.9% were 2 years below. The

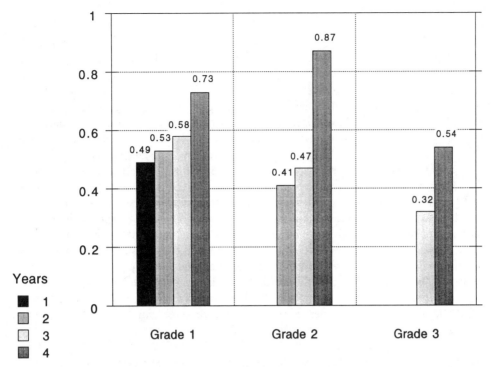

Figure 8.2. Effect Sizes Comparing Success for All and Control Schools According to Implementation Year

situation in the control group, however, was far worse. In these schools, 38% of third graders were at least a year below grade level and 11.7% were 2 years below. At the other end of the distribution, 18.1% of Success for All students (compared to 12.1% of controls) scored at least a year above grade level, and 4.9% (compared to only 1.9% of controls) scored at least 2 years above grade level.

Success for All and English Language Learners

The education of English language learners is at a crossroads. For many years, researchers, educators, and policymakers have debated questions of the appropriate language instruction for students who enter elementary school speaking languages other than English. Research on this topic has generally found that students taught to read their home language and then transitioned to English ultimately become better readers in English than do students taught to read only in English (Garcia, 1991; Willig, 1985; Wong-Fillmore & Valadez, 1986). More recently, however, attention has shifted to another question. Given that students are taught to read their home language, how can we ensure that they succeed in that language (see, for example, Garcia, 1994)? There is no reason to expect that children failing to read well in Spanish, for example, will later become good readers and successful students in English. On the contrary, research consistently supports the common-sense expectation that the better students in Spanish bilingual programs read Spanish, the better their English reading will be (Garcia, 1991; Hakuta & Garcia, 1989). Clearly, the quality of instruction in home-language reading is a key factor in the ultimate school success of English language learners, and must be a focus of research on the education of these children.

Even if all educators and policymakers accepted the evidence favoring bilingual over English-only instruction, there would still be large numbers of English language learners being taught to read in English. This is true because of practical difficulties of providing instruction in languages other than English or Spanish; teachers fully proficient in Southeast Asian languages, Arabic, and other languages are in short supply, as are materials to teach in these languages. Speakers of languages other than English or Spanish are among the fastest-growing groups in our nation's schools (U.S. General Accounting Office, 1994). Furthermore, many Spanish-dominant students are taught to read in English, either because of shortages of bilingual teachers, insufficient numbers of Spanish-dominant students in one school, parental desires to have their children taught in English, or other factors. For these reasons, a large percentage of English language learners will always be taught in English only, with instruction in English as a second language (ESL). As with bilingual programs, the quality of reading instruction, ESL instruction, and the integration of the two are essential in determining the success of English language learners being taught in English only.

There is remarkably little research evaluating programs designed to increase the Spanish reading performance of students in bilingual programs. Hertz-Lazarowitz, Ivory, and Calderón (1993) evaluated a bilingual adaptation of Cooperative Integrated Reading and Composition (BCIRC) in El Paso elementary schools starting in second grade. This program, an adaptation of the CIRC program that forms the basis of the upper-elementary reading program used in Success for All, involves having students work in small cooperative groups. Students read to each other, work together to identify characters, settings, problems, and problem solutions in narratives, summarize stories to each other, and work together on writing, reading comprehension, and vocabulary activities. Students in BCIRC classes scored significantly better than control students on the Spanish Texas Assessment of Academic Skills (TAAS) at the end of second grade, and as they transitioned to English in third and fourth grades they performed significantly better than control students on standardized reading tests given in English.

The first application of Success for All to English language learners began in Philadelphia's Francis Scott Key School, which serves a high-poverty neighborhood in which more than 60% of students enter the schools speaking Cambodian or other Southeast Asian languages. An adaptation of Success for All was designed to meet the needs of these children. This adaptation focused on integrating the work of ESL teachers and reading teachers, so that ESL teachers taught a reading class and then helped limited-English proficient students with the specific language and reading skills needed to succeed in the school's (English) reading program. In addition, a cross-age tutoring program enabled fifth graders, now fully bilingual in English and Cambodian, to help kindergartners succeed in the English program. The performance of students at Francis Scott Key has been compared to that of students in a matched comparison school each year, and the results have consistently favored Success for All for Asian as well as non-Asian students (Slavin & Yampolsky, 1991). This chapter reports the reading performance of the English language learners in Grades 3 through 5 at Key and its comparison school as of spring 1994, the end of the 6th year of program implementation (see Slavin & Madden, 1995).

As noted in Chapter 2, a Spanish adaptation of the Success for All reading program called Lee Conmigo ("Read With Me") was developed for use in Spanish bilingual programs in 1992. During the 1992 to 1993 school year the entire Success for All program (including Lee Conmigo for limited-English proficient students) was implemented in one Philadelphia school serving a predominately Latino (mostly Puerto Rican) student body. The first-year results showed the Spanish bilingual students to be performing substantially better than controls on individually administered tests of Spanish (Slavin & Madden, 1994). This chapter reports the results for the second graders who completed their 2nd year in Lee Conmigo (see Slavin & Madden, 1995).

A third evaluation of Success for All with English language learners was carried out by Dianda and Flaherty (1995) at the Southwest Regional Laboratory in Southern California. This study involved three schools. Fremont Elementary in Riverside, California, and Orville Wright Elementary in Modesto, are schools with substantial Spanish bilingual programs. The third, El Vista Elementary, also in Modesto, served a highly diverse student body

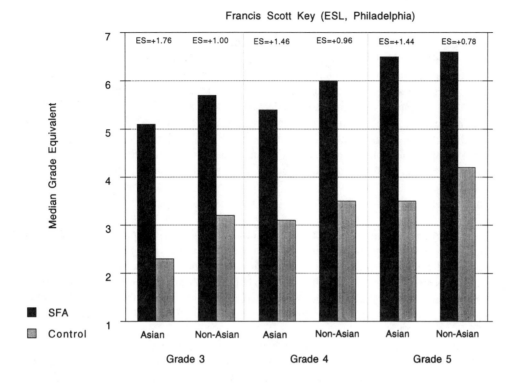

Figure 8.3. Acheivement Medians (Grade Equivalents and Effect Sizes) for Success for All Control Schools

speaking 17 languages using an ESL approach. Students in all three schools were compared to matched students in matched schools. In each case, students were assessed in the language of instruction (English or Spanish).

Francis Scott Key (ESL)

The program at Francis Scott Key was evaluated in comparison to a similar Philadelphia elementary school (see Slavin & Yampolsky, 1991). The two schools were very similar in overall achievement level and other variables. Of the comparison school's students, 33% were Asian (mostly Cambodian), the highest proportion in the city after Key. The percentage of students receiving free lunch was very high in both schools, although higher at Key (96%) than at the comparison school (84%).

The data reported here are for all students in Grades 3 through 5 in spring 1994. With the exception of transfers, all students had been in the program since kindergarten.

Results: Asian Students. The results for Asian students are summarized in Figure 8.3. Success for All Asian students at all three grade levels performed far better than control students. Differences between Success for All and control students were statistically significant on every measure at every grade level ($p < .001$). Median grade equivalents and effect sizes were computed across the three Woodcock scales. On average, Success for All Asian students exceeded control in reading grade equivalents by almost 3 years in third grade (median $ES = +1.76$), more than 2 years in fourth grade (median $ES = +1.46$), and about 3 years in fifth grade (median $ES = +1.44$). Success for All Asian students were reading more than a full year above grade level in Grade 3 and more than a half-year above in fourth and fifth grade, while similar control students were reading more than a year below grade level at all three grade levels.

Results: Non-Asian Students. Outcomes of Success for All for non-Asian students, also summarized in Figure 8.3, were also very positive in Grades 3 through 5. Experimental-control differences were statistically significant ($p < .05$ or better) on every measure at every grade level. Effect sizes were somewhat smaller than for Asian students, but were still quite substantial, averaging +1.00 in Grade 3, +0.96 in Grade 4, and +0.78 in Grade 5. Effect sizes were particularly large for the Passage Comprehension measure at all three levels. Success for All students averaged almost 2 years above grade level in third grade, more than a year above grade level in fourth grade, and about 8 months above grade level in fifth grade; at all grade levels, Success for All averaged about 2.5 years higher than control students.

Fairhill (Bilingual)

The bilingual version of Success for All, Lee Conmigo, was first implemented at Fairhill Elementary School, a school in inner-city Philadelphia. Fairhill serves a student body of 694 students of whom 78% are Hispanic and 22% are African American. A matched comparison school was also selected. Nearly all students in both schools qualified for free lunches. Both schools were Chapter 1 schoolwide projects, which means that both had high (and roughly equivalent) allocations of Chapter 1 funds that they could use flexibly to meet student needs.

Results. All students defined by district criteria as limited-English proficient at Fairhill and its control school were pretested at the beginning of first grade on the Spanish Peabody Picture Vocabulary Test (PPVT). Each following May, these students were tested by native-language speakers on three scales of the Spanish Woodcock (Bateria Woodcock de Proficiencia en el Idioma): Letter/Word Identification (Identificacion de Letras y Palabras), Word Attack (Analisis de Palabras), and Passage Comprehension (Comprension de Textos).

ANCOVA's controlling for pretests showed that at the end of Grade 2 Success for All students scored substantially higher than controls on every measure ($p < .01$ or better). Figure 8.4 summarizes mean grade equivalents and effect sizes. Control second graders scored far below grade level on all three scales. In contrast, Fairhill students averaged near grade level on all measures. Effect sizes on all measures were substantial. Fairhill students exceeded control by 1.8 standard deviations on Letter-Word Identification, 2.2 on Word Attack, and 1.3 on Passage Comprehension.

Fremont (Bilingual), Wright (Bilingual), and El Vista (ESL)

Data from first graders in the three California Success for All schools were analyzed together by Dianda and Flaherty (1995), pooling data across schools in four categories: English-dominant students, Spanish-dominant students taught in Spanish (Lee Conmigo in Success for All schools), Spanish-dominant students taught in English ("sheltered students"), and speakers of languages other than English or Spanish taught in English. The pooled results are summarized in Figure 8.5 (adapted from Dianda & Flaherty, 1995).

As is clear in Figure 8.5, all categories of Success for All students scored substantially better than control students. The differences were greatest, however, for Spanish-dominant students taught in bilingual classes (ES = +1.03) and those taught in sheltered English programs (ES = +1.02). The bilingual students scored at grade level, and more than 6 months ahead of controls. The sheltered students scored about 2 months below grade level, but were still 4 months ahead of their controls. Both English-speaking students and speakers of languages other than English or Spanish scored above grade level and about 2 months ahead of their controls.

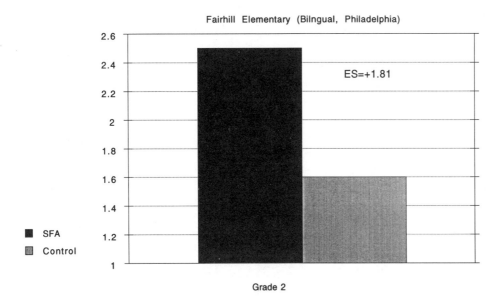

Figure 8.4. Spanish Reading Achievement Medians (Grade Equivalents and Effect Sizes) for Success for All and Control Schools, Spanish-Dominant Students

The effects of Success for All on the achievement of English language learners are substantially positive. Across three schools implementing Lee Conmigo, the Spanish curriculum used in bilingual Success for All schools, the average effect size for first graders on Spanish assessments was +0.88; for second graders (at Philadelphia's Fairhill Elementary) the average effect size was +1.77. For students in sheltered English instruction, effect sizes

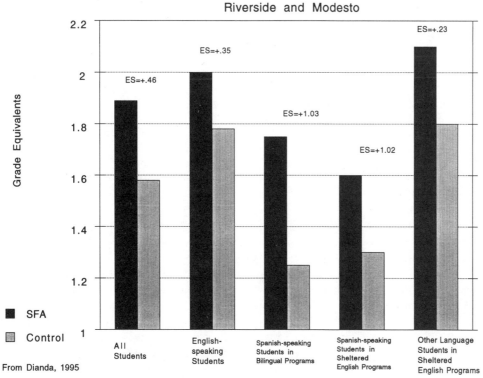

Figure 8.5. Achievement of Success for All and Control Students by Language Group
NOTE: From Dianda and Flaherty (1995).

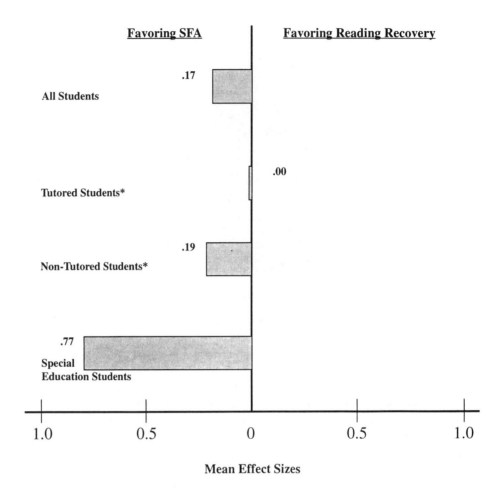

Figure 8.6. Comparison of Success for All and Reading Recovery Students in Mean Effect Sizes
NOTE: Adapted from Ross et al. (in press).
*Excludes special education students.

for all comparisons were also very positive, especially for Cambodian American students in Philadelphia and Mexican American students in California.

Comparing Success for All and Reading Recovery

Reading Recovery is one of the most extensively researched and widely used innovations in elementary education. Like Success for All, Reading Recovery provides one-to-one tutoring to first graders who are struggling in reading. Research on Reading Recovery has found substantial positive effects of the program as of the end of first grade, and longitudinal studies have found that some portion of these effects maintain at least through fourth grade (DeFord, Pinnell, Lyons, & Young, 1987; Pinnell et al., 1994).

Schools and districts attracted to Success for All are also often attracted to Reading Recovery, as the two programs share an emphasis on early intervention and a strong research base. Increasing numbers of districts have both programs in operation in different schools. One of the districts in the Success for All evaluation, Caldwell, Idaho, happened to be one of these. Ross, Smith, Casey, & Slavin (in press) used this opportunity to compare the two programs.

Reading Recovery tutoring is similar to that used in Success for All in that it is done by certified teachers and in that it emphasizes "learning to read by reading" and direct teaching of metacognitive skills. It is also, however, different in many important ways. Reading Recovery tutors receive substantially more training than do Success for All tutors. Reading Recovery tutoring sessions are longer than those used in Success for All (30 minutes vs. 20 minutes). Success for All places a great deal of emphasis on a linkage between tutoring and classroom reading instruction; tutors usually use the same books as those used in the reading class and emphasize the same objectives. Tutors in Success for All teach a reading class, so it is easy for them to maintain a consistency of approach. Reading Recovery does not emphasize coordination between tutoring and classroom instruction to this degree largely because the nature and quality of classroom reading instruction is not the central concern of the Reading Recovery program. Many schools using Reading Recovery, however, do provide classroom reading teachers with professional development to help them create supportive classroom environments that reinforce the strategies used in tutoring.

In Caldwell, two schools are using Success for All and one is using Reading Recovery. All three are very similar rural schools with similar ethnic make-ups (10% to 25% Hispanic, with the remainder Anglo), proportions of students qualifying for free lunch (45% to 60%), and sizes (411-451). The Success for All schools were somewhat higher than the Reading Recovery school in poverty and percentage Hispanic. In 1992 to 1993, one of the Success for All schools was in its 2nd year of implementation and the other was a new school that was in its first year (but had moved a principal and some experienced staff reassigned from the first school). Reading Recovery was in its 2nd year of implementation.

The study compared first graders in the three schools. Figure 8.6 summarizes the results. As is clear from the figure, students in the Success for All schools performed somewhat better than students in the Reading Recovery school overall (ES = +.17). Differences for special education students were substantial, averaging an effect size of +.77. Special education students were not tutored in the Reading Recovery school and were primarily taught in a separate resource room. These students scored near the floor on all tests. In contrast, Success for All special education students were fully mainstreamed and did receive tutoring, and their reading scores, although still low, showed them to be on the way toward success in reading.

Excluding the special education students, there were no differences in reading performance between tutored students in the Success for All and Reading Recovery schools (ES = .00). In light of earlier research, these outcomes suggest that both tutoring programs are highly effective for at-risk first graders.

The comparison of Success for All and Reading Recovery supports a common sense conclusion. Success for All, which affects all students, has positive effects on all students. Reading Recovery focuses on tutoring and therefore produces its effects on tutored students. These results suggest that Success for All may be most appropriate in schools serving many at-risk students, whereas Reading Recovery may be the better choice when the number of students at risk of reading failure is small. The results may also justify a merger of the two programs, combining the breadth and comprehensiveness of Success for All with the outstanding professional development of tutors provided by Reading Recovery. Such mergers of Success for All and Reading Recovery are being started in about a half dozen schools located around the United States.

Success for All and Special Education

Perhaps the most important goal of Success for All is to place a floor under the reading achievement of all children, to ensure that every child performs adequately in this critical skill. This goal has major implications for special education. If the program makes a substantial difference in the reading achievement of the lowest achievers, then it should reduce special education referrals and placements. Furthermore, students who have individual education plans (IEPs) indicating learning disabilities or related problems are typically treated the same as other students in Success for All. That is, they receive tutoring if they need it, participate in reading classes appropriate to their reading levels, and spend the rest of the day in age-appropriate, heterogeneous homerooms. Their tutor, reading teacher, or both are likely to be a special education teacher, but otherwise they are not treated differently. One-to-one tutoring in reading, plus high-quality reading instruction in the mainstream at the student's appropriate level, should be more effective than the small-group instruction provided in special education classes. For this reason we expect that students who have been identified as being in need of special education services will perform substantially better than similar students in traditional special education programs.

The philosophy behind the treatment of special education issues in Success for All is called "neverstreaming" (Slavin et al., 1991). That is, rather than waiting until students fall far behind, are assigned to special education, and then may be mainstreamed into regular classes, Success for All schools intervene early and intensively with students who are at risk to try to keep them out of the special education system. Once students are far behind, special education services are unlikely to catch them up to age-appropriate levels of performance. Students who have already failed in reading are likely to have an overlay of anxiety, poor motivation, poor behavior, low self-esteem, and ineffective learning strategies that are likely to interfere with learning no matter how good special education services may be. Ensuring that all students succeed in the first place is a far better strategy if it can be accomplished. In Success for All, the provision of research-based preschool, kindergarten, and first grade reading, one-to-one tutoring, and family support services are likely to give the most at-risk students a good chance of developing enough reading skills to remain out of special education, or to perform better in special education than would have otherwise been the case.

The data relating to special education outcomes clearly support these expectations. Several studies have focused on questions related to special education. One of the most important outcomes in this area is the consistent funding of particularly large effects of Success for All for students in the lowest 25% of their classes. Although effect sizes for students in general have averaged around +0.50 on individually administered reading measures, effect sizes for the lowest achievers have averaged in the range of +1.00 to +1.50 across the grades. As noted earlier in this chapter, across five Baltimore schools only 3.9% of third graders averaged 2 years behind grade level, a usual criterion for special education placement. In contrast, 11.7% of control third graders scored this poorly. Baltimore data have also shown a reduction in special education placements for learning disabilities of about half (Slavin et al., 1992). A recent study of two Success for All schools in Ft. Wayne, Indiana, found that over a 2-year period 3.2% of Success for All students in grades K through 1 and Grades 1 through 2 were referred to special education for learning disabilities or mild mental handicaps. In contrast, 14.3% of control students were referred in these categories (Smith, Ross, & Casey, 1994).

Taken together, these findings support the conclusion that Success for All both reduces the need for special education services (by raising the reading achievement of very low achievers) and reduces special education referrals and placements.

Another important question concerns the effects of the program on students who have already been assigned to special education. Here again, there is evidence from different sources. In the study comparing Reading Recovery and Success for All described previously, it so happened that first graders in special education in the Reading Recovery group were not tutored, but instead received traditional special education services in resource rooms. In the Success for All schools, first graders who had been assigned to special education were tutored one-to-one (by their special education teachers) and otherwise participated in the program in the same way as all other students. As noted earlier (recall Figure 8.6), special education students in Success for All were reading substantially better (ES = +.77) than special education students in the comparison school (Ross et al., in press). In addition, Smith et al. (1994) combined first-grade reading data from special education students in Success for All and control schools in four districts: Memphis (TN), Ft. Wayne (IN), Montgomery (AL), and Caldwell (ID). Success for All special education students scored substantially better than controls (mean *ES* = +.59).

Evaluation of Roots and Wings

Roots and Wings was developed much more recently than Success for All, and has therefore not been evaluated as extensively. An evaluation of the full Roots and Wings model in its pilot sites, however, shows strong evidence of effectiveness.

The pilot schools are located in rural St. Mary's County, Maryland. Three are in or near the town of Lexington Park, and one is in a completely rural area. An average of 48% of students in the four schools qualify for free or reduced-price lunches. The schools began program implementation in the 1992 to 1993 school year, but all program elements were not piloted until the 1994 to 1995 school year.

The assessment of Roots and Wings involves tracking changes over time on the Maryland School Performance Assessment Program (MSPAP), a state-of-the-art performance assessment in which third and fifth graders are asked to design and carry out experiments, write compositions in various genres, read and respond to extended passages, use mathematics to solve complex problems, and so on. Student responses are rated by state contractors against well-validated rubrics on a 5-point scale.

Figures 8.7 and 8.8 show gains over 3 years in MSPAP scores for third and fifth graders, respectively. The figures show substantial gains over that time period in the percentage of students scoring at or above "satisfactory" on all MSPAP scales. The overall state of Maryland also increased over this time period, but far less than the Roots and Wings schools. Averaging across the six scales, the percentage of Maryland third graders scoring satisfactory or better increased in 1993 to 1995 by 8.6 percentage points, in comparison to a gain of 18.9 for Roots and Wings schools. For fifth graders, the state gained an average of 6.4 percentage points, while Roots and Wings schools gained 13.0. This was true despite the fact that the Roots and Wings schools served many more children in poverty, had three times as many Title I students, and had mobility rates twice the state average.

The evaluation of Roots and Wings is important in documenting the positive effects of the program, of course, but it is also important for another reason. This is the first formal evaluation we have conducted using longitudinal data from a new state performance measure. States are moving toward the use of such performance measures, and current Title I legislation requires that schools adopt similar approaches to assess Title I programs by the year 2000. The demonstration that Roots and Wings affects performance measures also suggests that Success for All does so because the reading approaches used in the two programs are identical.

Conclusion

The results of evaluations of 23 Success for All schools in 9 districts in 8 states clearly show that the program increases student reading performance. In every district, Success for All students learned significantly more than matched control students. Significant effects were not seen on every measure at every grade level in every district, but the consistent direction and magnitude of the effects show unequivocal benefits for Success for All students. Pooling across all sites and analyzing at the cohort level (e.g., all first graders in a given school in a

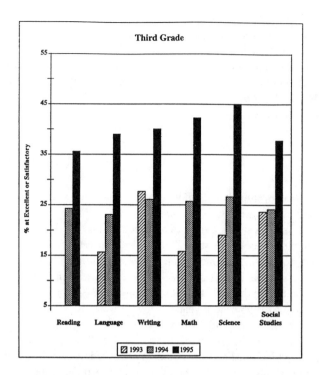

Figure 8.7. Roots and Wings: Saint Mary's County, Maryland School Performance Assessment Program, School Years 1993-1995

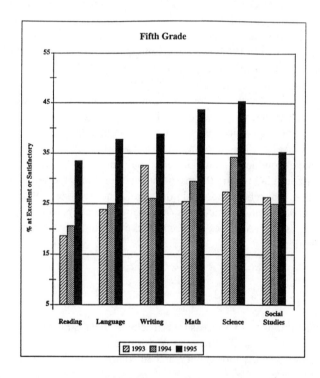

Figure 8.8. Roots and Wings: Saint Mary's County, Maryland School Performance Assessment Program, School Years 1993-1995

given year), there were significant positive effects on every measure at every grade level, 1 through 5. Follow-up studies show continuing program effects into sixth and seventh grades. This chapter also presents evidence showing particularly large impacts on the achievement of limited-English proficient students in both bilingual and ESL programs, and on both reducing special education referrals and improving the achievement of students who have been assigned to special education. It compares the outcomes of Success for All with those of another early intervention program, Reading Recovery.

The evaluation of Roots and Wings shows strong positive effects of this program on all six scales of a state performance measure given to third and fifth graders. This evaluation both supports the effectiveness of Roots and Wings and demonstrates that Success for All/Roots and Wings can have a significant impact on new performance measures.

The Success for All evaluations have used reliable and valid measures, individually administered tests that are sensitive to all aspects of reading: comprehension, fluency, word attack, and word identification. Performance of Success for All students has been compared to that of matched students in matched control schools, who provide the best indication of what students without the program would have achieved. The Roots and Wings evaluation showed important gains on the type of performance measures being adopted in many state assessment programs. Replication of high-quality experiments in such a wide variety of schools and districts is extremely unusual.

An important indicator of the robustness of Success for All is the fact that of the more than 150 schools that have used the program for periods of 1 to 7 years, only 6 have dropped out (in all cases because of changes of principals). Many other Success for All schools have survived changes of superintendents, principals, facilitators, and other key staff, major cuts in funding, and other serious threats to program maintenance.

The research summarized here demonstrates that comprehensive, systemic school-by-school change can take place on a broad scale in a way that maintains the integrity and effectiveness of the model. The 23 schools in 9 districts that we are studying in depth are typical of the larger set of schools currently using Success for All in terms of quality of implementation, resources, demographic characteristics, and other factors. Program outcomes are not limited to the original home of the program; in fact, outcomes tend to be somewhat better outside of Baltimore. The widely held idea based on the RAND study of innovation (Berman & McLaughlin, 1978; McLaughlin, 1990) that comprehensive school reform must be invented by school staffs themselves is certainly not supported in research on Success for All and Roots and Wings. Although the programs are adapted to meet the needs of each school, and although school staffs must agree to implement the program by a vote of 80% or more, Success for All and Roots and Wings are externally developed programs with specific materials, manuals, and structures. The observation that these programs can be implemented and maintained over considerable time periods and can be effective in each of their replication sites certainly supports the idea that every school staff need not reinvent the wheel.

There is nothing magic about Success for All or Roots and Wings. None of their components are completely new or unique. Obviously, schools serving disadvantaged students can have great success without a special program if they have an outstanding staff. Other prevention/early intervention models, such as Reading Recovery (Pinnell et al., 1994) and the School Development Program (Comer, 1988) also have evidence of effectiveness with disadvantaged children. The main importance of the Success for All and Roots and Wings research is not in validating a particular model or in demonstrating that disadvantaged students can learn. Rather, its greatest importance is in demonstrating that success for disadvantaged students can be routinely ensured in schools that are not exceptional or extraordinary (and were not producing great success before the program was introduced). We cannot ensure that every school has a charismatic principal or every student has a charismatic teacher. Nevertheless, we can ensure that every child, regardless of family background, has an opportunity to succeed in school.

The demonstration that an effective program can be replicated and can be effective in its replication sites removes one more excuse for the continuing low achievement of disadvantaged children. To ensure the success of disadvantaged students we must have the political commitment to do so, with the funds and policies to back up this commitment. Success for All and Roots and Wings do require a serious commitment to restructure elementary schools and to reconfigure uses of Title 1, special education, and other funds to emphasize prevention and early intervention rather than remediation. These and other systemic changes in assessments, accountability, standards, and legislation can facilitate the implementation of Success for All and other school reform programs. We must, however, also have methods known not only to be effective in their original sites, but also to be replicable and effective in other sites. The evaluations presented in this chapter provide a practical demonstration of the effectiveness and replicability of one such program.

Note

1. Portions of this chapter are adapted from Slavin et al. (in press).

9

Success for All, Roots and Wings, and School Reform

Success for All and Roots and Wings are clearly having a substantial impact on the schools that are implementing them. This is, of course, important in itself. The experience of developing and disseminating these programs, however, and in particular, the research on their outcomes, have important implications for school reform that go beyond these schools. Success for All/Roots and Wings provide what may be the best evidence available that well-structured, comprehensive programs can be replicated on a substantial scale and can ensure success for a large proportion of children who would otherwise need long-term remedial and special education services. This chapter discusses the implications of research on Success for All and Roots and Wings for compensatory education, for special education, and for school reform in general.

Can Success for All and Roots and Wings Be Replicated?

The practical or policy consequences of research on Success for All and Roots and Wings would be minimal if the program depended on conditions unlikely to be replicated in schools beyond our pilot sites. Yet this is certainly not true; the program currently exists in over 300 schools in 24 states and is continuing to expand. Clearly, successful implementation of the

217

program does not depend on the existence of hand-picked staff, charismatic principals, or proximity to Johns Hopkins University. The 300 schools are highly diverse and are located in all parts of the United States, from California to Alaska to Texas to Alabama to Indiana. This is not to say that every school serving disadvantaged students can successfully implement the program. It does require a clear commitment from the district, principal, and staff to a very different way of organizing their schools. It is our belief and experience, however, that with adequate support from their central administration, the majority of Title I elementary schools want to implement a program like Success for All and are capable of doing so.

The most important impediments to the widespread use of Success for All and Roots and Wings are not any lack of willingness or skill on the part of school staffs, but rather revolve around the cost of the program and around our ability to provide training and support to large numbers of schools. Chapter 7 describes how we are working to expand our training and support capacity by helping establish regional training sites and by helping develop school districts' own capacities to support the program.

The following sections discuss several questions relating to the cost of Success for All and Roots and Wings. First is a discussion of what the costs are. This is followed by discussion of mid to long-term savings brought about by the program, and a discussion of the effectiveness of Success for All in comparison to equally expensive alternatives.

Costs

Success for All and Roots and Wings have been implemented with widely varying constellations of resources. Most schools fund the program by reconfiguring existing Title I support sometimes supplemented by funds or personnel from special education, state compensatory education, funding from settlements in desegregation or school finance suits, or bilingual education or ESL programs. Recent analyses of our Success for All schools indicate that 75% of the funding is from Title I. Schools may obtain grants or other short-term funding to help them with the initial costs of training and materials, but most do not. None of the current Success for All schools have more than $25,000 beyond what they would have had without the program.

Table 9.1 shows estimated program costs for Success for All schools, exclusive of personnel and released time for training. First-year costs for Roots and Wings are the same as those for Success for All, because Roots and Wings schools typically implement the Success for All components in the first implementation year. In years 2 and 3, however, costs for Roots and Wings remain as high as those of the first year because MathWings and WorldLab are phased in during the 2nd and 3rd implementation years.

Some of the training and travel costs can be reduced by arranging to have more than one school in a district work together in implementing Success for All or Roots and Wings.

Staffing Needs

The number of staff needed in Success for All and Roots and Wings (other than classroom teachers) is typically the same as the staff already available in the school, but staff roles change significantly. In general, Title I (and often special education) staff become tutors, and one position is set aside for the facilitator. Table 9.2 shows typical staff configurations for Success for All/Roots and Wings schools of 500 students with various levels Title I eligibility (and corresponding levels of Title I funds).

The Success for All and Roots and Wings curriculum and instructional program could be used without tutors, family support staff, and other staff, and we have evidence that even without these resources it can increase student achievement. (Of course, student achievement will not increase as much as in the full model, especially for the most at-risk children.) At

TABLE 9.1   Costs of Implementing Success for All and Roots and Wings[a]

	Year 1	Year 2	Year 3
Sample Cost Estimates (for sample school of about 500 students)			
SFA	$45,000-$57,500**	$17,000-$21,000	$11,000-$14,000
R&W	$45,000-$57,500	$45,000-$52,000	$45,000-$52,000
Two or Three Schools conducting training together (per school)			
SFA	$41,000-$48,000**	$16,000-$19,000	$10,500-$13,500
R&W	$41,000-$48,000	$41,000-$44,000	$41,000-$44,000
Four or more schools conducting training together (per school)			
SFA	$37,000-$46,000**	$15,500-$17,500	$10,000-$13,000
R&W	$37,000-$46,000	$37,000-$42,000	$37,000-$42,000

a. Includes training and implementation visits, reporting of observations and discussions, telephone assistance, teacher's manuals and student copies of curriculum materials, conference registration for two staff members, travel expenses for SFA/R&W staff.

present, however, we are emphasizing dissemination to districts able to implement something close to our vision of a school in which very few students fail or require special or remedial education, and this requires tutors and other staff. In our experience, most high-poverty schools, especially Title I schoolwide projects, can implement Success for All or Roots and Wings using Title I and special education resources. Schools with fewer disadvantaged students and, therefore, fewer Title I dollars, often require funds from elsewhere: desegregation funds, state funds, foundation or government grants, and so on. Costs generally diminish over time as the need to provide remedial services for older children diminishes. We have found that it is not a good idea for schools to try to obtain grants to fund the *continuing* costs of the program, because they then have to continually fight to maintain their funding. Short-term grants, however, to help with start-up costs can be very helpful.

TABLE 9.2   Typical Staffing Needs (FTEs) for Success for All or Roots and Wings Schools at Different Title I Eligibility Levels

	Percentage of Students Eligible for Title I		
	75%	50%	25%
Facilitator	1.0	1.0	1.0
Tutors[a]	4.0	2.0	1.0
Family support specialist[b]	1.0	1.0	1.0

a. Certified teachers serve as tutors. High-quality paraprofessionals or retired teachers can be added to this number or substituted for some tutors if at least one certified teacher-tutor is available to supervise others and work with children with the most serious problems.
b. Social worker, counselor, or parent liaison.

Alternatives for Reducing the Costs of
Success for All and Roots and Wings

The variations in staff and other resources between different Success for All schools has enabled us to examine the contribution made by many key program elements to program outcomes. Our conclusion at present is that inexpensive forms of the program can significantly increase the achievement of students in general, but to guarantee the success of every child requires greater funding (see Chapter 8). In a study comparing schools with additional funding beyond Title I to schools just using their Title I resources, the fully funded schools had overall achievement effects only slightly better than those obtained in less well-funded locations, but they had more positive effects on the performance of the most at-risk students (those in the lowest 25% at pretest) and on such outcomes as retentions and special education placements (see Slavin, Madden, Karweit, Dolan, & Wasik, 1992). For the students with the greatest difficulties, the provision of adequate tutoring and family support services was crucial for success, but even a small number of such students in each school absorbed enormous person-hours.

Having adequate resources also enabled the schools to avoid the use of expensive alternative services, such as special education and retention. For example, a student who was struggling at the end of first grade might be promoted to second grade and given continued one-to-one tutoring and family support. In a school without adequate support services, the same child would likely be retained or referred to special education. Retention rates and special education placements for learning disabilities have been substantially reduced by the program (see Chapter 8), leading to savings that are not immediately apparent but that reduce real education costs in the long run in schools using Success for All and Roots and Wings.

Without question, the most important resources for the most at-risk students are the tutors. The effects of Success for All for the lowest 25% of students are closely associated with the number and quality of tutors. In most schools we have insisted on the use of certified teachers as tutors. In schools that cannot afford enough certified tutors, however, we have recommended a mix of certified, paraprofessional, and volunteer tutors. These schools have at least one (but usually two) certified teacher tutor who works with the students with the most severe and unusual reading problems and also supervises the paraprofessional tutors, the volunteer tutors, or both. Reducing the number of qualified tutors does reduce the capacity of the program to ensure success for all, but schools can still make a substantial difference in student achievement by implementing the curricular and instructional components of the program and using a mix of certified and noncertified tutors.

One goal of Success for All is to provide tutoring support in high-risk schools to 1 in every 5 first through third graders. Analyses of our sites indicate that 90% have tutoring ratios of between 1:5 to 1:10 students. In addition, 94% of the schools use all certified staff or certified staff paired with paraprofessionals. Tutoring is clearly the most variable component of Success for All implementations and is linked to the school district's ability to fully fund the program.

The impact of additional family support staff has been clearly seen on student attendance. Family support interventions have also been crucial for individual children who have had serious behavior problems, health problems, or other family-related problems, and family support plays an important role in finding alternatives to special education placements. The impact of family support on overall reading scores is probably small, but if Success for All is to truly mean *all,* family support is a critical component. Most schools, however, now create family support teams within their existing staff rather than adding staff for this purpose, so family support may not be a major factor in program cost. Our analyses of family support programs indicate that they vary widely from school to school depending on level of support, staffing patterns, and community involvement and needs.

Because all Success for All and Roots and Wings schools have facilitators, we cannot assess the contribution they make to program outcomes. Our experience tells us, however, that they are essential. The changes in instruction, curriculum, support services, and other features of the elementary program are so extensive that there must be someone whose sole job is to ensure that all elements of the program are well implemented, well coordinated with each other, and focused on the success of every child. We have experimented with half-time facilitators (who tutor in the afternoon), but we recommend against this in the early stages of program implementation. Most schools that started with half-time facilitators have moved to full-time facilitators.

To summarize, we believe based on our research to date that much of the overall impact of Success for All or Roots and Wings can be achieved through improvements in curriculum and instruction, with the provision of a full-time facilitator critical to success in implementation. For the lowest-achieving students, tutors are clearly essential, as is family support. When hard choices have to be made, we emphasize the importance of tutors and the facilitator in addition to curriculum change, professional development, and a basic family support program (at least guaranteeing attendance) as minimum requirements for an adequate implementation.

Savings Brought About by Success for All/Roots and Wings

Although the costs of Success for All or Roots and Wings must be primarily justified as an investment in children, it is important to note that the program typically brings about many savings.

Retentions. Many Success for All schools have substantially reduced their rate of retentions (Slavin et al., 1992). Reducing retentions has an important effect on educational costs. A retained first grader is receiving a very expensive intervention; one more year of first grade. Every time an elementary school retains 25 to 30 students it must eventually hire an additional teacher, supply an additional classroom, and so on. When Success for All started in 1987, retention rates in many urban districts often approached 15%. Over the last several years, research on the negative effects of retention (Shepard & Smith, 1989) have changed district retention policies. Most districts have lowered their retention rates, and therefore the cost savings brought about by Success for All's reductions in retention rates are not as large as when the program began.

Special Education. Success for All schools have been able to reduce special education placements for learning disabilities by about half. The additional cost of serving such students is approximately $3,500 per year. If over a period of years the number of children in special education for learning disabilities could be cut from 8% to 4%, the annual savings in a school of 500 students would be $70,000. In addition, reducing the number of assessments for special education (a national average of $1,800) from 8% to 4% would add a savings of $36,000 per year. Most schools report fewer referrals and the referrals they do receive tend to be more accurate, thereby reducing unnecessary assessments.

Supplanted Training and Materials. Success for All materials and training often take the place of regular staff development and materials. Therefore, the costs noted on Table 9.1 may not be additional costs to the school, but may replace current programs.

Long-Term Savings

The preceding discussion only deals with short- to midterm savings realized by the school or school system. To these savings must be added the likely savings to society over the long term in costs of welfare, police, prisons, and so on. The link between school success and life success, and between these and the need for expensive social services, is well established. To the degree that Success for All ultimately reduces delinquency, dropout, teen pregnancy, or other problems strongly associated with school failure in low-income communities, its savings to society could far outweigh any costs of implementation (see Barnett & Escobar, 1977). Research on prevention also suggests that the links between early school achievement and mental health will be strong.

Comparison With Alternative Interventions

Leaving aside the question of monetary savings, the cost-effectiveness of programs that are both more expensive and more effective than existing programs is hard to assess. Clearly, the effectiveness of schools serving disadvantaged students is far below what we can accept in our society. What we should be asking is what are the means of bringing disadvantaged students to acceptable levels of achievement, and only then ask which are the least expensive of the effective alternatives.

There are several approaches to early intervention that have objectives similar to those of Success for All or Roots and Wings and have costs in the same order of magnitude. As a point of comparison, recall from Chapter 8 that on average, Success for All students exceeded matched control students in reading by an effect size of +.53 at the end of first grade, +.43 at the end of third, and +.68 at the end of fifth grade. For the lowest achievers, the corresponding effects were +1.03 in first grade, +1.19 in third, and +1.29 in fifth. Also recall that special education referrals almost halved.

One often-proposed alternative is to reduce class size in the early grades to about 15. Studies of this usually find small positive effects. The largest effects ever found, in a Tennessee statewide study, were effect sizes of +.34 at the end of first grade and +.24 at the end of third (after 4 years of small class sizes). A follow-up study of fourth graders found lasting effects to be even smaller, +.14 (Nye, Zaharias, Fulton, Achilles, & Hooper, 1991). A similar statewide study in Indiana found much smaller effects (Farr, Quilling, Bessel, & Johnson, 1987); by the end of third grade, students who had been in small classes exceeded controls in reading by an effect size of only +.06. Studies in South Carolina, Virginia Beach, New York City, and Austin, Texas, have found effects of reduced class size closer to the small Indiana effects than the larger Tennessee findings (see Slavin, 1994). Clearly, Success for All is substantially more effective than simply reducing class size.

Another frequent solution to the problem of early reading delays is the use of transitional first grades, prefirsts, and other means of adding a year between kindergarten entry and the end of first grade. Such programs produce a short-lived boost to students' scores in comparison to their new (younger) classmates, but this effect rapidly fades in later years (Karweit, 1994b).

Other expensive alternatives have few if any effects on early reading. Among these are provision of instructional aides and IBM's Writing to Read computer program (Slavin, 1994).

The most successful alternatives to Success for All are programs that have elements in common with it. In particular, other one-to-one tutoring programs, such as Reading Recovery (Pinnell, 1989), have effects on low-achieving first graders similar to those of Success for All. Because Reading Recovery does not alter the school's program beyond first grade, however, the effects do not continue to grow; by the end of third grade, effect sizes average +.20 (Wasik & Slavin, 1993), in comparison to +1.19 for Success for All's low achievers.

High-quality preschool programs have had substantial immediate effects on students' IQs and language skills, moderate effects on retentions and special education placements, and important long-term effects on such outcomes as dropout and delinquency, but have had few effects on school achievement (see Berrueta-Clement, Schweinhart, Barnett, Epstein, & Weikart, 1984).

In sum, none of the major alternatives to Success for All that have been evaluated are as effective in increasing reading performance, and only the preschool studies have any evidence of reduced retentions or special education placements.

Success for All is a practical, replicable, and effective program for improving the performance of disadvantaged elementary students. It is expensive, but with reallocations of Title I, special education, and other funds, most school districts serving many disadvantaged student can afford a credible form of the model. Immediate and long-term savings introduced by Success for All may ultimately offset most of the program's cost. Success for All is considerably more effective than other, equally expensive approaches to early education such as reducing class size, providing instructional aides, and implementing computer-assisted instruction. For these reasons, Success for All appears to be a cost-effective means of bringing all children in disadvantaged schools to acceptable levels of reading performance. It could be considered a practical alternative to any school serving high-risk students. If it lives up to its current promise, Roots and Wings will extend its effect to all elementary subjects.

Implications of Success for All/ Roots and Wings for Compensatory Education[1]

Once upon a time (or so the story goes), there was a train company experiencing a high rate of accidents. The company appointed a commission to look into the matter, and the commission issued a report noting its major finding, which was that when accidents occurred, damage was primarily sustained to the last car in the train. As a result of this finding, the company established a policy requiring that before each train left the station, the last car was to be uncoupled! (Slavin, 1991).

All too often in its 25-year history, compensatory education has primarily pursued a "last car" strategy in providing for the needs of low-achieving students. The attention and resources of Title I and its predecessor, Chapter 1, have mostly gone into identifying and remediating the damage sustained by individual children. Yet the fault lies not in the children, but in the system that failed to prevent the damage in the first place, just as the damage to the last car was due to the train system and had nothing to do with the last car in itself.

The 1994 reauthorization of Chapter 1 as Title I has created unprecedented opportunities for high-poverty schools to fundamentally reform themselves. In particular, it reduced the free-lunch criteria for schools to qualify as schoolwide programs from 75% to 50%. Schoolwide programs can use their Title I resources flexibly to meet the needs of all children and to provide extended professional development for all staff. Integration of Title I services with Title VII services (bilingual education) and with special education also allows for significant reform. More than ever before, Title I schools can select programs that match their vision of excellence, and implement that program with adequate professional development, materials, and flexibility. Yet all too many Title I schools are still not taking advantage of the flexibility they have. They are continuing to invest in pull-out remedial teachers and instructional aides, neither of which has any demonstrated effect on student achievement (Puma, Jones, Rock, & Fernandez, 1993).

Title I can be much more than it has been in the past. It can be an engine of change in the education of disadvantaged children. It can ensure the basic skills of virtually all children; it can in essence help our nation's schools put a floor under the achievement expectations for all nonretarded children, so that all children will have the basic skills necessary to profit from regular classroom instruction. It can help schools move toward teaching of a full and appropriate curriculum for all students, but particularly for those who by virtue of being "at risk" too often receive a narrow curriculum emphasizing isolated skills. It can make the education of disadvantaged and at-risk students a top priority for all schools.

Preventing Early Reading Failure

Perhaps the most important objective of compensatory education is to ensure that children are successful in reading the first time they are taught, and never become remedial readers. The importance of reading success in the early grades is apparent to anyone who works with at-risk students. The consequences of failing to learn to read in the early grades are severe. For example, disadvantaged students who have failed a grade and are reading below grade level are extremely unlikely to graduate from high school (Lloyd, 1978). Retentions and special education referrals are usually based on early reading deficits.

Trying to remediate reading failure after it has occurred is very difficult, because by then students who have failed are likely to be unmotivated, to have poor self-concepts as learners, and to be anxious about reading. Reform is needed at all levels of education, but no goal of reform is as important as seeing that all children start off their school careers with success, confidence, and a firm foundation in reading. Success in the early grades does not guarantee success throughout the school years and beyond, but failure in the early grades does virtually guarantee failure in later schooling.

A growing body of evidence from several sources indicates that reading failure in the early grades is preventable. The outcomes summarized in Chapter 8 show that Success for All has been able to dramatically reduce the number of students who fail to learn to read. Reading Recovery (Pinnell, DeFord, & Lyons, 1988), which provides at-risk first graders with one-to-one tutoring from specially trained certified teachers, has been found to substantially increase these students' achievement and to sustain these improvements into the later elementary grades. Prevention of learning disabilities (Silver & Hagin, 1990), which provides tutoring to at-risk first and second graders, with a focus on perceptual skills often lacking in learning disabled students, has also had markedly positive effects on students at-risk for learning disabilities. This and other evidence suggests that reading failure is preventable for nearly all children, even a substantial portion of those who are typically categorized as learning disabled.

If reading failure *can* be prevented, it *must* be prevented. Title I is the logical program to take the lead in giving schools serving disadvantaged students the resources and programs necessary to see that all children learn to read.

Enhancing Regular Classroom Instruction

One of the most fundamental principles of Chapter 1/Title I has been that compensatory funds must be focused on the lowest-achieving students in qualifying schools. In principle this makes sense, in that it avoids spreading Title I resources too thinly. But in practice this requirement has led to many problems, including a lack of consistency or coordination between regular and Chapter 1 instruction, disruption of children's regular classroom instruction, labeling of students who receive services, and unclear responsibility for children's progress (Allington & Johnston, 1989; Allington & McGill-Franzen 1989; Stein, Leinhardt, & Bickel, 1989).

It is time to recognize that the best way to prevent students from falling behind is to provide them with top-quality instruction in their regular classrooms. A substantial portion of Title I funds should be set aside for staff development and adoption of programs known to be effective by teachers in Title I schools. For example, by hiring one less aide, schools could instead devote about $20,000 per year to staff development, a huge investment in terms of what schools typically spend, but a small one in terms of what many Title I schools receive. The educational impact of one aide could never approach that of thorough and intelligent implementation of effective curricula and instructional practices in regular classrooms throughout the school. For the cost of two aides, a school could pay all of the nonpersonnel costs of Success for All. For this amount of money, a school could pay for extensive inservice, in-class follow-up, and release time for teachers to observe each other's classes and to meet to compare notes, as well as purchase needed materials and supplies. The achievement benefits of effective classroom instruction all day would far outweigh the potential benefits of remedial service.

There are many examples of programs that have been much more successful for low-achieving students than remedial services. In reviews of the literature on effective programs for students at risk (Slavin, Karweit, & Madden, 1989; Slavin, Karweit, & Wasik, 1994), we identified several such programs, including a variety of continuous progress models, cooperative learning, and peer tutoring. Programs directed at improving classroom management skills also often increase achievement. Many of the exciting innovations in constructivist curriculum currently being discussed are not affecting poor schools, but could do so with the support of Title I funds. In addition to particular classroom methods, schoolwide change programs such as James Comer's (1988) School Development Program, Theodore Sizer's (1984) Coalition of Essential Schools, Henry Levin's (1987) Accelerated Schools model, and most of the New American Schools Development Corporation programs (as well as Success for All and Roots and Wings) can be funded by Title I if Title I is seen as a means of reforming high-poverty schools.

Success for All provides one demonstration of how a schoolwide emphasis on staff development and adoption of effective practices can be implemented under Title I funding and can greatly affect the learning of all students. Title I must help create a situation in which eligible schools are able to select from among a set of programs known to be effective and are then able to use their funds to obtain inservice, follow-up, and materials—whatever is needed to ensure top-quality implementation of whatever methods the schools have chosen.

Of course, Title I should not only be a staff development program. There is still a need for service targeted to individual children (for example, to provide tutoring to first graders having difficulty reading). Without major investment in staff development, however, those who provide Title I services will always be trying to patch up individual children's deficits without being able to affect the setting in which students spend the great majority of their day, the regular classroom. Under current regulations, schools can use a Title's I dollars for staff development, but this rarely goes into the kind of training, follow-up, and assessment needed to effectively implement validated programs. One-day workshops with no follow-up are far more typical.

Implications for Special Education Policy[2]

For more than 30 years, the most important debates in special education research and policy have revolved around the practice of mainstreaming, particularly mainstreaming of students with mild academic handicaps, such as those identified as learning disabled. From early on, most researchers and policymakers have favored mainstreaming academically handicapped students to the maximum extent possible (Leinhardt & Pallay, 1982; Madden & Slavin, 1983), and the passage of PL 94-142 in 1975 put the federal government squarely behind this effort. Since that time, students with academic disabilities have certainly spent more time in general education classes than they did before, but the number of students identified for special education services has risen dramatically. Since 1975, the proportion of students categorized as learning disabled has risen more than 250%, while the category of educable mental retardation has diminished only slightly (U.S. Department of Education, 1993).

Despite the increase in mainstreaming, significant proportions of both special and general education teachers have never been comfortable with the practice. The recent movement toward full inclusion, which includes an even broader range of students in general education classes, has increased this discomfort. At the school level, holding mainstreaming or inclusion in place is often like holding together two positively charged magnets; it can be done, but only if external pressure is consistently applied. General education teachers are quite naturally concerned about the difficulty of teaching extremely heterogeneous classes, and special education teachers, seeing themselves as better trained to work with academically handicapped students and more concerned about them, are often reluctant to send their students into what they may perceive as an inappropriate environment.

Solutions to the problems of mainstreaming academically handicapped children have generally been built around attempts to improve the capacity of the general classroom teacher to accommodate the needs of a heterogeneous classroom (Zigmond et al., 1995). For example, forms of individualized instruction (Slavin, 1984; Wang & Birch, 1984), cooperative and peer-mediated instruction (Jenkins, Jewell, Leceister, Jenkins, & Troutner, 1990; Slavin, Stevens, & Madden, 1988), and teacher consultation models (Idol-Maestas, 1981) are based on the idea that to fully integrate academically handicapped students, teachers need new programs and skills.

Improving the capacity of the general education classroom to meet diverse needs is an essential part of a comprehensive strategy to serve academically handicapped students, but it is not enough. The problem is that once a child is academically handicapped (or significantly behind his or her peers for any reason), neither mainstreaming nor special or remedial education are likely to bring the child up to age-appropriate achievement norms. For most academically handicapped children, mainstreaming may only be the least unappealing of many unappealing options.

The Success for All and Roots and Wings models propose a markedly different approach to the education of students who are likely to become academically handicapped. The key focus of these models is an emphasis on prevention and on early, intensive, and untiring intervention to bring student performance within normal limits. We call this approach "neverstreaming" because its intention is to see that nearly all children remain in the mainstream by intervening to prevent the academic difficulties that would lead them to be identified for separate special education services.

Success One Year at a Time

One key concept underlying neverstreaming is that instructional programs must help students start with success and then maintain that success at each critical stage of development.

First, all students should arrive in kindergarten with adequate mental and physical development. This requires investments in prenatal and infant and toddler health care, parent training, early stimulation programs for at-risk toddlers, effective preschool programs, and so on.

The next critical juncture is assurance that all students leave first grade well on their way to success in reading and other critical skills. This requires effective kindergarten and first grade instruction and curriculum, family support programs, one-to-one tutoring or other intensive interventions for students who are having difficulties in reading.

Actually, success in passing from each grade level to the next might be considered a critical requirement for neverstreaming at all levels; programs and practices must be directed toward doing whatever it takes to see that all children make it each year. As students move into second and third grade and beyond, this would mean continuing to improve regular classroom instruction, to monitor student progress, and to intervene intensively as often as necessary to maintain at-risk students at a performance level at which they can fully profit from the same instruction given to students who were never at risk.

The idea here is to organize school and nonschool resources and programs to relentlessly and systematically prevent students from becoming academically handicapped from their first day of school (or earlier) to their last (or later). Rather than just trying to adapt instruction to student heterogeneity, neverstreaming attacks the original problem at its source, attempting to remove the low end of the performance distribution by preventing whatever deficits can be prevented, intensively intervening to identify and remediate any remaining deficits, and maintaining interventions to keep at-risk students from sliding back as they proceed through the grades.

Is "Neverstreaming" Feasible?

For neverstreaming to be a viable concept, we must have confidence that prevention and early intervention can, in fact, bring the great majority of at-risk students to an acceptable level of academic performance and prevent unnecessary special education referrals. Several recent developments in research on programs for students at risk of academic difficulties have shown the potential of prevention and early intervention to keep students in the early grades from starting the process of falling behind that often ultimately results in assignment to special education. As noted earlier, there is a growing body of evidence to suggest that reading failure is fundamentally preventable for a very large proportion of at-risk students. Reading failure is a key element of the profile of most students identified as learning disabled (Norman & Zigmond, 1980).

The findings to date of the Success for All evaluations illustrate the potential of prevention and early intervention to keep students from falling far behind their agemates, to keep them from failing, and to keep them from being assigned to special education for learning disabilities. Most Success for All and Roots and Wings schools serve very disadvantaged student populations; many experience problems with truancy, inadequate health care, parental poverty, drug involvement, and other problems that are unusual even among urban schools. Yet, in these schools, even the lowest achievers are well on their way to reading, are being promoted, and are staying out of special education. More typical schools without many of these challenges should be able to ensure that virtually all nonretarded students are successful in reading and other basic skills and can therefore stay out of separate special education programs.

How Many Students Can Be "Neverstreamed?"

It is too early to say precisely what proportion of the students now identified as having academic handicaps can be neverstreamed, which is to say prevented from ever having learning deficits serious enough to warrant special education. It may be that as our knowledge and experience grow, it will become possible to avoid separate special education for the great majority of students currently categorized as learning disabled, about 5% of all students ages 6 to 17 (U.S. Department of Education, 1993), plus some proportion of those identified as mildly mentally retarded and behaviorally handicapped.

Looking at data from Success for All, it is clear that even the very lowest-achieving third graders are reading at a level that would allow them to participate successfully in regular classroom instruction. Only 4% of Success for All third graders scored 2 years below grade level, one third the proportion in the control schools. With continuing improvements in curriculum and instruction through the fifth grade, these third graders should all complete their elementary years with an adequate basis in reading, and this should greatly increase their chances of success in the secondary grades. There is no reason to believe that similar strategies in mathematics, spelling, writing, and other subjects would not have similar impacts, particularly to the degree that success in these areas depends on reading skills.

The number of students who can be neverstreamed is not only dependent on the effectiveness of prevention and early intervention, but also on the degree to which general education can become better able to accommodate student differences. For example, use of cooperative learning, individualized instruction, and other strategies can also increase the ability of classroom teachers to meet individual needs. In one sense, the idea of neverstreaming is to work from two sides at the same time; making the classroom better able to accommodate individual differences, and reducing the severity of deficits in the first place to make accommodation of differences much easier.

The Role of Special Education in a "Neverstreamed" World

At the policy level, one practical means of beginning to emphasize neverstreaming would be to require that no child be assigned to special education for a reading disability unless he or she had been given a year of one-to-one tutoring from a qualified tutor. This, plus other reforms in instruction and curriculum, would greatly reduce the number of children who end up with individual education plans (IEPs) indicating learning disability. There will, however, always be students who will continue to need top-quality special education services, such as those who are retarded or severely emotionally disturbed, as well as those with physical, speech, or language deficits and those with severe learning disabilities. The goal of Success for All is to keep special education "special." In a neverstreamed school, traditionally configured special education services would still be provided to these students, with an emphasis on prevention and early intervention and on providing services in the least restrictive environment. This approach allows special education to return to its focus on more severely impaired students, those truly in need of special services.

Special education also has a key role to play in providing consultation to classroom teachers on such issues as adapting instruction to accommodate diverse needs and learning styles, improving classroom management, and assessing students. For example, even students who are reading well may have learning and behavior problems that classroom teachers may need help to accommodate. Special education consultants might include among their responsibilities working with individual children for brief periods to learn how to succeed with them and then returning them to their teachers and tutors. Many of our Success for All and Roots and Wings schools involve special education teachers as reading teachers during the 90-minute reading period, often serving primarily identified students. This greatly improves the reading group options for students.

If neverstreaming were to become institutionalized on a broad scale, it would create a need for a new category of teachers—professional tutors. Effective tutoring is not simply a matter of putting one teacher with one student; there are several studies of tutoring that have found unsystematic forms of tutoring to have few effects on learning (see Wasik & Slavin, 1993). The education and supervision of tutors might take place under the auspices of special education.

Unresolved Issues

Clearly, there is much we would need to know to maximize the degree to which students at risk can be successfully neverstreamed. We need to experiment with alternative models of early prevention, early childhood education, beginning instruction in reading and other basic skills, tutoring, family support, inservice, and school change, to find ever more effective strategies in each of these areas, and to find optimal mixes of elements. One particular question of great importance is whether tutoring in reading and other basic skills is enough to keep all nonretarded students from falling behind, or whether instruction specific to neurological deficits needs to be provided for some students, either preventively or in the later grades.

At the policy level, many other issues must be resolved. First, we must have a consensus that investments in early education will pay off in the long run. Second, we must have a willingness to devote funds to prevention. This implies that there must be a willingness at the policy level to increase funds for early education for some period of time, because it would be irresponsible to strip funds away from remedial services for students already in the system to concentrate them on prevention and early intervention for younger students. In addition, regulatory changes encouraging preventive uses of special education, Title I, and other categorical monies (and most important, not punishing schools and districts that reduce their special education counts) would be needed.

At the moment, neverstreaming should be seen as a goal rather than a well-developed policy. If, however, this goal is to be realized, we need to focus our energies on research, development, evaluation, and demonstration to move toward a day when students with learning disabilities and other students at risk of academic handicaps can confidently expect what neither mainstreaming nor special education can guarantee them today: not only services, but success.

Success for All/Roots and Wings Within the School Reform Movement

We are in a time period in American society where there is tremendous pressure to reform our schools. This pressure comes from constituencies at the national, state, and local community level. Reform efforts range from modest supplements to traditional classroom instruction to radical "break the mold" approaches to school change.

Success for All and Roots and Wings have many components that have been implemented in isolation in many educational environments. They benefit from past research that documents effective instructional programs for children at risk. One does not have to dig too deeply to recognize how the model has benefited from the development and research of others. For example, our tutoring model has benefited from the research on Reading Recovery, our family support team from Comer's (1988) School Development Program, our cross-grade regrouping from research on the Joplin Plan, and of course our instructional approaches draw extensively on our earlier research on the benefits of cooperative learning. We have not tried to reinvent the educational wheel. We have, however, put together many existing "wheels" to create a vehicle to optimize success for every child.

Success for All and Roots and Wings are among a growing number of school restructuring efforts. In many ways, however, they are quite distinct from other reform efforts. What is different about our model is not so much the individual strategies, but the way these strategies are woven together as a comprehensive system of complementary parts. We start with effective instruction within the regular classroom. Next, a set of multistaged interventions are available whenever danger signs are noted. The model involves many changes in both the organization and curriculum of schools. It is based on the concept of "relentlessness," which implies always having a back-up strategy to ensure success. In the case of Success for All and Roots and Wings, we believe the whole is indeed greater than the sum of its parts.

This is a time when there is doubt that research-based school change can take place on a broad scale, when many policymakers believe that only "systemic" changes in standards, assessments, frameworks, and legislation can make a difference. Success for All, Roots and Wings, and other replicable school designs show that this is untrue. Systemic change is necessary and desirable, but it must be accompanied by professional development, materials, and school organization methods capable of enabling schools to confidently achieve to new, higher standards. Success for All and Roots and Wings provide one model of how standards and school-by-school reform can work together.

Next Stage of Development

Success for All and Roots and Wings are still in development and probably always will be. Over the past years we have gradually added new sites with the goal of exploring the effectiveness of the model in varying contexts. We are currently working to complete the development of the math and social studies/science elements of Roots and Wings. We are continuing many of the program elements and staff into the first year of middle school, including our family support activities and support of content-related reading in areas such as science and social studies. We are working to build dissemination capacity to work on a much larger scale without sacrificing program quality. Our goal is to build and maintain success as expansion occurs, as we move from more nurtured sites to more typical replications that inevitably lead to less contact and control from our development team.

Conclusion

Not more than 15 years ago, Ronald Edmonds (1981) put forth three assertions:

a. We can, whenever and wherever we choose, successfully teach all children whose schooling is of interest to us;

b. We already know more than we need to do that; and

c. Whether or not we do it must finally depend on how we feel about the fact that we haven't so far. (p. 23)

Edmonds's conclusions were based on his studies of effective and ineffective schools serving poor and minority children. His key assumption was that if the characteristics of effective schools could be implanted in less effective schools, all children could learn. Yet this transfer turned out not to be an easy one. Making a run-of-the mill school into an outstanding one takes much more than telling staffs the characteristics of outstanding schools.

The greatest importance of the research on Success for All and Roots and Wings is that it brings us closer to making Edmond's vision a reality. Only when we have confidence that we can take a typical school serving disadvantaged children and ensure the success of virtually every child, can we really force the essential political and policy question: Given that we know that we can greatly improve the educational performance of at-risk children, *are we willing to do what it takes to do so?*

The findings of research on Success for All, Roots and Wings, and related prevention and early intervention programs make it impossible to continue to say that the problems of education in the inner city cannot be solved. The Success for All/Roots and Wings schools, which include some of the most disadvantaged schools in the United States do not have hand-picked staffs or principals. If they can achieve success with the great majority of at-risk children, so can most schools serving similar children.

It takes money and time, but increasingly the money is already in place because schools are given increasing flexibility in using Title I and special education funds. We have demonstrated that with sustained efforts over time, significant change can occur for the vast majority of students. What is most needed is leadership, a commitment at every level of the political process to see that we stop discarding so many students at the start of their school careers.

If we had an outbreak of a curable disease, we would have a massive outpouring of publicity and funding to do whatever is necessary to cure it. *Reading failure is a curable disease.* If we are a caring nation, or even if we are only a self-interested but far-sighted nation, the knowledge that reading failure is fundamentally preventable must have a substantial impact on our policies toward education for at-risk children.

There is much more we need to learn how to do and much more we need to learn about the effects of what we are already doing, but we already know enough to make widespread reading failure a thing of the past. Next September, another 6 million children will enter kindergarten. If we know how to ensure that all of them will succeed in their early schooling years, we have a moral responsibility to use this knowledge. We cannot afford to let another generation slip through our fingers.

Notes

1. Portions of this section are adapted from Slavin (1991).
2. This section is adapted from Slavin et al. (1991).

References

Adams, M. J. (1990). *Beginning to read: Thinking and learning about print.* Cambridge: MIT Press.

Allington, R. L., & Johnston, P. (1989). Coordination, collaboration, and consistency: The redesign of compensatory and special education interventions. In R. E. Slavin, N. L. Karweit, & N. A. Madden (Eds.), *Effective programs for students at risk* (pp. 320-354). Boston: Allyn & Bacon.

Allington, R. L., & McGill-Franzen, A. (1989). School response to reading failure: Instruction for Chapter I and special education students in grades two, four, and eight. *Elementary School Journal, 89*(5), 529-542.

Barnett, W. S., & Escobar, C. M. (1977). The economics of early education intervention: A review. *Review of Educational Research, 57,* 387-414.

Berman, P., & McLaughlin, M. (1978). *Federal programs supporting educational change: A model of education change, Vol. VIII: Implementing and sustaining innovations.* Santa Monica, CA: RAND.

Berrueta-Clement, J. R., Schweinhart, L. J., Barnett, W. S., Epstein, A. S., & Weikart, D. P. (1984). *Changed lives.* Ypsilanti, MI: High/Scope.

Calkins, L. M. (1983). *Lessons from a child: On the teaching and learning of writings.* Exeter, NH: Heinemann.

Comer, J. (1988). Educating poor minority children. *Scientific American, 259,* 42-48.

DeFord, D. E., Pinnell, G. S., Lyons, C. A., & Young, P. (1987). *Ohio's Reading Recovery program: Vol. 7, Report of the follow-up studies.* Columbus: Ohio State University.

Dianda, M. R., & Flaherty, J. F. (1995, April). *Effects of Success for All on the reading achievement of first graders in California bilingual programs.* Paper presented at the annual meeting of the American Educational Research Association, San Francisco.

Durrell, D., & Catterson, J. (1980). *Durrell analysis of reading difficulty.* New York: Psychological Corporation.

Edmonds, R. R. (1981). Making public schools effective. *Social Policy, 12,* 56-60.

Epstein, J. L. (1989). Effects of teacher practices of parent involvement on student achievement in reading and math. In S. Silvern (Ed.), *Literacy through family, community, and school interaction* (pp. 88-108). Greenwich, CT: JAI.

Farr, B., Quilling, M., Bessel, R., & Johnson, W. (1987). *Evaluation of PRIMETIME: 1986-1987 final report.* Indianapolis, IN: Advanced Technology.

Garcia, E. E. (1991). Bilingualism, second language acquisition, and the education of Chicano language minority students. In R. R. Valencia (Ed.), *Chicano school failure and success: Research and policy agendas for the 1990s.* New York: Falmer.

Garcia, E. E. (1994, April). *The impact of linguistic and cultural diversity on America's schools: A need for new policy.* Paper presented at the annual meeting of the American Educational Research Association, New Orleans.

Glass, G. V., McGaw, B., & Smith, M. L. (1981). *Meta-analysis in social research.* Beverly Hills, CA: Sage.

Graves, D. (1983). *Writing: Teachers and children at work.* Exeter, NH: Heinemann.

Hakuta, K., & Garcia, E. E. (1989). Bilingualism and education. *American Psychologist, 44,* 374-379.

Haxby, B., Lasaga-Flister, M., Madden, N. A., Slavin, R. E., & Dolan, L. J. (1995). *Family support manual for Success for All/Roots and Wings.* Baltimore: Johns Hopkins University, Center for Research on the Education of Students Placed at Risk.

Hertz-Lazarowitz, R., Ivory, G., & Calderón, M. (1993). *The bilingual cooperative integrated reading and composition (BCIRC) project in the Ysleta Independent School District: Standardized test outcomes.* Baltimore: Johns Hopkins University, Center for Research on Effective Schooling for Disadvantaged Students.

Horwitz, R. I. (1987). Complexity and contradiction in clinical trial research. *American Journal of Medicine, 82,* 498-510.

Idol-Maestas, L. (1981). A teacher training model: The resource/consulting teacher. *Behavior Disorders, 6,* 108-121.

Jenkins, J. R., Jewell, M., Leceister, N., Jenkins, L., & Troutner, N. (1990, April). *Development of a school building model for educating handicapped and at-risk students in general education classes.* Paper presented at the annual meeting of the American Educational Research Association, Boston.

Karweit, N. L. (1994a). Can preschool alone prevent early reading failure? In R. E. Slavin, N. L. Karweit, & B. A. Wasik (Eds.), *Preventing early school failure: Research on effective strategies* (pp. 58-77). Boston: Allyn & Bacon.

Karweit, N. L. (1994b). Issues in kindergarten organization and curriculum. In R. E. Slavin, N. L. Karweit, & B. A. Wasik (Eds.), *Preventing early school failure: Research on effective strategies* (pp. 78-101). Boston: Allyn & Bacon.

Karweit, N. L., & Coleman, M. A. (1991, April). *Early childhood programs in Success for All.* Paper presented at the annual meeting of the American Educational Research Association, Chicago.

Karweit, N. L., Coleman, M. A., Waclawiw, I., & Petza, R. (1990). *Story Telling and Retelling (STaR): Teachers' manual.* Baltimore: Johns Hopkins University, Center for Research on Effective Schooling for Disadvantaged Students.

Leinhardt, G., & Pallay, A. (1982). Restrictive educational settings: Exile or haven? *Review of Educational Research, 52,* 557-578.

Levin, H. M. (1987). Accelerated schools for disadvantaged students. *Educational Leadership, 44*(6), 19-21.

Lloyd, D. N. (1978). Prediction of school failure from third-grade data. *Educational and Psychological Measurement, 38,* 1193-1200.

Madden, N. A. (1995). *Reading Roots: Teachers' manual.* Baltimore: Johns Hopkins University, Center for Research on the Education of Students Placed at Risk.

Madden, N. A., Livermon, B. J., & Rice, L. B. (1994). *Lee conmigo: Teachers' manual.* Baltimore: Johns Hopkins University, Center for Research on the Education of Students Placed at Risk.

Madden, N. A., Livingston, M., & Cummings, N. (1995). *Facilitators' manual for Success for All/Roots and Wings.* Baltimore: Johns Hopkins University, Center for Research on the Education of Students Placed at Risk.

Madden, N. A., & Slavin, R. E. (1983). Mainstreaming students with mild academic handicaps: Academic and social outcome. *Review of Educational Research, 53,* 519-569.

Madden, N. A., Slavin, R. E., Farnish, A. M., Livingston, M. A., Calderón, M., & Stevens, R. J. (1996). *Reading Wings: Teachers' manual.* Baltimore: Johns Hopkins University, Center for Research on the Education of Students Placed at Risk.

Madden, N. A., Slavin, R. E., Karweit, N. L., Dolan, L. J., & Wasik, B. A. (1993). Success for All: Longitudinal effects of a restructuring program for inner-city elementary schools. *American Educational Research Journal, 30,* 123-148.

Madden, N. A., Wasik, B. A., & Petza, R. J. (1989). *Writing From the Heart: A writing process approach for first and second graders.* Baltimore: Johns Hopkins University, Center for Research on Effective Schooling for Disadvantaged Students.

Matt, G. E., & Cook, T. D. (1994). Threats to the validity of research and syntheses. In H. Cooper & L. V. Hedges (Eds.), *The handbook of research synthesis* (pp. 503-520). New York: Russell Sage.

McLaughlin, M. W. (1990). The RAND change agent study revisited: Macro perspectives and micro realities. *Educational Researcher, 19*(9), 11-16.

National Center for Education Statistics. (1993). *Digest of education statistics.* Washington, DC: U.S. Department of Education, National Center for Education Statistics.

Norman, C., & Zigmond, N. (1980). Characteristics of children labeled and served as learning disabled in school systems affiliated with child service and demonstrated centers. *Journal of Learning Disabilities, 13,* 542-547.

Nye, B. A., Zaharias, J. B., Fulton, B. D., Achilles, C. M., & Hooper, R. (1991). *The Lasting Benefits study: A continuing analysis of the effect of small class size in kindergarten through third grade on student achievement test scores in subsequent grade levels.* Nashville: Tennessee State University.

Pinnell, G. S. (1989). Reading Recovery: Helping at-risk children learn to read. *Elementary School Journal, 90,* 161-182.

Pinnell, G. S., DeFord, D. E., & Lyons, C. A. (1988). *Reading recovery: Early intervention for at-risk first graders.* Arlington, VA: Educational Research Service.

Pinnell, G. S., Lyons, C. A., DeFord, D. E., Bryk, A. S., & Seltzer, M. (1994). Comparing instructional models for the literacy education of high-risk first graders. *Reading Research Quarterly, 29,* 8-38.

Puma, M. J., Jones, C. C., Rock, D., & Fernandez, R. (1993). *Prospects: The congressionally mandated study of educational growth and opportunity* (Interim report). Bethesda, MD: ABT Associates.

Ross, S. M., Smith, L. J., Casey, J., & Slavin, R. E. (in press). Increasing the academic success of disadvantaged children: An examination of alternative early intervention programs. *American Educational Research Journal.*

Schweinhart, L. J., Barnes, H. V., & Weikart, D. P. (1993). *Significant benefits: The High/Scope Perry preschool study through age 27.* Ypsilanti, MI: High/Scope.

Shepard, L. A., & Smith, M. L. (Eds.). (1989). *Flunking grades: Research and policies on retention.* Philadelphia: Falmer.

Silver, A. A., & Hagin, R. A. (1990). *Disorders of learning in childhood.* New York: John Wiley.

Sizer, T. (1984). *Horace's compromise: The dilemma of the American high school.* Boston: Houghton Mifflin.

Slavin, R. E. (1984). Team-assisted individualization: Cooperative learning and individualized instruction in the mainstreamed classroom. *Remedial and Special Education, 5*(6), 33-42.

Slavin, R. E. (1986). Best-evidence synthesis: An alternative to meta-analytic and traditional reviews. *Educational Researcher, 15*(9), 5-11.

Slavin, R. E. (1987). Ability grouping and student achievement in elementary schools: A best-evidence synthesis. *Review of Educational Research, 57,* 347-350.

Slavin, R. E. (1991). Chapter I: A vision for the next quarter century. *Phi Delta Kappan, 72*(8), 592-596.

Slavin, R. E. (1994). School and classroom organization in beginning reading: Class size, aides, and instructional grouping. In R. E. Slavin, N. L. Karweit, B. A. Wasik, & N. A. Madden (Eds.), *Preventing early school failure: Research on effective strategies* (pp. 122-142). Boston: Allyn & Bacon.

Slavin, R. E. (1995). *Cooperative learning: Theory, research, and practice* (2nd ed.). Boston: Allyn & Bacon.

Slavin, R. E. (1996). Neverstreaming: Preventing learning disabilities. *Educational Leadership, 53*(5), 4-7.

Slavin, R. E., Dolan, L. J., & Madden, N. A. (1994). *Scaling up: Lessons learned in the dissemination of Success for All.* Baltimore: Johns Hopkins University, Center for Research on the Education of Students Placed at Risk.

Slavin, R. E., Karweit, N. L., & Madden, N. A. (Eds.). (1989). *Effective programs for students at risk.* Boston: Allyn & Bacon.

Slavin, R. E., Karweit, N. L., & Wasik, B. A. (1994). *Preventing early school failure: Research on effective strategies.* Boston: Allyn & Bacon.

Slavin, R. E., & Madden, N. A. (1993, April). *Multisite replicated experiments: An application to Success for All.* Paper presented at the annual meeting of the American Educational Research Association, Atlanta.

Slavin, R. E., & Madden, N. A. (1994). *Implementing Success for All in the Philadelphia public schools* (Final report to the Pew Charitable Trusts). Baltimore: Johns Hopkins University, Center for Research on Effective Schooling for Disadvantaged Students.

Slavin, R. E., & Madden, N. A. (1995, April). *Effects of Success for All on the achievement of English language learners.* Paper presented at the annual meeting of the American Educational Research Association, San Francisco.

Slavin, R. E., Madden, N. A., Dolan, L. J., & Wasik, B. A. (1994). Roots and Wings: Inspiring academic excellence. *Educational Leadership, 52*(3), 10-13.

Slavin, R. E., Madden, N. A., Dolan, L., Wasik, B. A., Ross, S. M., & Smith, L. J. (1994). "Whenever and wherever we choose": The replication of Success for All. *Phi Delta Kappan, 75*(8), 639-647.

Slavin, R. E., Madden, N. A., Dolan, L., Wasik, B. A., Ross, S. M., Smith, L. J., & Dianda, M. R. (1996). Success for All: A summary of research. *Journal for the Education of Students Placed at Risk, 1,* 41-76.

Slavin, R. E., Madden, N. A., Dolan, L. J., Wasik, B. A., Ross, S. M., Smith, L. J., & Dianda, M. R. (in press). Success for All: A summary of research. *Journal of Education for Students Placed at Risk.*

Slavin, R. E., Madden, N. A., Karweit, N. L., Dolan, L., & Wasik, B. A. (1992). *Success for All: A relentless approach to prevention and early intervention in elementary schools.* Arlington, VA: Educational Research Service.

Slavin, R. E., Madden, N. A., Karweit, N. L., Dolan, L., Wasik, B. A., Shaw, A., Mainzer, K. L., & Haxby, B. (1991). Neverstreaming: Prevention and early intervention as alternatives to special education. *Journal of Learning Disabilities, 24,* 373-378.

Slavin, R. E., Madden, N. A., Karweit, N. L., Livermon, B. J., & Dolan, L. (1990). Success for All: First-year outcomes of a comprehensive plan for reforming urban education. *American Educational Research Journal, 27,* 255-278.

Slavin, R. E., Madden, N. A., & Stevens, R. J. (1989/1990). Cooperative learning models for the 3 Rs. *Educational Leadership, 47*(4), 22-28.

Slavin, R. E., Stevens, R. J., & Madden, N. A. (1988). Accommodating student diversity in reading and writing instruction: A cooperative learning approach. *Remedial and Special Education, 9,* 60-66.

Slavin, R. E., & Yampolsky, R. (1991). *Effects of Success for All on students with limited English proficiency: A 3-year evaluation.* Baltimore: Johns Hopkins University, Center for Research on Effective Schooling for Disadvantaged Students.

Smith, L. J., Ross, S. M., & Casey, J. P. (1994). *Special education analyses for Success for All in four cities.* Memphis, TN: University of Memphis, Center for Research in Educational Policy.

Stein, M. K., Leinhardt, G., & Bickel, W. (1989). Instructional issues for teaching students at risk. In R. E. Slavin, N. L. Karweit, & N. A. Madden (Eds.), *Effective programs for students at risk* (pp. 145-194). Boston: Allyn & Bacon.

Stevens, R. J., Madden, N. A., Slavin, R. E., & Farnish, A. M. (1987). Cooperative integrated reading and composition: Two field experiments. *Reading Research Quarterly, 22,* 433-454.

Stevens, R. J., & Shaw, A. H. (1990). *Listening comprehension.* Baltimore: Johns Hopkins University, Center for Research on Effective Schooling for Disadvantaged Students.

U.S. Department of Education. (1993). *Fifteenth annual report to Congress on the implementation of the Individual with Disabilities Education Act.* Washington, DC: Author.

U.S. General Accounting Office. (1994). *Limited English proficiency: A growing and costly educational challenge facing many school districts.* Washington, DC: Author.

Wang, M. C., & Birch, J. W. (1984). Comparison of a full-time mainstreaming program and a resource room approach. *Exceptional Children, 51,* 33-40.

Wasik, B. A., Bond, M. A., & Waclawiw, I. (1995). *Early learning: Teachers' manual for prekindergarten and kindergarten.* Baltimore: Johns Hopkins University, Center for Research on the Education of Students Placed at Risk.

Wasik, B. A., & Madden, N. A. (1995). *Success for All tutoring manual.* Baltimore: Johns Hopkins University, Center for Research on the Education of Students Placed at Risk.

Wasik, B. A., & Slavin, R. E. (1993). Preventing early reading failure with one-to-one tutoring: A review of five programs. *Reading Research Quarterly, 28,* 178-200.

Willig, A. C. (1985). A meta-analysis of selected studies on the effectiveness of bilingual education. *Review of Educational Research, 55,* 269-317.

Wong-Fillmore, L., & Valadez, C. (1986). Teaching bilingual learners. In M. C. Wittrock (Ed.), *Handbook of research on teaching* (3rd ed., pp. 648-685). New York: Macmillan.

Zigmond, N., Jenkins, J., Fuchs, L. S., Deno, S., Fuchs, D., Baker, J. N., Jenkins, L., & Couthino, M. (1995). Special education in restructured schools: Findings from three multiyear studies. *Phi Delta Kappan, 76*(7), 531-540.

Index

CORWIN
PRESS

The Corwin Press logo—a raven striding across an open book—represents the happy union of courage and learning. We are a professional-level publisher of books and journals for K-12 educators, and we are committed to creating and providing resources that embody these qualities. Corwin's motto is "Success for All Learners."